PILGRIMAGE AND LITERARY TRADITION

In this original and wide-ranging book, Philip Edwards examines the theme of pilgrimage in the works of a variety of major writers, including Shakespeare, Conrad, T. S. Eliot, Yeats and Heaney. Edwards considers the original and early uses of the terms 'pilgrim' and 'pilgrimage' in life and literature, and demonstrates the importance, vitality and flexibility of pilgrimage as a literary theme over the centuries. The emphasis is almost wholly on post-Reformation writers, analysing the theme of pilgrimage in major works where previously it has not been thought to exist, and marking an important departure from traditional studies of the pilgrim and pilgrimage in literature. With the character of Hamlet central to the discussion, Edwards argues the emergence in Shakespeare of a new tragic vision of pilgrimage, which perhaps had its beginnings in ancient Irish literature. This is a ground-breaking and unusual study, which encompasses centuries under a common, and vital, theme.

PHILIP EDWARDS is Emeritus Professor of English Literature at the University of Liverpool. A renowned scholar of Shakespeare and Renaissance drama, he edited the New Cambridge Shakespeare edition of *Hamlet* (1985). He is also the author of numerous books on other periods in literature, including *Threshold of a Nation* (1979) on English and Irish drama, and *The Story of the Voyage* (1994). He has contributed essays to many books on Shakespeare, Irish literature, voyages and exploration, and has written extensively for various journals including *Shakespeare Survey*.

PILGRIMAGE AND LITERARY TRADITION

PHILIP EDWARDS

CAMBRIDGE
UNIVERSITY PRESS

PUBLISHED BY THE PRESS SYNDICATE OF THE UNIVERSITY OF CAMBRIDGE
The Pitt Building, Trumpington Street, Cambridge, United Kingdom

CAMBRIDGE UNIVERSITY PRESS
The Edinburgh Building, Cambridge, CB2 2RU, UK
40 West 20th Street, New York, NY 10011–4211, USA
477 Williamstown Road, Port Melbourne, VIC 3207, Australia
Ruiz de Alarcón 13, 28014 Madrid, Spain
Dock House, The Waterfront, Cape Town 8001, South Africa

http://www.cambridge.org

First published 2005

Printed in the United Kingdom at the University Press, Cambridge

Typeface Fournier 12.5/14 pt.   *System* LATEX 2ε [TB]

A catalogue record for this book is available from the British Library

ISBN 0 521 84762 1 hardback

For Matthew, Charles, Richard and Catherine

Contents

Illustrations

Acknowledgements

This book originated in a paper given at the triennial conference of the International Association of University Professors of English at Durham in 1998, on the metaphor of pilgrimage in the poetry of Southwell, Herbert and Vaughan. In acknowledging some of the assistance I have had in writing this book I must single out Anne Barton, who encouraged me to continue, and Brendan Kennelly, who has been unstinting in his support and in his generous supply of books about Irish writers and pilgrimage. I also thank former colleagues Helen Wilcox, David Mills and Philip Davis for their help, and John Gossage, John Hodgkinson, Linda Kelly, Derek Longmire and Antoinette Quinn for encouragement and assistance of various kinds. I owe much to the British Academy and the Huntington Library for an award which allowed me to spend a month working at the Huntington in California.

I acknowledge the permission of the Bodleian Library, Oxford, to quote two poems from the Rawlinson MSS on pp. 26–7 and 32–3, and the permission of the authors and Random House Group to quote from the work of David Lodge and Robert Crawford. I thank A. P. Watt Ltd (on behalf of Michael B. Yeats) and Scribner (Simon and Schuster) for permission to quote from the poems of W. B. Yeats. I am also grateful to Harvard University Press and the Trustees of Amherst College for permission to quote poems by Emily Dickinson. I have myself edited the quotations from Shakespeare's plays; line references are those of the Riverside Shakespeare.

Introduction

This book is about the theme of pilgrimage in a number of writers, English, Irish and American, from Shakespeare and Ralegh to Seamus Heaney and David Lodge. There is some discussion of *Piers Plowman* and the *Ancrene Wisse* in the first chapter, and of St Brendan and the Irish *peregrini* in later chapters; otherwise the emphasis is on post-Reformation literature.

I make no pretence of offering a history of 'pilgrimage literature' as a whole, even in English only, though the studies which follow are intended to clarify that history, and establish an understanding of what we may mean by a literary tradition of pilgrimage. I am, naturally, mainly concerned with the use of pilgrimage as a metaphor for a religious life or dedication, but metaphoric and non-metaphoric usages of 'pilgrimage' are hard to separate. Definition, or an attempt at it, is a prime necessity, and in my first chapter I try to disentangle the roots and stems of meaning in the words 'pilgrim' and 'pilgrimage', umpire the debate between reality and metaphor, consider the arguments about 'true' and 'false' pilgrimage, and mark the difference between those pilgrims who travel hopefully towards a shrine and those others, the *peregrini*, who (as it were) travel from the shrine, either to worship God in the solitude of cave or desert or sea, or else to go abroad to found monasteries and spread the truth. I hope that the definitions I reach are at the same time generous and strict; the course that the book takes is dependent on this initial investigation of meaning.

The major uncertainty in devotional poets of the seventeenth and nineteenth centuries about the value of the imagery deriving from the fundamental metaphor of Christian life as a pilgrimage, as seen in the Epistle to the Hebrews, is the subject of two of my chapters,

beginning with Southwell and culminating in the ironic and sometimes caustic treatment which traditional Christian metaphors receive
in Emily Dickinson's poems. My examination of the pilgrimage theme
in Shakespeare stresses not only how important the concept of pilgrimage was to him (whatever his own religious persuasion) but also how
misunderstanding of the meaning of the word pilgrimage and mis-
reading of Shakespeare's text have concealed the importance of the
issue of pilgrimage in the later tragedies. A recurring issue in the book
is what might be implied by the snatch of the old Walsingham ballad
sung by the mad Ophelia in the fourth act of *Hamlet*.

> How should I your true love know
> From another one?
> By his cockle hat and staff
> And his sandal shoon.

The scallop or cockle shell was worn as a badge by pilgrims who had
been to the shrine of St James at Compostela in Spain; it later became
part of the traditional pilgrim's dress, along with the broad-brimmed
hat, the staff, the scrip or satchel, the water bottle – all given lapidary
status in the opening of *The Passionate Man's Pilgrimage* ('Give me my
scallop shell of quiet'; see Chapter Four). I argue that Ophelia's fleeting
reference to her estranged lover as a pilgrim is not only important for
an understanding of *Hamlet*, but is also a kind of turning point in the
post-medieval era in the literary use of the pilgrimage motif, marking
the moment when the shadow of tragic doubt is cast over the pilgrim's
mission.

Deprived by Latimer and Thomas Cromwell of pilgrimage on
land, England took pilgrimage to sea. I am unable to accept Samuel
Purchas's grounds for redefining pilgrimage as voyaging, and, in particular, colonising America. This endeavour involved the long-lived
exploitation of the early Irish *peregrinus*, St Brendan, as an explorer
and discoverer of North America. It also led, very directly, to a confusion between metaphor and reality in applying the term 'pilgrims'
to the Mayflower settlers. I suggest that two writers from a much later
period, Conrad and T. S. Eliot, 'challenge' the Purchas view: Conrad
in *Heart of Darkness* with his 'pilgrims' on the bank of the river waiting

for the boat to take them to their loot, and Eliot in his finest pilgrimage poem, *Marina*, restoring New England to its purely metaphorical role of Promised Land. Eliot's religious poetry, in its well-known fusion of movement and stillness in *Four Quartets*, also provides a reconciliation of opposed imperatives in the contention about the appropriateness of the pilgrimage metaphor to a life of Christian commitment.

A main distinction between pilgrimage literature in England and Ireland is that in Ireland pilgrimage was never wholly suppressed, so that the Irish writer's contact with it has been real. The pilgrimage to Lough Derg, where Jesus is supposed to have shown St Patrick the entrance to Purgatory, has been a very rich source of literary accounts since Carleton's time, accounts in which self-examination about the virtue and value of pilgrimage is to the fore. Yeats's poem 'The Pilgrim', set to the music of an old ballad, is important in this respect, and it has been unduly neglected. But my main discussion concerning the Lough Derg writings has to be of Heaney's *Station Island*. This 1984 collection is heavily dependent on Heaney's 1983 translation of the early Irish work *Buile Suibhne* (as *Sweeney Astray*). Like most people I came to this extraordinary series of poems and prose passages about the mad bird-man through Heaney's translation, and it was Heaney's inspired comparison, in his Introduction, of Sweeney's language with that of Poor Tom in *King Lear* that helped me to see that the mad outsider King Sweeney was the type and symbol of the *peregrinus* whom I needed, and that I was justified in finding the *peregrinus* figure in Shakespeare's late tragedies. My immersion in *Buile Suibhne* has however led me to a paradoxically critical view of the direction of *Station Island*.

Bunyan's *Pilgrim's Progress* has only a subliminal presence in this book, but it comes out of the shadows for the discussion on doubt which is the subject of my concluding chapters. It is a largely comic novel, David Lodge's *Therapy*, which introduces Kierkegaard into the more or less continuous dispute between faith and doubt on the issue of pilgrimage. His hero, Laurence Passmore, feels that Kierkegaard's irrational 'leap into the void', which alone justifies faith, could explain and countenance what is happening to Margaret in her 'absurd' pilgrimage to Compostela. Many years ago I felt that in Kierkegaard's irrational 'leap' lay the only way of understanding *Hamlet*, and I urged people to accept not that Hamlet was right to overcome his doubts about his visitor from Purgatory, but that he might possibly be right (see p. 209). It is in this arena of *possibility* that I see the real strength of pilgrimage literature. It is an arena full of uncertainty and doubt about pilgrimage itself, considered as a means of access to the divine, but just as pilgrimage 'on the ground' has survived a history of corruption and abuse, so pilgrimage in literature, even more resourceful, has insistently reasserted itself as faith and belief have inevitably ebbed away, and remains a dominating image of search for the impossible – or rather for possibility. In what may be the strongest of all the pilgrimage poems of the age of unbelief, 'Sailing to Byzantium', Yeats uses the extraordinary phrase 'the artifice of eternity'. 'Gather me', pleads his pilgrim-speaker, 'into the artifice of eternity'. Yeats said of his poem, in a late broadcast, that 'I symbolise the search for the spiritual life by a journey to that city' (Byzantium). What the poem's speaker looks for in Byzantium is a symbol or image of the spiritual life, a thing of art which may suggest to the world he has left behind a sense of that which outgoes the limits of ordinary experience. 'Eternity', in so far as it means a life beyond this life, 'from whose bourn no traveller returns', is necessarily an artifice, an imagined possibility conveyed by image and metaphor. 'Sailing to Byzantium' as a whole is in itself a triumphant example of the use of the metaphor of pilgrimage to create that world of possibility.

CHAPTER I

Peregrinus

What do we mean by 'pilgrim' and 'pilgrimage'? For centuries past it has normally been understood that a pilgrimage is a journey, expected to be long and arduous, to a sacred place or a shrine, where the pilgrim hopes by a rite of communion to obtain spiritual benefit or divine assistance, or forgiveness, or a physical cure. Or the pilgrim may wish to give thanks for such assistance already received. This practice of making visits to sacred places, for various kinds of benefit, pre-dates Christianity, and is widespread in many religions.[1] It seems to be a universal urge. But curiously there are no pilgrims of this sort in the English Bible. The word occurs a number of times, but always with a different signification. The most important of these occurrences is in the Epistle to the Hebrews, 11:13–14. Here is the passage in the Authorised Version. The writer of the Epistle (his identity is not known) is speaking of those who lived before the coming of Christ, particularly Abraham, who was commanded by God to travel from his home 'unto a land that I will show thee'.

These all died in faith, not having received the promises, but having seen them afar off, and were persuaded of them, and embraced them, and confessed that they were strangers and pilgrims on the earth.

For they that say such things declare plainly that they seek a country.

These two verses have had a huge influence on the meaning of the word 'pilgrim' and on its allegorical uses over the centuries. John Wycliffe, or one of his disciples, translated this passage in the middle of the fourteenth century as follows. These worthy people 'knowlechide

---

[1] See, for example, Simon Coleman and John Elsner, *Pilgrimage Past and Present: Sacred Travel and Sacred Space in the World Religions* (London: British Museum Press, 1995).

that thei weren pilgryms, and herboryd men on the erthe' ('herboryd men' means 'harboured men', i.e., lodgers). Tyndale took over the word 'pilgrims' but emended the phrase to 'strangers and pilgrims'. And this phrase remained through all English versions, the Great Bible, the Geneva Bible, the Bishops' Bible, the Authorised Version and the Revised Version of 1881.[2]

'Strangers and pilgrims' is the Greek ξένοι καὶ παρεπίδημοί (xenoi kai parepidemoi). The Vulgate version is *peregrini et hospites*. Both these phrases suggest travellers who are temporarily residing in a territory which is not their own. Martin Luther (working from the Greek) accurately rendered the phrase as 'Gäste und Fremdlinge' [visiting strangers]. Though a French Bible of 1561 reads 'estrangers & pelerins', later versions are 'étrangers et voyageurs' and 'étrangers et forains'. The English Revised Standard Version of 1946 threw out the word 'pilgrims' and gave the phrase as 'strangers and exiles'. The New English Bible of 1961 reads 'strangers or passing travellers'. The New Revised Standard Version of 1989 has 'strangers and foreigners'.

Clearly, later translators have found the word 'pilgrims' confusing, though it was the direct rendering of '*peregrini*' ('pélerin' in French, 'pellegrino' in Italian, 'Pilger' in German, etc). Latin had no special word for one who journeyed to a sacred place, and the words '*peregrinus*' and '*peregrinatio*' had a basic set of meanings which are applicable in this passage and were correctly rendered by Luther and the later translators. '*Peregrinus*' meant a wanderer, a traveller from foreign parts, an alien, and it is in these senses that it is used in the Epistle to the Hebrews to translate the Greek, given above. The pre-Christian worthies considered themselves as exiles as they made their way through this world and this life. That the word 'pilgrim' meant just that is clear from a Lollard tract formerly attributed to Wycliffe: 'Euery citizen of the hevenli countre is a pilgrime of this world for al tyme of this present lijf.'[3]

---

[2] See *The New Testament Octapla*, ed. L. A. Weigle (New York: Thomas Nelson, 1962).
[3] *The Lanterne of Light*, ed. L. M. Swinburn, Early English Text Society, os 151 (London: Kegan Paul, Trench, Trübner, and Oxford University Press, 1917), pp. 85–6. Cf. Jonathan Sumption, *Pilgrimage: An Image of Mediaeval Religion* (Totowa, N.J.: Rowman and Littlefield, 1975; London: Faber and Faber, 2002), p. 300.

The author of the Epistle was transposing the sense of exile which suffuses the Old Testament – the Jews seeing themselves as a displaced people, enforced wanderers in search of the Promised Land, longing for a return to Zion, or Jerusalem – and allying it with the spirit of alienation from the life around them which inspired the early Christians, dedicated to a wholly new purpose. In doing this, he was pushing the word which means exile and was rendered as 'pilgrim' towards that same 'normal' definition which I gave at the head of this chapter. For the very word *exile* requires the concept of a homeland, to which the exile longs to return. 'For they that say such things', viz. that they are strangers and exiles, 'declare plainly that they seek a country' (11:14, AV). Abraham 'looked forward to the city that has foundations, whose architect and builder is God' (11:10, NRSV). And that city is firmly identified with the spiritual destination of the new Christians. 'But ye are come unto mount Sion, and unto the city of the living God, the heavenly Jerusalem, and to an innumerable company of angels' (12:22, AV). 'For here have we no continuing city, but we seek one to come' (13:14, AV). So those who are, metaphorically, *peregrini* (exiles or temporary residents or 'sojourners') are also (by extension of the metaphor) pilgrims in the narrower sense, being spiritual travellers to a heavenly destination. By means of this passage, *peregrini* became pilgrims in the customary sense, and all wayfaring pilgrims of the future became exiles.

The Epistle to the Hebrews was the bedrock for early Christian ideas on pilgrimage, and we need to explore further the implications of this central passage. But first there is another epistle to look at, another fundamental passage in which the Vulgate use of '*peregrini*' was expanded to embrace the concept of pilgrimage. This is the first Epistle of Peter, 2:11. 'Dearly beloved', writes the author, 'I beseech you as strangers and pilgrims, abstain from fleshly lusts, which war against the soul.' So the Authorised Version. The Greek phrase for 'strangers and pilgrims' was παροίκους καὶ παρεπιδήμους (paroikous kai parepidemous), [foreign residents and strangers]. The Vulgate reads *advenas et peregrinos*. The New English Bible has 'aliens in a foreign land'. The New Revised Standard Version gives us 'aliens and exiles'. It is still a matter of debate to whom the Epistle is addressed.

Who are these Christians scattered in 'Pontus, Galatia, Cappadocia, Asia, and Bithynia'? They may include Christian converts who have gone from Palestine to live in Asia Minor in the diaspora after the killing of Stephen; they may include converted Jews who were already living in Asia Minor, or perhaps converted pagans from those parts. Insofar as they were Palestinian Jews they were indeed *peregrini*, aliens and exiles in a double sense: away from their homeland and also separated from their neighbours by their faith. But all of them were aliens and exiles by reason of their religion; they did not belong to the society in which they resided, they belonged to Christ. There is no suggestion in the text itself, whatever the early commentators thought was implied, that they were *peregrini* in that they were metaphorically pilgrims bound for heaven. Peter urges them 'to abstain from fleshly lusts'. It has been suggested that they were to refrain from carnal desire because they were embarked on a divine pilgrimage.[4] The injunction seems much more pragmatic. Their purity is their mark and their distinction. They are 'a peculiar people' (1 Peter 2:9, AV), and they are to show their distinction by maintaining their holiness among unbelieving pagans, who may by their example learn to glorify God (2:12).

It is the argument of Dee Dyas's important book, *Pilgrimage in Medieval English Literature, 700–1500* (2001), that the idea of 'life-pilgrimage' (that is, life conceived as a pilgrimage towards a heavenly destination) was embedded in the Bible and dominated the concept of pilgrimage in the early Christian centuries. She shows that what she calls 'place-pilgrimage' (that is, actual journeys to holy shrines) did not really begin among Christians until the late third century. Life-pilgrimage has both the precedence and the superior value; place-pilgrimage is secondary and subordinate. In her Conclusion she writes: 'it has become clear that the *primary* meaning of pilgrimage within Christian thought is concerned with the journey of individual believers through an alien world to the homeland of heaven' (p. 247). Elsewhere she writes: 'The place-oriented pilgrimages which

---

[4] See Dee Dyas, *Pilgrimage in Medieval English Literature 700–1500* (Cambridge: D. S. Brewer, 2001), pp. 24–5.

multiplied so quickly during the fourth century ideally formed a part of that longer eternal journey' (p. 64).

Quite rightly, therefore, Dee Dyas questions the ordinary assumption that place-pilgrimages are literal journeys and that life-pilgrimage is a metaphor (p. 245). On the contrary, she argues, the journey of the soul towards union with Christ is the reality, and the physical journey to a shrine may be seen as a metaphor – 'a miniature version of that longer, more complex journey which every soul must choose to undertake' (p. 246). Dyas is anything but dogmatic on this question – which is the reality and which is the metaphor? – but it seems essential to pursue the matter further.

The 'eternal journey' of the Christian soul was indeed the ultimate reality. Territorial pilgrims were acting out scenes which copied *in parvo* the desired structure of their whole lives. The renunciation of friends and family, and the commitment to strange and hostile territory in order to reach the relics of a saint, might well be thought a metaphor for the moral dedication and struggle of a whole Christian life. As Duffy argues, 'Late medieval men and women were . . . well aware of the symbolic value of pilgrimage as a ritual enactment and consecration of their whole lives.'[5] Nevertheless, the manner in which the destiny of the Christian soul was defined was also metaphorical. The image of territorial pilgrimage was supplied by the earliest readers to texts in which they thought it inhered, though, as we have seen, these texts did not expressly declare it.

It will be granted that in the Epistle to the Hebrews the condition of exile in which the newly converted Christians found themselves is a metaphor – and that this metaphor is within the text. Spiritual alienation was given its meaning by being grounded in the literal situation of the Jewish people. And, as an exile longs for home, the Christian longs for union with Christ. The new covenant was explained metaphorically: an ethereal transposition of a known physical state. There is no doubt that what the Christians believed they had access to was the higher reality, but that higher reality was forced to find

---

[5] Eamon Duffy, *The Stripping of the Altars: Traditional Religion in England, c. 1400– c. 1580* (New Haven and London: Yale University Press, 1992), p. 192.

expression in the concreteness of the common experiences of life – in this case the condition of exile. The ease of movement between the physical and the spiritual is remarkably evident in the doubtfulness of the commentators on the Petrine epistle whether those *peregrini* who are to abstain from fleshly lusts are geographical exiles or spiritual exiles. And as spiritual apartness finds itself in the metaphor of physical exile, so the passage of the soul of the spiritual exile to its ultimate solace was voiced as a journey.

The words of Christ prepare us for the metaphor of the journey in which the author of Hebrews conveyed the struggle and hope of the new covenant. 'Seek, and ye shall find; knock, and it shall be opened unto you . . . Strait is the gate, and narrow is the way, which leadeth unto life' (Matthew 7:7, 14). And when Thomas grasps as it were a portion of the meaning of this metaphoric language, Christ magnificently drives home its fullness.

Thomas saith unto him, Lord, we know not whither thou goest; and how can we know the way?

Jesus saith unto him, I am the way, the truth, and the life; no man cometh unto the Father, but by me. (John 14:5–6)

The metaphoric Christian journey in Hebrews was a journey with a holy destination. The *peregrini* who undertook this journey were, metaphorically, exiles and 'sojourners'. It seems inevitable that the metaphorical language of the epistle should become extended, and that the journey should be characterised in terms of the territorial journey of the pilgrim to a sacred shrine. For this to be the case, 'pilgrimage' would need to share with 'exile' a real state on the ground (as it were) before it could be used as a symbol.

It will be said that for the original readers of the epistle, who established so firmly the understanding that the progress of the Christian soul was a pilgrimage, there were no pilgrimages 'on the ground' to serve as metaphoric fodder for the concept of life-pilgrimage. But the sweat and trudge along the exhausting road to a sacred place where lies a hope of relief is too deeply embedded in human life for it *not* to be available as a metaphor. The drift of the epistle is to present the new covenant of Christianity as a spiritual replacement of existing physicality. 'For Christ is not entered into the holy places made with hands, which are the figures of the true; but into heaven itself' (Hebrews 9:24). The physical objects of an outworn religion are only figures or symbols of truth. Yet they were needed, in order to express the idea of the truth which outwent them. And this is the case with pilgrimage – even if in those early years of Christianity the practice was unknown. Truth drew its strength from the language of what it despised and sought to replace.

This substitution becomes of the first importance when, from the fourth century, pilgrimage first to the Holy Land and then over the years to a thousand other places considered to be holy became a dominant reality in Christian life. The growth of pilgrimage in Europe makes an astounding story.[6] The international centres of the Holy Land and Rome, and the tomb of St James at Compostela in north-west Spain, plus in England the main shrines of Thomas à Becket at Canterbury and the Virgin at Walsingham in Norfolk, formed but a small fraction of the shrines of the multiplicity of saints whose intercession was sought in the length and breadth of every country. The dynamic tension between the spiritual journey and the physical journey which supplied its language grew increasingly exacerbated and bad tempered. There was a kind of warfare between the actuality of stumbling along the dusty road towards the tomb of a distant saint and the actuality of the spiritual life of dedication which could only express itself in the language of the humble physicality which it denounced. The opponents of territorial pilgrimage in the early Christian centuries and the Middle Ages were vociferous and articulate. Their burden was that Christ was not best sought in a far-off shrine but in the mind and the heart. 'God is in all places' said St Augustine in the fourth century,[7] echoing St Gregory of Nyssa, who said that travel brought no-one closer to God. Much later St Anselm urged pilgrims to forget the geographical Jerusalem and begin the way to the heavenly Jerusalem.

---

[6] Lucidly told by Diana Webb in her two books, *Pilgrims and Pilgrimage in the Medieval West* (London and New York: I. B. Tauris, 1999) and *Pilgrimage in Medieval England* (London and New York: Hambledon and London, 2000).

[7] For most of these references, see Giles Constable, 'Opposition to Pilgrimage in the Middle Ages', *Studia Gratiana* 19 (1976), 125–46.

In *The Canterbury Tales*, Chaucer's fictional Parson, who is actually on his way to Canterbury with the other pilgrims, says to his fellows that he hopes 'To shewe yow the wey, in this viage, / Of thilke parfit glorious pilgrymage / That highte Jerusalem celestial.'[8] And early in the fifteenth century, Thomas à Kempis wrote, 'Many run to divers places to visit the memorials of Saints departed . . . but behold, Thou art Thyself here present with me on Thine altar, my God, Saint of Saints'.[9]

It became a commonplace, among the Lollards for example, to denounce territorial pilgrims for their ignorance of *true* pilgrimage, which was the journey of life towards heaven. William Thorpe, interrogated in 1407 before Archbishop Arundel, said, 'I call them true pilgrims which travel towards the bliss of heaven . . . hating and fleeing all the seven deadly sins.'[10] This illustrates the fundamental paradox within the tropical language of Christian endeavour and aspiration. True pilgrims are not real pilgrims. Real pilgrims, that is territorial pilgrims, are engaged in a false activity. To be 'true' you have to masquerade under the colours of an activity which you denounce as false. The only way of describing the true activity seems to be by borrowing the language of a false activity.[11]

What becomes absolutely clear is that the spiritual experience is felt to be quite inadequately and ineptly described in the language which belongs to the misguided earthly pilgrim. The teeming richness of pilgrimage as a metaphor at all periods will often seem to lie in this very tension I have been describing between the physical journey and the spiritual quest which uses the language of the physical journey. The questioning of the adequacy of the territorial experience as an account of the spiritual experience, the

---

[8] The Parson's Prologue, lines 49–51. Quotation taken from *Works of Geoffrey Chaucer*, ed. F. N. Robinson, 2nd edn (London: Oxford University Press, 1968), p. 228.

[9] Thomas à Kempis, *Of the Imitation of Christ*, Book 4, Chapter 1, viii. Quotation taken from the Oxford University Press edition of 1906, p. 190.

[10] Sumption, *Pilgrimage*, p. 300; Webb, *Pilgrimage in Medieval England*, p. 243.

[11] There is a welcome relief from the abuse of actual pilgrimage in *The Pylgrimage of Perfection* (1526), attributed to W. Bonde, which constantly explains the meaning of the Christian metaphor in terms of the experiences of pilgrims to the Holy Land. See for example Book 2, Chapter 4.

repudiation of the essential metaphor, begins early, and doesn't seem to end.

The crucial sentence from the first epistle of Peter, discussed above, is quoted in its Latin form in the English instructions for nuns known as *Ancrene Wisse*, dated 1190–1210.[12] The author at this point is closely following a sermon by St Bernard of Clairvaux (1090–1153). He translates *aduenas & peregrinos* as 'elþeodie & pilegrimes' [foreigners and pilgrims]. The author's purpose is to accept what he takes to be Peter's metaphor of Christians as pilgrims and to commend it, but then to show its insufficiency, and provide a better comparison. A good Christian is indeed like a good pilgrim in concentrating wholly on his destination, and in carrying nothing with him save essentials for his journey. Indeed, the spiritual pilgrim is the best kind of pilgrim, for whereas the real pilgrim is satisfied with the bones of St James or St Giles, the spiritual pilgrim is on the way to find God himself. The further we go, however, the more we find the weakness of the comparison. Earthly pilgrims on their way to a shrine get distracted and held up. All sorts of hindrances prevent them from accomplishing their journey. A better image for Christians to employ is that of dying to this world and living in Christ. And better than that is the image of hanging in anguish and shame on the cross of Christ.

The severest challenge in English medieval literature to the validity of the metaphor of pilgrimage for the life of the committed Christian must be Langland's *Piers Plowman*. Langland is so hostile to real pilgrims that we might suppose he would have no time anyway for pilgrimage as a metaphor. But that is not the reason why pilgrimage, as metaphor or allegory, is a recurrent feature of his poem, and keeps evaporating, disintegrating, collapsing – and reappearing.

In Passus v the assembled folk want to find Truth, but don't know the way there (lines 510–13).[13] A 'real' pilgrim appears, plastered with

---

[12] See Geoffrey Shepherd's edition of *Ancrene Wisse* for Nelson's Medieval and Renaissance Library (London: Nelson, 1959), pp. XXIII and 3.

[13] I use the second Everyman edition by A. V. C. Schmidt, *The Vision of Piers Plowman: A Critical Edition of the B-Text* (London: Dent, 1995). Where quotations are followed by translations these are based on Schmidt's World's Classics translation *Piers Plowman: A New Translation of the B-Text* (Oxford: Oxford University Press, 1992).

souvenirs of his visits to the Holy Land, Rome, Galicia and other places. They ask him if he knows the way to Truth.

> 'Nay, so me God helpe!' seide the gome thanne.
> I seigh never palmere with pyk ne with scrippe
> Asken after hym er now in this place.   (534–6)

('Heavens, no!' the fellow replied. 'I've never seen any pilgrim go looking for him with staff and scrip: never, I can tell you, and nowhere!')

Piers the ploughman now enters the poem. He knows Truth; he has been tilling Truth's land, sowing his seed and minding his animals for forty years. Piers's activities, based at his home, are both real and allegorical. He feeds his neighbours and the poor with food and also with what Truth teaches him. Piers counters the journeys undertaken by the pilgrim with the proposal of a more profitable journey. 'Ac if ye wilneth to wende wel, this is the wey thider' (560). The Passus ends with Piers's description of the journey and the reaction of his awed listeners. Piers makes it a very realistic journey through field and ford, brook and hill, but every place to be negotiated is a recommendation of good conduct. Honour your parents, do not take the Lord's name in vain, do not steal, bear no false witness. Piers's journey is not in the least a Bunyanesque struggle to push oneself forward through the difficulties facing a Christian. It's more a series of biblical injunctions hung up like clues in a treasure hunt. That's until we reach the destination, which seems to give point to the journey-metaphor before it explains why it was so feeble. This is a castle, 'a court as cler as the sonne' (585), whose gatekeeper is Grace.

> And if Grace graunte thee to go in in this wise
> Thow shalt see in thiselve Truthe sitte in thyn herte
> In a cheyne of charite[.]   (605–7)

The end of Piers's 'journey' is to find that Truth sits in your own heart. Piers counters the travel which is offered by the 'paynim' pilgrim (516) with the fancy of a better journey, which is not a journey at all, and which denies the suitability of the journey metaphor, because what Christian insight and Christian instruction have to offer in the stronghold of the Christian faith is a new discovery of the self.

Despite the deep ambiguity of the travel which Piers has just narrated to the assembly, he now offers to lead the expedition to Truth! But first he has to plough his half-acre.

> 'And I shal apparaille me,' quod Perkyn, 'in pilgrymes wise
> And wende with yow I wile til we fynde Truthe.'
>
> (Passus VI, 57–8)

The pilgrim's garments which Piers assumes, however, are his own working-clothes, and he goes on ploughing his land with the assistance of the other pilgrims. He promises that he *will* go on the pilgrimage, but he soon makes it clear that

> I wol worship therwith Truthe by my lyve,
> And ben His pilgrym atte plow for povere mennes sake.
>
> (101–2)

(I shall honour Truth while I live, and be his pilgrim by ploughing the earth for the benefit of the poor.)

So of course the story of the pilgrimage as a required journey fizzles out. It has never really had a chance as a metaphor of Christian development in competition with the metaphor of home-keeping husbandry. And to cap the moral, Passus VII begins with Truth rewarding Piers with an absolute pardon, and a command to stay at home and plough his land.

The poem has already established the insufficiency of the metaphor of the travelling pilgrim as an equation for the spiritual development of the Christian, but it has a very long way to go to show that Piers's achievement, fine though it is, is not the summation of Christian endeavour. The poem has to engage its dreamer in the prolonged enquiry for the nature not only of Dowel, but of Dobet and Dobest.

In Passus XIII pilgrimage emerges again, but in a different form. We meet Patience, a poor hermit dressed in pilgrim's clothes (29–30). He seems to be cast in the shape of the Irish *peregrini* whom I shall be discussing shortly – devout men who had chosen exile either to achieve holiness in solitude or to become missionaries in foreign parts. So when Conscience teams up with him (216) the pair set off, 'pilgrymes as it were', to carry the word of God to the common people. They are pilgrims in an older sense, *peregrini*, wandering exiles and missionaries.

But even in this much more limited sense, not expressing the great allegory of pilgrimage as the progress of the soul, the poem has little use for the image. The missionaries meet Everyman in the shape of Haukin the wafer-seller, and the pilgrimage disappears in the extensive treatment of Haukin's past, present and future.

Pilgrimage reappears, in its third and final guise, right at the end of the poem's protracted exploration of the true nature of holiness, which has involved the elevation of Piers into an image of Christ on earth. Conscience resolves to search for Piers, who embodies the truth of salvation in a way the church and the clergy cannot.

> 'By Crist!' quod Conscience tho, 'I wole bicome a pilgrym,
> And walken as wide as the world lasteth,
> To seken Piers the Plowman!'   (Passus XX, 381–3)

So in the end the pilgrimage becomes a quest, a search for the true meaning of Christianity in human life. Pilgrimage becomes the duty of the painful search which Langland himself has tried to carry out. It is not the difficult progress towards the known shrine but the journey to discover the shrine which real pilgrims and clergy evade. The end is not known except through the journey. Langland bestows immense strength on the metaphor of pilgrimage by questioning its usefulness.

Langland had many followers in succeeding centuries, as we shall see: writers who set against the imagery in which Christ urged men and women to follow him through a gate and along a path to a heavenly destination that other imagery blessing those who wait in patience and humility.

Behold, I stand at the door, and knock: if any man hear my voice, and open the door, I will come in to him, and will sup with him, and he with me. (Revelation 3:20)

There are those writers, Henry Vaughan chief among them,[14] who are more strongly attached to the image of waiting than to the image of travelling. They feel that there is altogether too much self-confidence in pilgrims who believe that once they have overcome the difficulties of their journey their future is assured. There is indeed more than

---

[14] See Chapter Four.

a hint of the heresy of the fourth-century Welshman Pelagius in the idea of pilgrimage. Pelagius believed that all were qualified for the kingdom of heaven, and that the grace of God was in proportion to human merit. Reward was therefore extended to those who exerted themselves. The pilgrim sets out to achieve his or her goal, and to receive the reward for that achievement. Set against this image of striving forward is Vaughan's love of preparing oneself in stillness for the visitation of the Lord, or indeed not going forward but retreating to the fast-receding home of the soul glimpsed in childhood. So the metaphor of pilgrimage in Vaughan tends to be an anti-pilgrimage metaphor.

To jump five hundred years, we shall find, in a later chapter, Emily Dickinson still asking about the fitness of the imagery of the pilgrim's progress.

> Will there really be a "Morning"?
> Is there such a thing as "Day"?
> Could I see it from the mountains
> If I were as tall as they?
>
> Has it feet like Water lilies?
> Has it feathers like a Bird?
> Is it brought from famous countries
> Of which I have never heard?
>
> Oh some Scholar! Oh some Sailor!
> Oh some Wise Man from the skies!
> Please to tell a little Pilgrim
> Where the place called "Morning" lies![15]

I return now to the history of *peregrinus*. For some centuries after Christ, the words '*peregrinus*' and '*peregrinatio*' had three bundles of meanings, which tended to overlap. At one extreme there are the

[15] Johnson 101 / Franklin 148. For the numbering of Emily Dickinson's poems, see Chapter Six, note 9. In line 5, Dickinson does not mean that water-lilies have feet. She means feet as beautiful as water-lilies. In *OED* (s. v. lily 4d) it is explained that 'lily-feet' was a Chinese term of admiration for women with bound feet. Christina Rossetti uses the phrase 'lily feet' in line 7 of 'The Convent Threshold' (see *The Complete Poems*, ed. R. W. Crump and Betty S. Flowers (Harmondsworth: Penguin, 2001), p. 56).

Latin non-religious meanings of wandering, and of being in a foreign land. At the other extreme we have 'pilgrim' and 'pilgrimage' in the strict sense of journeying to worship at a shrine. In between is the initial Christian connotation, of being an outcast on account of one's faith, journeying towards posthumous union with Christ. This last came to have a special meaning, literal and figurative at the same time, of travelling into exile in order to live a stricter life of spiritual commitment. These *peregrini* in the third sense were chiefly associated with Ireland. Diana Webb remarks that for the Venerable Bede, whose *History of the English Church* was completed in 731, 'true *peregrinatio* was self-exile for the love of God, which did not necessarily involve a known or defined destination'.[16] *Peregrini* might be hermits or they might be missionaries. They might set off in curraghs to find some remote place for the life of the solitary, or travel to lands where they might teach and proselytise.[17] Bede tells us much about St Fursa, 'a holy man from Ireland', 'of very noble Irish descent', *cupiens pro Domino . . . peregrinam ducere uitam* (anxious to live the life of a *peregrinus* for the Lord's sake). He came to East Anglia, where he was received by the king; he preached the gospel and converted many. He built a monastery, but resolved to end his life as a hermit. Forced to flee by invasions, he sailed to France, where, after building another monastery, he died.[18]

In writing of the Irish *peregrini* in his indispensable book *Pilgrimage: An Image of Mediaeval Religion*, Jonathan Sumption spoke of 'the idea of the aimless wanderer' and 'the popularity of aimless pilgrimage'.[19] But is the word 'aimless' right for those whose wanderings were inspired by and dedicated to the service of God? Their journeys may have been, at least at first, undirected, but the aim was clear enough: to leave the direction and destination to God. Nora

[16] Webb, *Pilgrimage in Medieval England*, p. 4.

[17] See Gwyn Jones, *The North Atlantic Saga* (London: Oxford University Press, 1964), pp. 5–6; T. M. Charles-Edwards, 'The Social Background to Irish *Peregrinatio*', *Celtica* 11 (1976), 43–55.

[18] *Bede's Ecclesiastical History*, ed. B. Colgrave and R. A. B. Mynors (Oxford: Clarendon Press, 1969), pp. 268, 274–6.

[19] Sumption, *Pilgrimage*, pp. 95, 97.

Chadwick has written very movingly about 'the special form of sanctity practised by the saints of the Celtic Church – poverty, asceticism,
solitude, contemplation'.[20] The ideals of *peregrinatio*, which led to the
formation of the great independent monasteries of Ireland, lost out
to the Rome-inspired church organisation at the Council of Whitby
in 663, but they are summed up in the *Old Irish Life of St Columba*
quoted by Nora Chadwick. True Christians are 'to leave their country
and their land, their wealth and their worldly delight for the sake of
the Lord of the Elements, and go in perfect pilgrimage in imitation
of Him'. This exile may be understood in both an allegorical and a
literal sense. A man may leave his fatherland 'in zeal of heart, though
not in body, being detained under authority in his own land', but this
allegorical exile is a second best. Those 'of the perfect pilgrimage'
leave their country altogether 'in body and soul'.[21] *Peregrinatio* as
exile was much more fruitful than *peregrinatio* as travel to a shrine,
and indeed the latter could be spurned as the Irish poet spurned it:
'To go to Rome / is much trouble, little profit; / The King whom
thou seekest there, / Unless thou bring Him with thee, thou wilt not
find.'[22]

An understanding of 'pilgrim' as *peregrinus* or wanderer continued to exist for centuries. The English reformers of the 1530s interestingly invoked the 'wandering' element in *peregrinus* in order to
denounce 'wandering to pilgrimages' in their Injunctions.[23] A pilgrimage can be either too much or too little of a purposeful journey.
A curious example of pilgrimage with the sole meaning of *peregrinus* as exile is the first quatrain of one of John Donne's Holy
Sonnets.

> Oh my blacke Soule! now thou art summoned
> By sicknesse, deaths herald, and champion;
> Thou art like a pilgrim, which abroad hath done
> Treason, and durst not turne to whence hee is fled . . .[24]

[20] Nora K. Chadwick, *The Age of the Saints in the Early Celtic Church* (London: Oxford
   University Press, 1963), p. 37.
[21] *Ibid.*, p. 83.   [22] *Ibid.*, p. 84.   [23] Duffy, *Stripping of the Altars*, pp. 407, 450.
[24] Quoted from John Donne, *The Divine Poems*, ed. Helen Gardner (Oxford: Clarendon
   Press, 1952), p. 7.

The word 'abroad' in the third line is in a thoroughly misleading position. The pilgrim is an exiled wanderer who has committed treason *at home*, has gone abroad and dare not return.

Dictionary definitions of the seventeeth and eighteenth centuries have different shades of interest in the complexity of the word 'pilgrim'. Thomas Blount, in *Glossographia* (1656), and Samuel Johnson, in his *Dictionary* of 1755, both give priority to the Latin meaning of '*peregrinus*', wanderer, consigning the 'common' acceptance of a devotional mission to a subordinate position. Blount says of 'pilgrim', 'one that travels into strange Countreys, commonly taken for him that goes in devotion to any holy place'. Johnson says: 'A traveller; a wanderer; particularly one who travels on a religious account'. However, Edward Phillips, in his *New World of English Words* (1658), had come down exclusively for 'one that travelleth out of devotion through strange Countries to visit holy places', and he was followed, in almost the same words, by John Kersey in his *Dictionarium* of 1708, and by Nathan Bailey in *Dictionarium Britannicum* (1730). In William Crakelt's humble version of John Entick's *Spelling Dictionary* for 'Artificers, Tradesmen, and Foreigners' (?1784) we find bluntly 'one who visits the shrines of saints'.[25] It was left to the incomparable Noah Webster, in his *American Dictionary* of 1828, to sort out the entanglements, as follows.

Pilgrim. 1. A wanderer: a traveler; particularly, one that travels to a distance from his own country to visit a holy place, or to pay his devotion to the remains of dead saints.
    2. In *Scripture*, one that has only a temporary residence on earth. Heb. xi.
Pilgrimage. 1. A long journey, particularly to some place deemed sacred and venerable, in order to pay devotion to the relics of some deceased saint . . .
    2. In *Scripture*, the journey of human life. Gen. xlvii.

It is evident that the multiplicity of meanings in '*peregrinatio*' has continued to cause problems. In his very popular translation of St Augustine's *Confessions* (written about AD 397) for the New American

---

[25] My copy is 1801, but Crakelt's first edition (*Entick's New Spelling Dictionary*) appeared in 1784. The first 'Entick' was published in 1764.

Library, Rex Warner translated *quamdiu peregrinor abs te*, which occurs when Augustine is speaking to God, with the words 'as long as I am on pilgrimage away from you'.[26] That is misleading. Augustine is clearly echoing 2 Corinthians 5:6: εἰδότες ὅτι ἐνδημοῦντες ἐν τῷ σώματι ἐκδημοῦμεν ἀπὸ τοῦ κυρίου. The Vulgate version is *scientes quoniam dum sumus in corpore peregrinamur a Domino*. The Authorised Version runs: 'knowing that, whilst we are at home in the body, we are absent from the Lord'. Augustine is not talking of being on a pilgrimage; so long as he is alive, he is travelling away from the Lord.[27]

In 1292 it was still necessary for Dante to worry about the confusion that lay within the word 'pilgrim'. In the last but two of the sections of *La Vita Nuova* (variously XL or XLI) he was led to his reflections by seeing a group of pilgrims who had come from a distant country to Florence on their way to Rome, to see the handkerchief of St Veronica, with its imprint of Christ's face. Well, he writes, I call them pilgrims, *peregrini*, in the broad sense of the term. After all, these people are travellers outside their own country. But properly this word '*peregrini*' is confined to those who travel to Galicia, to the shrine of St James at Compostela. For St James, dying far away from his own homeland, was truly an alien and an exile. Others who travel in the service of the Highest should also be given the names which are appropriate to the places they visit. Those who go overseas to the Holy Land we call palmers, *palmieri*, because of the branches of palm they bring back. Those who go to Rome we call *romei*, and it's to Rome that these people whom I call *peregrini* are going. It would seem that Dante is on the point of giving up the struggle to preserve the Latin *peregrinus* from the invading sense of pilgrim as shrine-visitor, but at least wants to keep it for that kind of pilgrim for whom it has some propriety. It is interesting that the word '*romei*', which had a long life in Italy, gave

[26] St Augustine, *The Confessions*, trans. Rex Warner (New York: The New American Library, 1963), p. 214 [X, 5].

[27] Samuel Purchas, however, in his inclusive definition of pilgrimage (see Chapter Five), included travel away from God: 'Thus is Mans whole life a Pilgrimage, either from God, as *Cains*, or from himself as *Abels*' (*Purchas His Pilgrimes* (1625), Book 1, Chapter 2).

us the name of the character who provides the most intense pilgrimage imagery in Shakespeare's works.

The first two cantos of *Childe Harold's Pilgrimage*, published in 1812, present a pilgrim in full Latin dress as wanderer and outsider. The 'Childe' is Byron's curious choice to present in Spenserian stanzas his own travels in Spain, Albania, Greece and so on in 1809–11. Harold, 'a shameless wight', who 'through Sin's long labyrinth had run' feels 'the fulness of satiety', and resolves to leave his native land, which he has come to loathe. This brooding sinner – 'Apart he stalk'd in joyless reverie' – requires a 'change of scene'. All this in the first six stanzas. Though this persona adumbrates the Byronic hero of the Eastern Tales, 'the wandering outlaw of his own dark mind' (III, 3), he is not really essential for Byron's travelogue, and has to be forcibly recalled: 'But where is Harold? Shall I then forget / To urge the gloomy wanderer o'er the wave?' (II, 16). In the much more mature meditations which make up the third and fourth cantos of the poem, published after Byron had indeed exiled himself from England (1816 and 1818), the Childe is more or less forgotten, and, so far as he enters the poem, gets in the way of Byron's development of his own persona.[28] He is affectionately despatched, however, now wearing 'his sandal-shoon and scallop shell', at the end of Canto IV, 'But where is he, the Pilgrim of my song . . .? . . . He is no more – these breathings are his last.' Byron's *peregrinus* is idiosyncratic and undeveloped, but those breathings were not his last. From him grew his major studies in alienation, in *Manfred*, and above all in *Cain* (1821). Cain kills his conformist brother in an unwitting frenzy, when Lucifer's words have confirmed and deepened his own doubts of God's dealings with mankind, and he is condemned to spend his life as a wandering fugitive. There is certainly a hint, in Byron's portrayal of his majestic outlaws, of that dichotomy in the Latin word '*sacer*', by which it can mean either sacred or accursed. The idea that, rather than promoting received religion, a pilgrim might actually be questioning it, in search of an alternative fulfilment, runs the risk of stretching the definition of

[28] See Vincent Newey, 'Authoring the Self: *Childe Harold* III and IV', in *Byron and the Limits of Fiction*, ed. B. Beatty and V. Newey (Liverpool: Liverpool University Press, 1988), pp. 148–90.

pilgrimage to breaking point.[29] The title of 'pilgrim' in those circumstances ought to be reserved for those outsiders genuinely in quest of alternative shrines: a different form of sacredness. All the same, alienation is one of the most significant strands of meaning in the words 'pilgrim' and 'pilgrimage'. The alienation from conventional thought and behaviour, which for the early Christians was their distinguishing mark and in Bunyan's way of thinking remained so, might well become the mark of those who rebelled against Christianity when that became conventional. For me, the symbol of a Christianity which has become ossified into an unimaginative orthodoxy is St Ronan, the bishop who in the early Irish work *Buile Suibhne*, translated by Seamus Heaney as *Sweeney Astray*, puts a dreadful curse upon his opponent, the bird-man king of Dal-Arie.[30] Of course, the king on whom the curse falls, Sweeney (a *peregrinus* if anyone is), was also a Christian, but in the wanderings of his exile his faith deepens to a level unimaginable by St Ronan. Another religious 'exile' is the speaker of the unrivalled pilgrim-poem, *The Passionate Man's Pilgrimage* (1604) ('Give me my scallop shell of quiet'), a Catholic awaiting execution for his faith – as I understand the poem.[31]

There are many strands in the word 'pilgrim', and they all need to be kept in mind. It is a useful initial grouping to think of two kinds of pilgrim, and the metaphorical nimbus around each: first the pilgrim who journeys to a shrine, hoping for communication with higher powers, and second the pilgrim whom I call *peregrinus*, who has already received illumination and now travels to deepen and spread that illumination either as a solitary or as a missionary.

---

[29] This is not to quarrel with the excellent critical analyses in Barry Qualls's book, *The Secular Pilgrims of Victorian Fiction* (Cambridge: Cambridge University Press, 1982).
[30] See Chapter Eight.   [31] See Chapter Four.

CHAPTER 2

Walsingham

Early in his reign, Henry VIII made a pilgrimage to the shrine of Our Lady of Walsingham in northern Norfolk. He halted at the chapel of Houghton St Giles, a mile and a half away, took off his shoes and walked the rest of the way barefoot. Perhaps he was praying for a son and heir. In January 1511 he was back at Walsingham, presumably to give thanks, immediately after the birth of Prince Henry. The child did not live, but Henry and Queen Katharine continued their benefactions to the shrine until the 1530s.[1]

King Henry was continuing a long tradition of royal patronage towards Walsingham. The shrine had been founded about the year 1130, when the widow Richelde de Fervaques built a chapel to resemble the House of the Annunciation in Nazareth – which her son Geoffrey had recently visited. This son founded a priory at Walsingham about the year 1150, and the Austin canons took charge of the shrine. The chapel originally contained a statue of the Angel Gabriel, but its glory and its fame were due to a statue of the Virgin and Child. King Henry II was a frequent visitor to the shrine and made many benefactions, including in 1246 twenty marks for a golden crown for the statue of the Virgin. His son Edward I made almost annual visits and there are records of the pilgrimages of Edward II, Edward III and Richard II. Visits by Henry V and Henry VI are recorded, and in 1487 Henry VII 'came to the place called Walsingham where he prayed devoutly before the image of the Blessed Virgin Mary . . . that he might be preserved from the wiles of his enemies'.[2]

---

[1] My chief authority for the history of Walsingham is J. C. Dickinson, *The Shrine of Our Lady of Walsingham* (Cambridge: Cambridge University Press, 1956).

[2] So Polydore Vergil, quoted by Dickinson, *Shrine of Our Lady*, pp. 41–2.

Walsingham was a shrine of major importance, the objective of thousands of unrecorded pilgrimages, and with the gifts of royalty, the aristocracy and ordinary people its possessions and wealth increased enormously. Erasmus visited the shrine in 1512 or soon after, and wrote about his experience in 1526, as a dialogue between the gently sceptical Menedemus and the fervent pilgrim Ogygius, who sought from the Virgin 'the health of his family, the increase of his estate, a long and happy life in this world, and eternal happiness in the next'.[3] Menedemus is particularly unimpressed by the Milk of the Virgin, which the priory had acquired.

Inevitably a shrine as notable as Walsingham was to the fore in the attacks of the Reformation, when the indignation of centuries against abuses perceived in the theory and practice of pilgrimage added fuel to the fires.[4] In 1534, the prior and canons signed a deed accepting Henry VIII as head of the English Church and rejecting the authority of the Pope. There were visitations, valuations, investigations. Smaller monasteries were dissolved in 1536. The northern rising of 1536, the Pilgrimage of Grace (originally the Pilgrimage *for* Grace), was force-fully and effectively put down, but in the spring of 1537 rumours of 'a great insurrection like to be among the King's subjects about Walsyngham' brought a brutal response, and George Gysburghe was drawn, hanged, beheaded and quartered at Walsingham, with nine others sharing the same fate at other places in Norfolk.[5] By January 1538, as the prior later informed Thomas Cromwell, the statue of Our Lady and the gold and silver about it had been taken away by the royal commissioners. A woman was carted and stocked in Walsingham that winter for spreading rumours that the statue was continuing to work miracles.[6] The statue had been taken to London where Cromwell him-self took charge of it, with others, at Chelsea. Hugh Latimer wrote to Cromwell in June urging the destruction of these images which

---

[3] Erasmus, *Pilgrimages to Saint Mary of Walsingham and Saint Thomas of Canterbury*, ed. J. G. Nichols (1849), p. 11.

[4] The abuses of theory included the doctrine of Purgatory and the veneration of images; the practical abuses included the multiplication of saints, shrines and relics, and the stories of miracles of healing.

[5] Dickinson, *Shrine of Our Lady*, pp. 63–4.

[6] Eamon Duffy, *The Stripping of the Altars: Traditional Religion in England, c. 1400–c. 1580* (New Haven and London: Yale University Press, 1992), p. 403.

had been collected. 'Our great Sibyll' of Worcester (in Latimer's own diocese) 'hath been the devil's instrument to bring many (I fear) to eternal fire', he wrote. He suggested that 'she herself, with her old sister of Walsingham' – and three others he names – 'would make a jolly muster in Smithfield; they would not be all day in burning'.[7] The statue was destroyed soon afterwards. On 4 August 1538, the prior of Walsingham and his canons, facing the royal commissioners in the chapter-house of the priory, signed the deed surrendering their house with all its possessions to the king.[8]

It can't have been long after this that an unknown poet composed his lament for the destruction of the Walsingham shrine. It survives in a manuscript copy now in the Bodleian.[9]

> In the wrackes of Walsingam,
>   Whom should I chuse
> But the Queene of Walsingam
>   To be guide to my muse?
>
> Then thou, Prince of Walsingam,
>   Graunt me to frame
> Bitter plaintes to rewe thy wronge,
>   Bitter wo for thy name.
>
> Bitter was it, Oh, to see
>   The seely sheepe
> Murdred by the raveninge wolves,
>   While the sheephards did sleep.
>
> Bitter was it, Oh, to vewe
>   The sacred vyne,
> Whiles the gardiners plaied all close,
>   Rooted up by the swine.
>
> Bitter, bitter, Oh, to behould
>   The grasse to growe
> Where the walles of Walsingam
>   So statly did shewe.

[7] *Sermons and Remains of Hugh Latimer*, ed. G. E. Corrie (Parker Society, 1845), p. 395.
[8] Dickinson, *Shrine of Our Lady*, p. 66.
[9] Text by permission of the Bodleian Library, University of Oxford; Rawlinson Poet. 219, f.16r–v. I have modernised the punctuation and divided the original into quatrains. In l. 13 the MS reads 'wewe'; in l. 20 'sheue'; in l. 41 'or'.

Such were the works of Walsingam
    While shee did stand;
Such are the wrackes as now do shewe
    Of that holy land.

Levell, levell with the ground
    The towres doe lye,
Which with their golden glitteringe tops
    Pearsed once to the skye.

Where weare gates no gates ar nowe;
    The waies unknowen
Where the presse of peares did passe,
    While her fame far was blowen.

Oules do scrike[10] wher the sweetest himnes
    Lately weer songe;
Toades and serpents hold ther dennes
    Wher the palmers did thronge.

Weepe, weepe, O Walsingam,
    Whose dayes are nightes;
Blessings turned to blasphemies,
    Holy deeds to dispites.

Sinne is where our Ladie sate,
    Heaven turned is to hell;
Sathan sittes wher our Lord did swaye;
    Walsingam, Oh, farewell.

Since we are concerned with images, it is worth pausing on the vehemence of Latimer's hostility to images, though his were of wood and stone and ours are of words.[11] In his sermon to the Convocation of the Clergy in 1536 he spoke of 'dead images' which were 'set up, only to represent things absent', and he inveighed against the practice of clothing these images of saints 'with silk garments . . . with precious gems and jewels . . . as who should say, here no cost can be too great'. This at a time of 'scarceness and penury', when 'we see Christ's faithful

---

[10] I.e., Owls do shriek.
[11] For the debate on images, with a very large bibliography, see Colin Morris and Peter Roberts, *Pilgrimage: The English Experience from Becket to Bunyan* (Cambridge: Cambridge University Press, 2002), esp. p. 5.

and lively images . . . to be an hungred, a-thirst, a-cold, . . . wrapped in all wretchedness'. People are led to believe that devotion to dead images is 'more acceptable to God than works of mercy', and that to behold an image 'though it be but a Pater-noster while' is more efficacious than 'reading and contemplation in scripture' for seven years' space.[12]

These images are images of saints. Saints in themselves did not have the power imputed to them by pilgrims. 'They be not our mediators by way of redemption', Latimer writes. 'The blood of martyrs hath nothing to do by way of redemption.' 'Christ alone is our mediator', and 'we may pray to God ourselves'.[13] And now 'images of saints are called saints'. But 'dead images are not to be prayed unto'. They are not true persons. To pray to a statue is to take the dead for the living, the image for the substance, the absent for the present, the shadow for the substance, the estuary for the source, the false for the true – and thus the devil for God. These images do have their potency! It is essential, he told Convocation, 'to take utterly away these deceitful and juggling images'.[14]

For Latimer the prime symbol of the great error of confusing the real and the unreal was to kiss an image. The Injunctions of 1538 express their revulsion in the phrase 'kissing or licking' images or relics.[15] Among the impostures of Rome listed by Latimer are 'osculares for kissers'.[16] 'Osculares' was not otherwise known to the *Oxford English Dictionary*, but it assumed it was the same as 'osculatory': 'A painted, stamped, or carved representation of Christ or the Virgin, formerly kissed by the priest and people during Mass.'

In almost everything he said against images, Latimer was rehearsing themes and ideas initiated by the Lollards which had become well-worn by reiteration for the best part of a century and a half. The attack on images is regarded by Margaret Aston as fundamental to Lollardy.[17] For Wycliffe, images themselves were not so offensive as the worship of them, but succeeding generations were not so soft, and

[12] *Sermons by Hugh Latimer*, ed. G. E. Corrie (Parker Society, 1844), pp. 36–7.
[13] Latimer, *Sermons and Remains*, pp. 233–4.   [14] Latimer, *Sermons*, p. 55.
[15] Duffy, *Stripping of the Altars*, p. 407.   [16] Latimer, *Sermons*, pp. 49–50.
[17] Margaret Aston, *Lollards and Reformers: Images and Literacy in Late Medieval Religion* (London: Hambledon Press, 1984), pp. 135–92.

the thunder of the decalogue – 'Thou shalt make thee no graven image of any manner likeness that is in heaven above'[18] – accompanied the insistence of the New Testament that God 'dwelleth not in temples made with hands'.[19] The only image of God was the human person He had created, and to decorate dead images with gold was to insult the suffering of that living image. It was claimed that St Augustine himself had condemned the revolting practice of kissing statues.[20] Some reformers tried to limit the attack on images to sculpture, but a defender of images such as Bishop Pecocke had no difficulty in pointing out that there was no possible point of arrest in the slide towards the image-making of painting and weaving – and writing.[21] Not only in his attack upon images but also in his preferred way of disposing of them was Latimer voicing well-worn arguments. Burning had long been recommended on Old Testament authority, and as a quick means of disproving miraculous intervention.[22]

The most vigorous defence of images at this time is in the first two books of Sir Thomas More's *Dialogue Concerning Heresies* (1529), which provides arguments against Lutheran attacks on 'praying to saints, worshipping of images, and going on pilgrimages'. We live in a world of representation, argued More. Representation is fundamental to language and fundamental to worship. 'All the wordes that be eyther wrytten or spoken be but ymages representyng the thinges that ye wryter or speker conceyveth in his mynde.'[23] A pilgrim doing reverence to an image was not 'fyxynge his fynall intente in the ymage'.[24] The name of Jesus is to be reverenced and held in honour, but 'that name of Jesus is nothyng els but a worde whiche by wrytyng or by

---

[18] Deuteronomy 5:8, as in *Tyndale's Old Testament* (1530), ed. D. Daniel (New Haven and London: Yale University Press, 1992).

[19] Acts of the Apostles 7:48; 17:24.   [20] Aston, *Lollards and Reformers*, p. 151.

[21] *Ibid.*, p. 183; cf. Diana Webb, *Pilgrimage in Medieval England* (London and New York: Hambledon and London 2000), p. 248.

[22] Aston, *Lollards and Reformers*, pp. 169–70.

[23] Thomas More, *Dialogue Concerning Heresies*, in *The Complete Works of Sir Thomas More*, vol. VI, pt. I, ed. T. M. C. Lawler *et al.* (New Haven and London: Yale University Press, 1981), p. 46. The development of More's views in later editions of the *Dialogue* is expounded by Margaret Aston in *England's Iconoclasts*, vol. I (Oxford: Clarendon Press, 1988), pp. 173–88.

[24] More, *Dialogue*, p. 45.

voyce representeth unto the herer the person of our Savyor Christ . . .
Why and with what reason can they dyspyse a fygure of hym carved
or paynted . . .?'[25]

Those who attacked images made of stone commonly used images
made of words. As we have seen,[26] Lollards were given to describing
the experience of the soul as a pilgrim's journey. Appearing before the
Archbishop of Canterbury in 1431, Thomas Bagley said, 'I believe that
every traveller is a pilgrim on earth; the end of his pilgrimage ought to
be the celestial fatherland . . .'[27] It is perhaps to Latimer's credit that,
when this arch-enemy of images set about creating a similar parable
of pilgrimage, his imagination faltered and failed. He began a sermon
in Lincolnshire in 1552 with the following words.

Dearly beloved in our Saviour Christ, I have to tell you at this present time
of a certain pilgrimage: but ye shall not think that I will speak of the popish
pilgrimage, which we were wont to use in times past, in running hither and
thither to Mr John Shorn,[28] or to our Lady of Walsingham. No, no; I will not
speak of such fooleries, but I will speak of such a pilgrimage, which our Saviour
Christ himself taught us, being here present with us, with his own mouth.
Therefore, whosoever will come to the eternal felicity, must go that pilgrimage;
else he shall never attain thereunto.[29]

This is to be a pilgrimage 'of eight miles, or of eight days' journeys',
but these eight miles turn out to be the Beatitudes of the Sermon on
the Mount, beginning with 'Blessed be the poor'. Latimer eschews all
images of journeying, and what he has to say is entirely injunction and
preachment. Until, that is, we reach the end of the 'eight days'. 'Now
ye have heard which is the way to heaven, what manner a pilgrimage
we must go.' Now 'the questmonger . . . shall have his reward of God'.
This curious word 'questmonger' is used only in a derogatory way by
Langland and others. Latimer himself uses the word several times in
another sermon,[30] and it seems to refer to a kind of professional juror,
a legalist open to bribes. Here the questmonger is one who insists that

---

[25] *Ibid.*, p. 39–40.   [26] See above, p. 12.
[27] Webb, *Pilgrimage in Medieval England*, p. 247.
[28] John Shorn or Schorn was rector at North Marston in Buckinghamshire in the early
fourteenth century. His shrine was greatly valued by those who sought a cure for the
ague.
[29] Latimer, *Sermons*, pp. 474ff.   [30] *Ibid.*, pp. 379–80.

the allegory of pilgrimage is to be taken literally. He has performed the journey and reached the destination (eternal felicity). Latimer has to undeceive him and show that doctrinally the metaphor of destination does not work. It is not the merits of the journeying Christian that count, but the merits of Christ.

Then shall the end be, *Merces vestra erit multa in coelis*; 'Your reward shall be great in heaven.' *Merces*, 'Reward.' This word soundeth as though we should merit somewhat by our own works: for reward and merit are correspondent, one followeth the other; when I have merited, then I ought to have my reward. But we shall not think so: for ye must understand, that all our works are imperfect.

Only faith and belief can secure the reward of everlasting life. But Latimer cannot deny his pilgrim the benefits of his good works. So, he argues, every man shall be rewarded for his good works *in* everlasting life, but not *with* everlasting life (my italics). Latimer's allegory of a pilgrimage is a pilgrimage in name only. He has no use for images of the journey, and the image of arrival is so misleading that the expectations it arouses have to be explained away.

In spite of the attacks on the false expectations of ignorant and deluded pilgrims, it looks as though it is not pilgrimage itself that is the enemy of the reformers but the images to which the pilgrims are drawn. It is these statues that are evil, and the erroneous theology in which they prosper. These graven images have to go, and with them the shrines which house them, and the whole support system of the church which maintains them. It was the contention of Sir Thomas More that the abuse of pilgrimage did not condemn the whole practice. The issue was, he said, 'whether yᵉ thyng yᵗ we speke of as prayeing to sayntes, goyng in pylgrymage, and worshypyng relykes and ymages may be done well. Not whether it may be done evyll. For if it may be well done, then though many wold mysse use it, yet doth all that nothynge mynyshe yᵉ goodnes of the thynge selfe.'[31] That was written in 1528. A few years afterwards, however, the shrines were destroyed, the abbeys and monasteries closed, and, its life-blood cut off, pilgrimage died.

Judging from the popularity of the music in Elizabethan times, and the number of late versions and allusions, the old Walsingham ballad, in

[31] More, *Dialogue*, p. 235 (see note 23).

which a deserted lover asks a pilgrim returning from the shrine whether he has seen the absent loved one, must have been very well known. But no early version exists. The best-known version is one copied into a commonplace book, now in the Bodleian, to which the copyist appended the initials 'Sir W. R.' (presumably Sir Walter Ralegh).[32]

Lover   As you went to Walsingam,
                To that holy lande,
            Met you not with my true love
                By the way as you went?

Pilgrim How shall I know your trew love   5
                That have mett many one
            As I went to the holy lande
                That have come, that have gone?

Lover   She is neyther whyte nor browne
                Butt as the heavens fayre;   10
            There is none hath a form so devine
                In the earth or the ayre.

Pilgrim Such a one did I meet, good Sir,
                Suche an Angelyke face,
            Who lyke a queene, lyke a nymph did appere   15
                By her gate, by her grace.

Lover   She hath left me here all alone,
                All alone as unknowne,
            Who sometymes did me lead with her selfe
                And me lovde as her owne.   20

Pilgrim What's the cause that she leaves you alone
                And a new waye doth take,
            Who loved you once as her owne
                And her joye did you make?

---

[32] Text by permission of the Bodleian Library, University of Oxford; from Rawlinson Poet. 85, f. 123r–v (see illustration 1). Peter Beal, in his *Index of English Literary Manuscripts*, vol. 1, 1450–1625, Parts 1–2 (London: Mansell; New York: Bowker, 1980), Part 2, p. 378 (RaW 4), says that the notebook is 'a miscellany compiled by a Cambridge student, possibly Sir John Finett (1571–1641) of Fordwich, Kent; c. 1586–91'. I have divided the poem into quatrains, modernised the punctuation and made two slight emendations. I have also indicated the speakers in the dialogue as I understand them; there are other ways of reading the poem (see p. 36).

Lover	I have lovde her all my youth,	25
	Butt now ould, as you see,	
	Love lykes not the fallyng frute	
	From the wythered tree.	

Pilgrim	Know that love is a careless chylld	
	And forgetts promysse paste,	30
	He is blynd, he is deaff when he lyste,	
	And in faythe never faste.	

His desyre is a durelesse contente
And a trustless joye,
He is wonn with a world of despayre 35
And is lost with a toye.

Lover	Of women kynde suche indeed is the love,	
	Or the word Love abused,	
	Under which many chyldish desyres	
	And conceytes are excusde.	40

Butt Love is a durable fyre
In the mynde ever burnynge;
Never sicke, never ould, never dead,
From itt selfe never turnynge.

It will be seen that this differs from the received version of Ralegh's poem, as it is given in the editions of Ralegh's poetry by Agnes Latham and Michael Rudick,[33] as well as in countless anthologies. Both Latham and Rudick print a different first stanza, as follows.

As you came from the holy lande
Of Walsinghame,
Mett you not with my true love
By the way as you came?

Latham writes that this stanza is a 'correction' of the one I have given; Rudick states that the original stanza has been 'cancelled'. A glance at the photograph (illustration 1) will show that the original stanza has

---

[33] *The Poems of Sir Walter Ralegh*, ed. Agnes Latham (London: Routledge and Kegan Paul, 1951), pp. 22–3; and *The Poems of Sir Walter Ralegh: A Historical Edition*, ed. Michael Rudick (Tempe, Ariz.: Arizona Center for Medieval and Renaissance Studies in conjunction with the Renaissance English Text Society, 1999), pp. 16–17. Subsequent quotations from Ralegh's 'The Ocean to Cynthia' are from Latham's edition, with modernised spelling.

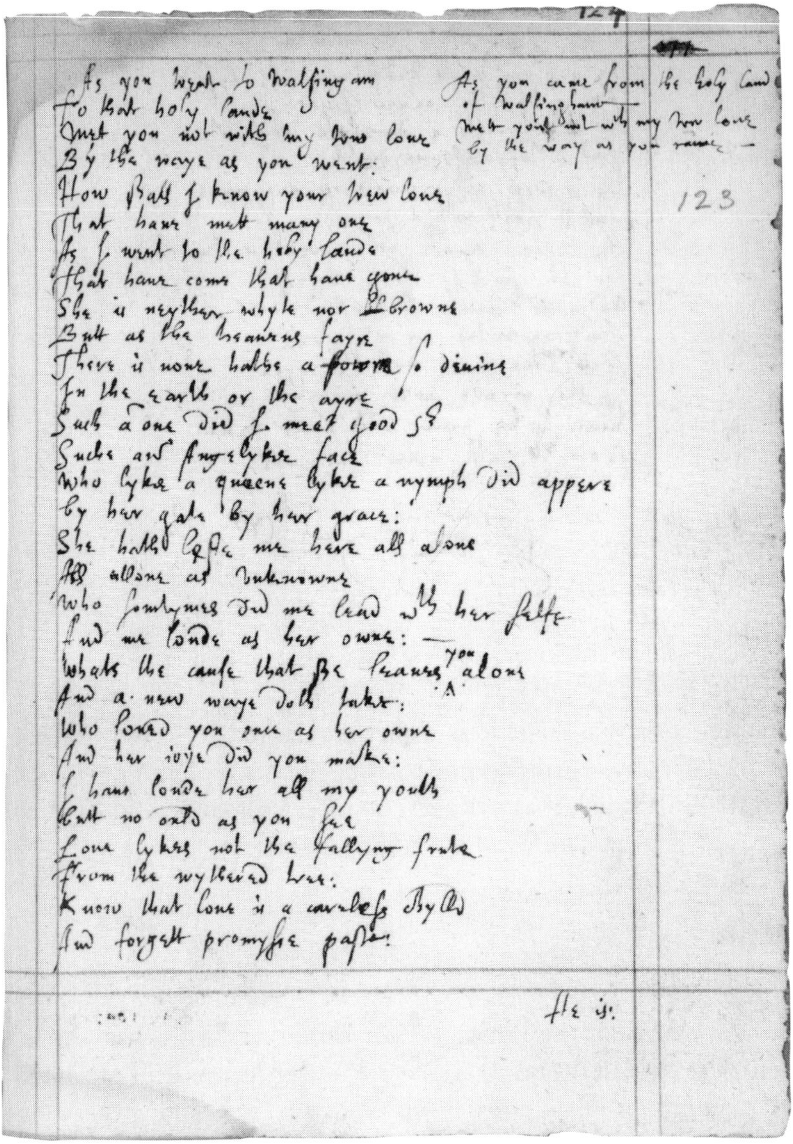

Illustration 1. The Walsingham Ballad. Bodleian Library, Oxford.

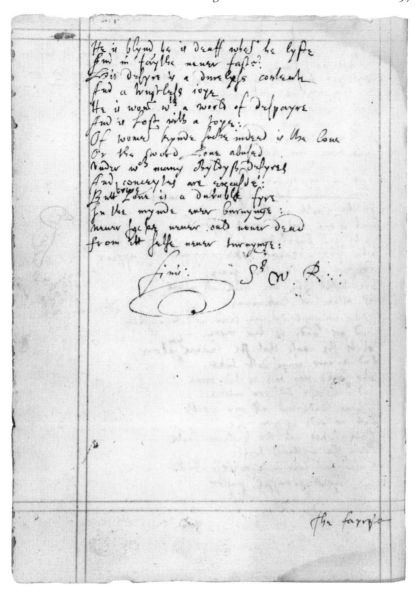

Illustration 1. (*cont.*)

not in fact been deleted. The new stanza has been written in smaller writing alongside the old. There is a second difference in my version; in line 41 the received text reads, 'But true love is a durable fire'. It will be seen from the photograph that the word 'true' has been inserted afterwards. Because both the writing and the pen seem to be slightly different, I take it that 'true' was not the correction of an omission, but a later addition.

I speculate that the copyist wrote out the poem as he had it before him (and as I have given it) and added, on whatever authority, the initials W. R. He then came across a very similar version of the poem, possibly the version that is printed in Thomas Deloney's *The Garland of Good Will*. (The latter was entered in the Stationers Register in 1593, but no edition earlier than 1631 survives.)[34] This gives the version of the first stanza as Latham and Rudick print it ('As you came from the holy land / Of Walsingham . . .'). I suggest that the copyist thought that this version, with its superior rhyme scheme, was worth noting and wrote it out without cancelling the other version. He probably noticed that the two versions are in conflict, because in line 7 of the original we have a repetition of '*went to* the holy land'. The Deloney version resolves this with its own repetition of 'came from' in line 7.

I have no doubt that the poem is Ralegh's, but my confidence depends on the distribution of the dialogue between the two speakers as I have indicated it. If we take it, as I think we must, that the pilgrim speaks the eighth and ninth stanzas ('Know that love is a careless chylld' down to 'And is lost with a toye') and that the lover responds with the final two stanzas, the ballad has a close relation with that long, rambling, inchoate masterpiece 'The Ocean to Cynthia', which is taken to express Ralegh's misery at the queen's rejection of his devotion. A courtier's personal commitment to his monarch is in that longer poem expressed in terms of the passionate and total commitment of a lover to his mistress. The mistress is not only of 'angel-like appearance' (line 112) but by her grace and absolute power had seemed to outgo

---

[34] There is another version, much like Deloney's, in a Huntington Library MS transcribed by Josephine W. Bennett in 'Early Texts of Two of Ralegh's Poems from a Huntington Manuscript', *Huntington Library Quarterly* 4 (1940–1), 473–4.

subjection to time and 'frail mortality', one 'whom love hath chose for his divinity' (188). But, after years of such worship, his adoration has had to admit its uncertainty. 'Yet hath her mind some marks of human race' (202). He is utterly rejected, and now –

> Writes in the dust, as one that could no more,
> Whom love and time and fortune had defaced
> (91–2)

There is no real progress in the poem. It endlessly debates the enigma of Cynthia, woman or goddess, whom he has served in all obedience, and who has now cast him out. Yet 'I powerless was to alter my desire;/ My love is not of time or bound to date' (300–1). His love is unquenchable, though its object flickers, vanishes, reforms and vanishes again before his gaze.

The similarity, in idea, in imagery and in vocabulary, between the short ballad of Walsingham and the 522-line poem to Cynthia, is remarkable. But what does the short poem say, being a dialogue with a veteran pilgrim who has just visited the shrine at Walsingham, which the long poem does not say? The question is, who gets the better of the interchange, the pilgrim or the lover? Within the ballad, the pilgrim, a figure from the past, confident in what an image of the Virgin means, is not given space to explain or commend *his* devotion – he doesn't need to; it's taken for granted. He only presents, as a consolation to the deserted lover, the case against human love, 'in faith never fast', 'won with a world of despair and lost with a toy.' The lover accepts the case, but argues that this scepticism applies only to the ordinary love of a man for a woman, and in the splendidly defiant last stanza describes something else.

> Butt Love is a durable fyre,
>   In the mynde ever burnynge;
> Never sicke, never ould, never dead,
>   From itt selfe never turnynge.

It is understandable that someone looking at the poem as it originally stood in the manuscript wanted to distinguish this 'love' and wrote in the word 'true'. But in the previous stanza the lover has made clear that ordinary love for women is an abuse of the word 'love'. The love he has for the queen is above this. Yet the queen whom he loved, and who returned his love, has now left him for others, behaving (in the standards of the poem) as a woman does. In so far as she is a woman, his beloved has gone, and with her the love that was between them. Even so, he had recognised in her something more than human – 'as the heavens fair . . . a form so divine' – and the pilgrim had recognised it too – 'an angel-like face . . . like a queen'. It must be this vestige of divinity that he continues to love, though its human embodiment has parted from him. But what *can* that mean?

The long poem 'The Ocean to Cynthia' never escapes from bewilderment, from the impossibility of resolving the incompatibles in the lover's situation: the beauty and majesty of Cynthia, the strength and truth of his adoration of her, the completeness of her renunciation of him, the hopelessness of his present plight. 'She is gone, she is lost! She is found, she is ever fair!' (493). There are glimpses of light like this, immediately extinguished. The poem is always trying to assert that a love as deep as his can never disappear – but its object is always vanishing. The last line is 'Her love hath end; my woe must ever last.' There is nothing here of the defiant final asseveration of the ballad, only the fleeting recognition, 'my love is not of time, or bound to date'.

There is no hint in that final stanza of the ballad that the lover has been converted to the divine love inspiring the pilgrim. The past cannot be recovered. By the time this version of the old ballad was written the shrine had been destroyed and with it the devotion that flowed through the image it contained. There is no possibility that what the poet meant by the durable fire of love was the image-free devotion of Latimer. A new image had been set up in the waste land, the image of Queen Elizabeth, head of the church in England, and the object of every poet's devotion. Ralegh himself is almost the symbol of the liberated intellect of the Reformation, a man of advanced views welcoming the approach of the new science, suspected indeed of 'atheism', enthusiastically and theatrically espousing the cause of Protestant England's nationalism and imperialism, spearheaded by a queen who was head of the English church. Yet Ralegh was a mass of contradictions, and perhaps he has in the ballad and in 'The Ocean to Cynthia' used what he sees as the betrayal of his devotion to the monarch to portray the hopelessness of substituting the queen for an image of the Virgin and Child. The ballad's last stanza reveals the inadequacy of what the Protestant mind had to offer to replace the certainties it had banished. The speaker in the poem has accepted a human image in place of the graven image to which the pilgrim bows, but this new object of devotion has shown an all too human face and disappeared, leaving the devotee to search for her while at the same time he climbs an uncertain neo-platonic ladder to protest that his unquenchable love belongs to a new idea and not to its image. It cannot be clear to the lover himself what he means by that 'durable fire from itself never turning'. The veteran pilgrim is tied to an old idea, whose images were burned at Smithfield, but in Ralegh's ballad he may get the best of the argument.

The next version of the ballad we have to consider is the one sung by Ophelia in her madness (*Hamlet*, Act 4 Scene 5, from line 21). What follows is based on the First Folio.

> *Enter Ophelia distracted.*
> *Ophelia.* Where is the beauteous majesty of Denmark?
> *Queen.* How now *Ophelia?*
> *Ophelia.* How should I your true love know
>   From another one?
>   By his cockle hat and staffe
>   And his sandal shoone.
> *Queen.* Alas sweet lady, what imports this song?
> *Ophelia.* Say you? Nay, pray you marke.
>   He is dead and gone lady,
>   He is dead and gone.
>   At his head a grasse-greene turfe,
>   At his heeles a stone.
>
> *Enter King.*
> *Queen.* Nay, but *Ophelia* –
> *Ophelia.* Pray you marke.
>   White his shrowd as the mountaine snow –
> *Queen.* Alas, looke heere my lord.
> *Ophelia.* Larded with sweet flowers,
>   Which bewept to the grave did not go,
>   With true-love showers.

Here the abandoned lover is a woman; her beloved has left her, and she believes he has gone on a pilgrimage; another pilgrim whom she questions has seen him – and seen his grave. I think it is very likely that all these elements were in the lost early version of the Walsingham ballad. That is to say, that it was a 'lover's complaint', a woman addressing a pilgrim returning from Walsingham, asking him for news, since she thinks her beloved had also been heading that way. That 'dead and gone' belongs to the original is suggested by the very free reworking of the old ballad by Robert Sidney (Sir Philip's brother). In his rather lengthy poem a woman interrogates a pilgrim returning from the east about her beloved, 'the knight that loves me best'. The pilgrim replies,

> Such a one I saw lady,
>   I once saw such a one,
> But him no more see shall I,
>   He is now dead and gone.[35]

Ophelia sings only fragments of the Walsingham ballad – she misses out the famous opening stanza – but it is richly suggestive that in her madness she should identify herself with a woman whose lover has parted from her to make his vows as a pilgrim.[36] It is the shaft of reason we expect in Shakespeare's scenes of madness. No more than a deep, scarcely conscious intuition on Ophelia's part, it portends not only a new understanding of Hamlet and the play, but also a new definition of pilgrimage.

The relationship between Hamlet and Ophelia is a perplexing and distressing element in Shakespeare's tragedy. At the beginning of the play they seem deeply in love. Ophelia tells her father that of late the prince has 'made many tenders / Of his affection to me', and has 'given countenance to his speech . . . / With almost all the holy vows of heaven' (1.3.99–100, 113–14). *She* is deeply in love. The quality of Hamlet's affection is harder to assess. His letter to Ophelia, which Polonius forces from her and reads out to the king, sounds affected and contrived, even as it affirms his love for her. 'That I love thee best, O most best, believe it' (2.2.120). By this stage, Polonius, believing that

---

[35] *The Poems of Robert Sidney*, ed. P. J. Croft (Oxford: Clarendon Press, 1984), p. 185.
[36] For helpful background about this, see Peter J. Seng, *The Vocal Songs in the Plays of Shakespeare* (Cambridge, Mass.: Harvard University Press, 1967), pp. 131–42.

the prince is only trifling with his daughter, has forbidden Ophelia to see Hamlet or receive any token from him, and she has obeyed him.

Ophelia knows nothing of Hamlet's encounter with the Ghost, who, seeming to be the spirit of his dead father released from Purgatory, tells his son his horrifying tale of adultery and murder, and demands revenge against the murderer, his brother Claudius. She knows nothing of this, nor of Hamlet's solemn vow of remembrance, nor of his proposal 'to put an antic disposition on' (1.5.172). But Hamlet's new life, so to call it, after his shattering meeting with the Ghost, is soon made known to her. She tells her father that Hamlet has burst into her closet, his clothes disordered, with an extraordinary look on his face, 'as if he had been loosèd out of hell', and, without speaking, has taken hold of her, gazed at her, then backed out again, with 'a sigh so piteous and profound / As it did seem to shatter all his bulk, / And end his being' (2.1.75–98).

It is not enough to say that the explanation of Hamlet's cruelty towards the young woman he has claimed to love is that she, in obedience to her father, has repelled him. The real reason (though nothing justifies his behaviour) lies deeper.

Hamlet's worst verbal abuse of Ophelia is in the 'nunnery' scene (3.1). Ophelia's response to his onslaught is that he is mad. 'Oh what a noble mind is here o'erthrown!' We know that Hamlet is not mad. His 'madness' is a cloak to conceal himself, his knowledge and his plans. But, in concealing himself, what does this master of irony reveal about himself? Here is the central passage.

Hamlet . . . I did love you once.
Ophelia Indeed my lord you made me believe so.
Hamlet You should not have believed me, for virtue cannot so inoculate our old stock but we shall relish of it. I loved you not.
Ophelia I was the more deceived.
Hamlet Get thee to a nunnery – why wouldst thou be a breeder of sinners? I am myself indifferent honest, but yet I could accuse me of such things that it were better my mother had not borne me. I am very proud, revengeful, ambitious, with more offences at my beck than I have thoughts to put them in, imagination to give them shape, or time to act them in. What should such fellows as I do, crawling between earth and heaven? We are arrant knaves all, believe none of us. Go thy ways to a nunnery.
(3.1.114–26)

Beneath the rant of the pretending madman lies a judgement on himself which is entirely unexpected. 'What should such fellows as I do,
crawling between earth and heaven?' Although the dominant meaning
of this is, 'What on earth are fellows like me up to?', it also takes its
place among the questions in which Hamlet pleads to know what he
is to do, the most famous of which is 'To be, or not to be, that is the
question'. When he first saw the Ghost, he asked, 'Say, why is this?
Wherefore? What should we do?' This kind of query puts us in mind
of the 'Man cloathed with Rags' whom Bunyan's dreamer beheld at
the start of *The Pilgrim's Progress*, who 'brake out with a lamentable
cry; saying, *what shall I do?*' The man in rags, with a great burden
on his back, found the answer to his question in the instruction to go
through a little wicket gate and begin his pilgrimage. It is not impossible that Hamlet also is looking for a gate. The burden on Christian's
back was his sins. What prompts Hamlet to declare in his supposed
madness, 'I could accuse me of such things that it were better my
mother had not borne me . . . with more offences at my beck than I
have thoughts to put them in . . . What should such fellows as I do,
crawling between earth and heaven? We are arrant knaves all'. This
farrago is designed to bewilder Ophelia, but it has a dangerous content
of Hamlet's true thoughts. In his first soliloquy (1.2.129–59) Hamlet
loftily blamed women for their moral weakness – 'frailty, thy name
is woman' – instancing his mother's sexual incontinence, her sexual
appetite. In the soliloquy which begins this third act ('To be, or not to
be . . .'), he raises himself above all sinners and protests that suicide
is the only way out of sin for a right-thinking person. But now, with
one of his mercurial changes, and in the ventriloquism of his antic
disposition, he is no longer pharisaical, and he includes himself in the
rottenness of the world, subject to the same temptations and failings
as everyone else.

Bunyan's Christian could only undertake *his* pilgrimage as a reluctant and sorrowful celibate (see Chapter Nine), and it is worth pursuing
the comparison to suggest that in order to fulfil his vow to his father,
which it seems he has interpreted as a duty to cleanse society – 'The
time is out of joint: O cursed spite / That ever I was born to set it right' –
Hamlet has also taken the path of celibacy, and has declared it twice

to the one person who has the power to make him take the other path: once in his invasion of Ophelia's closet, with the sigh which seemed to Ophelia to 'end his being', and now in this 'nunnery' scene, when he supposes himself alone with her.

'I did love you once', he says, but (he goes on) Ophelia should not have believed him, because 'virtue cannot so inoculate our old stock but we shall relish of it'. 'Inoculate' means to engraft, and 'our old stock' is our sexual appetite, which cannot be altered, Hamlet argues, by high-minded thoughts about the nobility of love. 'I loved you not.' It was not 'love' that moved him but the old, basic, universal sexual desire. So it is with the deepest seriousness beneath his 'madness' that Hamlet goes on to tell Ophelia that the only way that she can avoid the dictates of her nature – which will otherwise lead her to sin and to be the progenitor of sinners – is to enter a nunnery. There has been much misunderstanding of this scene since it was realised that in Elizabethan slang 'nunnery' could mean 'brothel'. 'Nunnery' could, and more generally did, mean a nunnery, a community of women dedicated to celibacy and chastity.

Of course we find it hateful for Hamlet to take this view of humanity, and to charge Ophelia so savagely. It makes it no better that he carries off his abuse of her as the rant of a madman. Presumably Shakespeare thought his behaviour hateful too; he charts the shifting judgement of his creature with frightening impartiality. All the same, what Hamlet appears to be proclaiming, through the distortion of his assumed role, is a view of humankind, engulfed in sin, particularly sexual sin, which was a view fundamental in Christian history, and certainly fundamental in the pre-Reformation ideal of society.

Ophelia bravely discounts what Hamlet is saying as sheer madness: his 'most sovereign reason' is 'out of time and harsh' (3.1.151–2). Later, when her father has met his death at the hands of this young man, everything seems different in the real madness which destroys *her* 'most sovereign reason'. She sings two songs, first snatches of the Walsingham ballad, and then a ballad for St Valentine's day, in which a maid knocks at her lover's window. He gets up and lets her in – 'Let in the maid that out a maid / Never departed more'.

> By Gis and by Saint Charity,
>   Alack and fie for shame,
> Young men will do't if they come to't –
>   By Cock, they are to blame.
>
> Quoth she, 'Before you tumbled me,
>   You promised me to wed.'
> 'So would I ha' done, by yonder sun,
>   And thou hadst not come to my bed.'
>
> (4.5.54–66)

In this ballad Ophelia does not, as some argue, hint at 'what actually happened' between herself and Hamlet. As history, it is as false as the first ballad, in which her lover has gone to be a pilgrim. A protected virgin acknowledges the truth of what Hamlet told her, acknowledges her own sexual longings, and faces what they might have led to. In accepting the 'truth' about her own nature, kept from her by the hypocrisy of her upbringing, she veers from one extreme to the other. How far she understands what she is saying and implying in her craziness is hard to say, but madness and insight are never far apart in Shakespeare. 'A document in madness' is what Laertes calls his sister's speech: by 'document' he means a lesson, or a warning. For the sake of the play, we have to heed the implication of Ophelia's songs. And the implication is that Hamlet has abused her and abandoned her because he has taken a vow as a pilgrim takes a vow. A new self has supervened, renouncing her as a potential whore as he has renounced himself as a potential seducer. Ophelia 'accepts' both the renunciation and the valuation. She glimpses that Hamlet's new life will lead to his death. It certainly leads to her own.

The nature of Hamlet's vow, and his erratic and doubt-ridden endorsement of it, is the subject of later chapters. What Ophelia has done in going to the old Walsingham ballad and applying it to her own circumstances is, quite unintentionally, to locate, in Hamlet, a new *peregrinus*, alienated and doomed.

CHAPTER 3

Shakespeare's pilgrims

The only real pilgrimage in Shakespeare occurs in a play which was not admitted into the First Folio: *Pericles, Prince of Tyre*. The language of the play is partly obscured in the murky waters of the surviving text, but there can be little doubt that one of the most adventurous of Shakespeare's late romances is there for us to rescue. The extraordinary story of endless misfortunes evolving into a happy outcome is presided over by Diana, goddess of chastity, and Neptune, god of the sea. Pericles has sought a bride at Antioch, but found incest instead. Pursued by Antiochus, he is shipwrecked and cast ashore at Pentapolis, where he wins Thaisa. Another voyage and another storm – in which Thaisa dies in childbirth and is buried at sea. But, her body being washed up at Ephesus, she is brought back to life by the mysterious art of Cerimon, and she retires to Diana's temple to lead the life of a nun. Pericles, supposing himself a widower, leaves his infant daughter Marina to be fostered. When she is fourteen, Marina survives a murderous attack by her foster-mother, but is kidnapped and sold into a brothel at Mytilene. She resists every attack on her virginity, and wins the protection of the ruler, Lysimachus. Pericles has been told that his daughter is dead, and he collapses into catatonic despair. When his ship puts into Mytilene, Lysimachus suggests that the remarkable young woman he has rescued from the brothel might help to cure him. So father and daughter are reunited. Diana then appears to Pericles in a vision.

> My temple stands in Ephesus. Hie thee thither,
> And do upon mine altar sacrifice. (5.1.240–1)

At Ephesus Pericles is reunited with Thaisa, and Thaisa with both her husband and her daughter.

The pilgrimage from Mytilene to Ephesus would not be much of a journey, a hundred miles or so by sea. The emphasis is entirely on the visit to the shrine, where Pericles tells his story and is recognised by one of the nuns – his wife, Thaisa. This pilgrimage is unique in Shakespeare, but the persuasion to believe that the incident is indeed Shakespeare's is strong. The ancient story of Apollonius of Tyre, the source of *Pericles*, with its magical conclusion in the temple of Diana at Ephesus, had been in Shakespeare's mind at the time of his earliest comedies, when he boldly used the romance as a frame in *The Comedy of Errors*. In that play, Antipholus of Syracuse, whose search for his brother is a pilgrimage of sorts, finally takes refuge in a holy place at Ephesus, here called a priory or an abbey, where all confusions are sorted out, and in the abbess the twins discover their long-lost mother, and Egeon his wife.

The Comedy of Errors is a Christian play, even though the Syracusans (with biblical authority) view Ephesus as a place of sorcery and witchcraft.[1] 'Here we wander in illusions', says Antipholus of Syracuse. 'Some blessèd power deliver us from hence!' (4.3.43–4). The power which delivers them is Christian not pagan. Diana makes no appearance in the play. What power does Diana of Ephesus represent in *Pericles, Prince of Tyre*?

It has been argued by F. Elizabeth Hart[2] that an Elizabethan audience would understand that Diana of Ephesus was 'distinct from Ovid's Diana, the chaste huntress and goddess of the moon', being rather an eastern mother-goddess having links with Cybele, 'a dual personification of the earth and moon, representing nature and fertility, cosmic as well as earthly time, and the life-and-death cycles of both human and vegetative existence'.

It is true that the text of *Pericles* is remarkably innocent of any allusion to Christianity or to Christian providence. But it is equally

---

[1] See Acts of the Apostles 19.
[2] F. Elizabeth Hart, 'Cerimon's Rough Music in *Pericles*, 3.2', *Shakespeare Quarterly* 51 (2000), 313–31.

true that the consistently invoked Diana stands for chastity and bears the traditional attributes of the goddess as they were recognised in the Christian era. The chastity she espouses is certainly a wide Spenserian concept, but that does not mean that Shakespeare knew of the famous many-breasted statue of Artemis at Ephesus – Artemis is what the Greek New Testament gave for the Vulgate's Diana of the Ephesians – or that Lucina, appearing twice in the play as goddess of childbirth (1.1.8 and 3.1.10), could be one of Diana's names. Possibly Shakespeare's awareness, from Acts of the Apostles 19, of the separateness from Christianity of the worship of Diana of the Ephesians gave him the freedom to create an image of the goddess as a controlling figure in the play, but she does not seem to me to import the pagan worship recounted by Elizabeth Hart.

The Diana of the text is the protectress of all women who honour chastity as virgins or married women and mothers. Thaisa, a mother who believes she has lost both husband and child, commits herself to celibacy as a 'votaress' of Diana, and dons a 'vestal livery'. Both she and her daughter Marina, who as a virgin metaphorically wears the 'silver livery' of Diana (5.3.7), are to find their fulfilment not in celibacy but in marriage. At Dian's altar, where he promises 'night-oblations', Pericles is reunited with his wife and accepts the marriage of Marina to Lysimachus.

At Mytilene, the inhabitants had been celebrating the annual feast in honour of the god Neptune, to whose capricious but in the end secondary power Pericles has been subject throughout the play. Marina, born at sea, inspired and protected in the brothel by Diana, is linked with the magus Cerimon who restored her mother to life – 'this man / Through whom the gods have shown their power' (5.3.59–60). Her art brings new life to her father, 'begets' him, in the electric words of this sometimes banal text. She joins him in his pilgrimage to the shrine of Diana at Ephesus, where their reward is the 'nativity' of which the abbess had spoken at the end of *The Comedy of Errors* – 'Go with me – / After so long grief, such nativity!' (5.1.406–7). The same kind of reunion and restoration has taken place at a shrine in the same town in two plays, of very different calibre, separated by years of writing.

Both plays depend on journeys, and journey's end in both is a holy place. Both the early play and the late play are prodigiously theatrical, and the ways in which loss and death are circumvented belong to the arts of the theatre more than to theology. Nevertheless, pilgrimage, overt in the later play, is subliminal in the earlier. A sense of the sacred emerges from the farcical mistakes of the earlier play and the romantic disasters of the later, and sets on both an unexpected seal of mystery and reverence.

Shakespeare treats pilgrimage with respect everywhere except in the second part of *Henry VI*, Act 2 Scene 1. There, at St Albans, with the royal party hawking and the nobles quarrelling, the townspeople break in, acclaiming the miracle that has restored sight to Simpcox. Simpcox is brought before them, with the holy monarch thanking God who gives light in darkness to believing souls. Simpcox says he was born blind and that St Alban appeared to him in a dream at his home in Berwick offering help if he visited his shrine. But he is exposed as a fraud by the good Duke Humphrey, who finds Simpcox has no problem in naming colours, and he is whipped out of town. The immediate source of the story seems to be Foxe's *Acts and Monuments*, where it is an example of the fraud and hypocrisy of the Catholic church, but Foxe took it from Sir Thomas More, who was concerned with the damage that fraudulent 'miracles' did to the accounts of true divine intervention at the shrines of saints.[3]

There is a false pilgrimage of a very different sort in *All's Well that Ends Well*, when Helena, in her distress at the results of her 'ambitious love' in obtaining Bertram for a husband as the king's gift to her for curing him, resolves to leave the France which Bertram will not return to while his unwanted wife is there. 'Come thou home, Rossillion . . . I will be gone' (3.2.120, 122). She doesn't speak of a destination; she just wants to get out of his way. But in the letter which she leaves behind for the Countess she writes as follows.

---

[3] Geoffrey Bullough, *Narrative and Dramatic Sources of Shakespeare*, vol. III (London: Routledge and Kegan Paul; New York: Columbia University Press, 1960), p. 60. Eamon Duffy, *The Stripping of the Altars: Traditional Religion in England c. 1400 – c. 1580* (New Haven and London: Yale University Press, 1992), pp. 196–7.

I am Saint Jaques' pilgrim, thither gone.
Ambitious love hath so in me offended
That barefoot plod I the cold ground upon
With sainted vow my faults to have amended.

(3.4.4–7)

She even contemplates her own death 'to set him free' (line 17). The strange thing is that she next turns up in Florence, where she has heard that Bertram has gone (3.2.68). The famous shrine of St Jaques or St James is of course Santiago de Compostela in Galicia in north-west Spain. The assumption that Shakespeare and/or Helena meant that shrine seems confirmed by later references to 'Saint Jaques le Grand' (3.5.34) and 'great Saint Jaques' (3.5.95). The shrine at Compostela, supposed to be the burial place of the apostle, was the third holiest site in Christendom after Jerusalem and Rome and was visited by tens of thousands of pilgrims every year (including Margery Kempe and the Wife of Bath). It is scarcely credible that Shakespeare did not know that Santiago de Compostela was in north-west Spain and therefore due west of Roussillon, in south-east France, where the play is set. To get to Florence Helena would need to go a long way east, in precisely the opposite direction. One might assume that Helena's declaration of her intention to the Countess was simply a blind to conceal her real intention to seek out Bertram. This after all is what is said in the sources. In the story as told by both Boccaccio and Painter, Helena announced that she was going to spend the rest of her days making pilgrimages and doing good works, and then, dressed as a pilgrim, she set straight off for Florence to find Bertram. It was Shakespeare who inserted the shrine of St Jaques, and he seems to insist that it is near Florence for, when Helena meets in Florence the Widow who keeps a lodging-house for pilgrims, the Widow guesses she has come from France and invites her to join several other pilgrims staying with her who are 'to great Saint Jaques bound' (3.5.95). It is in the Widow's company that Helena comes across Bertram, and this encounter seems quite accidental.

There are numerous solutions to this much-discussed problem. Shakespeare's geographical ignorance, for example, or if not his ignorance his indifference. But something strange is going on here, stranger than Bohemia's famous sea-coast in *The Winter's Tale*. Geographical indifference in Shakespeare's tragicomedies can take unexpected shapes, helping to create that shifting balance between fantasy and truth which is the property of these plays. Shakespeare magnified the importance of Helena's pilgrimage by specifying Santiago, and he disengaged it from reality by locating the shrine somewhere near Florence. He left Helena's motives and intention open, between on the one hand penance and possible death, and on the other the conquest of Bertram. If there was a bland indifference to geography in placing the shrine of St Jaques near Florence, the proximity of the two destinations – St Jaques and Bertram – emphasises the rivalry of the two pilgrimages.

Helena is aware from the beginning of this rivalry between God and Bertram as the object of her devotion. In the first scene, learning that Bertram is going to Paris to serve the king, Helena speaks of her secret love for a person so high above her in social status –

> But now he's gone, and my idolatrous fancy
> Must sanctify his relics.   (1.1.97–8)

She resolves to follow him, and tells his mother of her love.

>   I confess
> Here on my knee, before high heaven and you,
> That before you, and next unto high heaven,
> I love your son . . .
>   Thus Indian-like,
> Religious in mine error, I adore
> The sun, that looks upon his worshipper,
> But knows of him no more.
>   (1.3.191–4, 204–7)

In Paris she cures the king, and just before she claims Bertram as her reward, she says –

> Now Dian, from thy altar do I fly,
> And to imperial Love, that god most high,
> Do my sighs stream.   (2.3.74–6)

But Bertram repudiates the wife who has been foisted on him, and refuses to return to Rossillion and acknowledge Helena until she can show him a child 'begotten of thy body that I am father to'. And so begins the second pilgrimage, to St Jaques the Great, as we have seen. But as soon as Helena sees Bertram, and learns from the Widow of his plan to seduce the Widow's daughter, all her energy goes into outwitting Bertram and claiming him as her husband. She takes the place of the daughter, Diana, in bed, so that when Bertram thinks he is seducing the young Florentine girl he is actually consummating his marriage. On-stage (4.3), we find two of Bertram's fellow-officers, knowing his plan to seduce Diana, discussing his conduct. They are identified in the Folio as '*two French Captaines*', and referred to as '*Cap. G*' and '*Cap. E*'.

> *Cap. G.* Sir, his wife some two months since fled from his house. Her pretence is a pilgrimage to Saint Jaques le Grand, which holy undertaking with most austere sanctimony she accomplished; and there residing, the tenderness of her nature became as a prey to her grief; in fine, made a groan of her last breath, and now she sings in heaven.
> *Cap. E.* How is this justified?
> *Cap. G.* The stronger part of it by her own letters, which makes her story true even to the point of her death. Her death, which could not be her office to say is come, was faithfully confirmed by the rector of the place.
> *Cap. E.* Hath the count all this intelligence?
> *Cap. G.* Ay, and the particular confirmations, point from point, to the full arming of the verity. (4.3.47–62)

The word 'pretence' in the second sentence of this extract had the predominant meaning of 'intention' or 'expressed purpose', but it could also have its modern meaning of 'pretext' or 'false motive' (*OED*, 3 and 3b). It does not help us to decide the seriousness of Helena's initial purpose. But to whom were these letters written? How did this lord or captain get his knowledge of them? And who is this 'rector' who has falsely certified Helena's death? Here is indeed a false pilgrimage. Do we blame Shakespeare or Helena for this attention to the details of a mendacious story to assist the outwitting of Bertram?

The liberties which have here been taken with holy matters resemble the misrepresentations made by the Duke in *Measure for Measure* as he manoeuvres to circumvent Angelo. Shakespeare creates problems for us by imposing moral responsibilities on the characters of his tragicomedies as he involves them in the manipulation of events towards the fortunate conclusions which the plays demand. Helena could hardly have escaped reproof from some of the older members of the original audience for the lies about the 'most austere sanctimony' with which she accomplished the 'holy undertaking' of her pilgrimage. The pilgrimage to the shrine of St Jaques le Grand had become of no importance to Helena because she had returned to a quite different pilgrimage, to Bertram, the proper completion of which was to her a matter of much greater significance. The play, however, questions the value of what she takes to be the higher pilgrimage.

It is of some significance in this connection that Bertram shares with Helena a belief in the need to shift objectives from the divine to the sexual. The maid on whom Bertram's eyes fall and whom he proposes to seduce is named by Shakespeare Diana. She has no name in the source. The name surprises Bertram.

Bertram. They told me that your name was Fontybell.
Diana. No, my good lord, Diana.
Bertram.   Titled goddess,
    And worth it, with addition! But, fair soul,
    In your fine frame hath love no quality?
    If the quick fire of youth light not your mind,
    You are no maiden but a monument.   (4.2.1–6)

Almost everyone who witnesses or reads *All's Well that Ends Well* is dissatisfied by the ending of the play: dissatisfied by the meanness of Bertram, the objective of Helena's pilgrimage, and uncomfortable with Helena's devices for obtaining what she wants. The outcome of her striving seems a tawdry and uncertain triumph. It reflects back on her endeavours, and labels her devotion idolatry, as she feared it was; her pilgrimage a misplaced dedication.

There is an undercurrent in the play about the capacity for salvation or damnation in every person. It runs through the choric language of the officers in 4.3. 'The web of our life is of a mingled yarn, good and ill together.' 'As we are ourselves, what things are we! . . . Merely our own traitors.' It runs through the otherwise supererogatory offerings of the clown Lavatch in 4.5, when, admitting his service of 'the prince of the world', he surprisingly claims that he is 'for the house with the narrow gate', though most will opt for 'the flow'ry way that leads to the broad gate and the great fire'.

It is true that Helena is granted special powers, almost beyond the human, in *All's Well*. Of the act of healing in the second act, she says, with more modesty than arrogance, 'Heaven hath through me restored the king to health.' She shares with Marina the power to restore and rejuvenate the old. It may be supposed then that in pursuing Bertram her mission is in some sense to save him and redirect him to a new and better life. Her role, in pursuit of love, would therefore be that of both pilgrim and saint. The question is how far the play of *All's Well* as a whole recognises Helena's love-pilgrimage as a respectable and viable alternative to the more traditional pilgrimage with which Shakespeare has placed it in competition by means of displacing the shrine of St Jaques le Grand. It certainly seems that the age-old question of the place of sexual love within Christian piety was given a new sharpness by the suppression of that devotion which a pilgrim might offer to God through a saint. Ralegh's treatment of the Walsingham ballad seems to show the failure of the attempt to renegotiate the object of devotion, and include sexual love within divine love. Astrophil, in the fifth sonnet of Sir Philip Sidney's sequence *Astrophil and Stella* (?1582), finds little satisfaction in the exclusively metaphorical journey remaining for the Protestant pilgrim, and puts the claims of sexual love in opposition to it. The one pilgrimage appeals to the head, while the feeling of the heart lies elsewhere. It is true, the lover says, that 'the heavenly part / Ought to be king' –

> True, that on earth we are but pilgrims made,
> And should in soule up to our countrey move:
> True, and yet true that I must *Stella* love.[4]

Elsewhere Sidney wrote, 'Leave me O Love which reachest but to dust',[5] contrasting sexual love with 'eternal love'. Where are we

---

[4] Sir Philip Sidney, *Poems*, ed. W. A. Ringler (Oxford: Clarendon Press, 1962), p. 167.
[5] *Ibid.*, p. 161.

to find the 'durable love' of Ralegh's ballad? It swings between Sidney's rejection here and the enthusiasm of his creature Astrophil. The pendulum also swings in Hamlet's treatment of Ophelia. 'I loved Ophelia', he says eventually and uselessly over her grave (5.1.236). Helena's pilgrimage in *All's Well* swings violently towards the securing of Bertram. 'Securing' is perhaps the right word. Her pregnancy, founded upon the deception of an unwilling person, must diminish and question the triumphant ending of her quest. Salvation by means of penitence and supplication on the one hand and salvation by human love on the other are not necessarily incompatible, but the parallel lines of the two kinds of pilgrimage along which Helena travels may never meet.

There could hardly be a greater contrast with the relationship between Helena and Bertram than the relationship between Romeo and Juliet in the play which Shakespeare wrote some years earlier. Their love is spontaneous and mutual, fully and naturally consummated. Its ending, in disaster and death, does not really reflect back on or qualify their passion. In this earlier tragedy there is no parallel of pilgrimages, no preference or disparagement. But in Shakespeare's most renowned use of the trope of love-as-pilgrimage there is a perfect balance between the two devotions, sexual and spiritual. In Act 1 Scene 5, Romeo is gatecrashing Capulet's feast in hope of seeing Rosaline, but he meets Juliet.

Romeo. If I profane with my unworthiest hand
　　This holy shrine, the gentle sin is this,
　　My lips, two blushing pilgrims, ready stand
　　To smooth that rough touch with a tender kiss.
Juliet. Good pilgrim, you do wrong your hand too much,
　　Which mannerly devotion shows in this,
　　For saints have hands that pilgrims' hands do touch,
　　And palm to palm is holy palmers' kiss.
Romeo. Have not saints lips, and holy palmers too?
Juliet. Ay, pilgrim, lips that they must use in prayer.
Romeo. O then, dear saint, let lips do what hands do:
　　They pray, grant thou, lest faith turn to despair.
Juliet. Saints do not move, though grant for prayers' sake.
Romeo. Then move not while my prayer's effect I take.

Thus from my lips, by thine, my sin is purged.
                    [*Kissing her*]
Juliet. Then have my lips the sin that they have took.
Romeo. Sin from my lips? O trespass sweetly urged!
   Give me my sin again.   [*Kissing her again*]
Juliet.   You kiss by th' book.

(1.5.93–110)

The light-heartedness with which Romeo exploits the image of pilgrimage to express his feelings for Juliet and win a kiss from her might
look like irreverence, making fun of an abolished ritual as he sophis-
tically bends it in order to achieve his reward. But the banter could
hardly exist without a basic respect. If Romeo mocks pilgrimage, he
mocks his love for Juliet. The force of the exchange depends on the
sincerity of a pilgrim's reverence for the image of a saint. The genuineness of the emotion which is growing between Romeo and Juliet
has to be balanced by the genuineness of reverence for the saint. Each
justifies the other. If the reverence is belittled, the love is belittled,
and vice versa. The two are interlocked as the quatrains of the sonnet
are interlocked in the dialogue. Romeo (whose name means pilgrim)
faces Juliet as though she were the statue of a saint in its shrine. If his
tone is light and teasing, he is not mocking the humility of the pilgrim
who hopes for the intervention of the saint on his behalf. The play
is set in a Catholic country, and Juliet, whose role is (as so often) to
cool the exaggerated rhetoric of Romeo,[6] knows the proper actions
and expectations of a supplicant. Her acceptance of the kiss, which is
an acceptance of her role as a substitute for the worshipped saint, is
therefore all the more impressive. She will shortly tell Romeo that he
is the god of her idolatry (2.2.114; anticipating Helena). She is quite
aware of the exchange which is being made. The dialogue turns upon
the devotional practice of not only touching but kissing the saint's
statue, the practice which was so offensive to the reformers. Romeo
pretends he would profane the holy image by touching it, suggesting
it would be less of a sin to touch it with his lips. Juliet argues that

[6] See Philip Edwards, 'The Declaration of Love', in *Shakespeare's Styles*, ed. P. Edwards,
I.-S. Ewbank and G. K. Hunter (Cambridge: Cambridge University Press, 1980),
pp. 39–43.

touching would express quite sufficient devotion, and that if lips are to be used they are to be used in prayer. Romeo presses the case for lips. Hands pray as well as touch, and lips can do the same. It is with Romeo's 'They pray, grant thou' that the similitude between Juliet and the saint has to 'fail'. For what Juliet has to grant as a reward for the supplication is the very kiss which Romeo offers as supplication. That is what Romeo means by taking his 'prayer's effect' in kissing her. The kiss is both the prayer and the reward for the prayer. The two objects of devotion, one divine, the other human, are in some confusion here. Romeo optimistically claims that his sin – the sin motivating every penitent pilgrim – is purged by kissing his saint. Juliet, more realistically, says that she thereby has received his sin. But she accepts his second kiss. In thus equalising the sexual and the religious Shakespeare is not ridiculing either.

In the second line of this passage from *Romeo and Juliet* Shakespeare uses the word 'shrine' to signify both the image of his saint and the person of Juliet. It is a peculiarity of his writing that when he is employing the metaphor of pilgrimage in the context of human love he makes this portmanteau of the holy place, the statue therein and the person worshipped. The fusion of place, image and person is clear in *The Merchant of Venice*. Morocco says this of Portia.

> From the four corners of the earth they come
> To kiss this shrine, this mortal breathing saint.
> (2.7.39–40)

This uncommon, possibly unique, usage of 'shrine' helps us with a difficult passage in *Cymbeline* in which Iachimo relates how they had taunted Posthumus by praising the women of Italy

> for feature, laming
> The shrine of Venus or straight-pight Minerva,
> Postures beyond brief nature[.]   (5.5.163–5)

Iachimo must mean that Italian women make Venus herself look lame: Venus, that is, as she is known from her statue, even though such a statue outdoes nature. Shakespeare's mind in all these passages contains at the same instant the holy place, the image of the saint and the person of the saint. Latimer excoriated the worship of 'dead images', but for Shakespeare, apparently, not only the images but the places in which they were located were alive with the presence of the person worshipped.

The word 'pilgrimage' itself in Shakespeare is often glossed as meaning no more than 'the course of one's life', with reference made to Genesis 47:9, which in the Geneva Bible reads thus: 'And Jacob said unto Pharaoh, The whole time of my pilgrimage is an hundreth and thirty yeres.' The flattened gloss ('course of one's life') may therefore accord with the original meaning but it ignores the history of the phrase in Christian usage and with it Shakespeare's much more evocative and pregnant signification. Once again the amplitude and hospitality of the word *'peregrinus'* has been at work. The Vulgate version of Jacob's account is *dies peregrinationis meae centum triginta annorum sunt*. The word *'peregrinatio'* here seems to belong to the concept of life as the temporary dwelling of one exiled from his promised home. The New English Bible and the New Revised Standard Version render the phrase 'the years of my earthly pilgrimage' as 'the years of my earthly sojourn', picking up 'sojourn' from the Greek text of the Pentateuch, ἅς παροικῶ (has paroiko), [where I dwell *or* sojourn]. As in the Epistles, the concept of life as the wandering of an alien has been promoted into the metaphor of the Christian pilgrim, travelling to his heavenly home. Curiously, however, the word *peregrinatio*, having been up-graded to mean a pilgrimage to heaven, became so overused that it wore down again to mean no more than 'the course of one's life'. Hence the gloss on 'pilgrimage' in most Shakespearian editions. But to attribute this neutral and worn-down meaning to Shakespeare is to risk misunderstanding a number of important passages, for in Shakespeare the word almost always means a purposeful and dedicated journey towards a desired destination.

In a powerful scene in the first part of *Henry VI*, invented by Shakespeare and historically impossible (2.5), Richard Plantagenet, future Duke of York, visits the old rebel Mortimer, who is dying in gaol. He learns from him how the present discord in the state stems from the dispute over the succession to Richard II. Understanding

now what his own mission in life must be, he addresses the body of
Mortimer.

> In prison hast thou spent a pilgrimage,
> And like a hermit overpassed thy days.
>
> (2.5.116–17)

'Pilgrimage' here means much more than the course of a whole lifetime.
There is an opposition in this passage between a pilgrim and a hermit.
Mortimer's imprisonment has forced him into the inactivity of the
hermit, and so he has 'overpassed' the days which might have been
spent in a pilgrimage – which here would mean the bid to assert his
family's claim to the throne. To this bid Richard Plantagenet now
dedicates himself.

In *A Midsummer Night's Dream*, Theseus warns Hermia that if she
doesn't obey her father and marry Demetrius she must abjure the
society of men and enter a nunnery. He pulls back in his warnings
of the direness of this punishment ('chanting faint hymns to the cold
fruitless moon') to admit, as it were, that there is another view of this
celibacy.

> Thrice blessed they that master so their blood
> To undergo such maiden pilgrimage.
>
> (1.1.74–5)

The Riverside edition glosses 'maiden pilgrimage' as 'journey through
life as a virgin'. But it seems clear that Shakespeare is here using
(anachronistically) the time-honoured Christian metaphor of the
dedicated journey to heaven. A similar requirement that a pilgrimage
have a destination is found when time's pilgrimage is alluded to, in
Lucrece (960), and in *Romeo and Juliet* (4.5.45) when Lady Capulet
speaks, thinking Juliet is dead.

> Most miserable hour that e'er time saw
> In lasting labour of his pilgrimage.

Time, pictured as a pilgrim pursuing his long weary journey, is striving
to attain the end-point of his travel, when 'time must have a stop' and
eternity succeeds.

In *Measure for Measure*, Angelo ignores Escalus's plea for compassion towards Claudio.

> See that Claudio
> Be executed by nine tomorrow morning.
> Bring him his confessor, let him be prepared,
> For that's the utmost of his pilgrimage.
>
> (2.1.33–6)

Here commentators seem to agree that by 'the utmost of his pilgrimage' Angelo means the limit of life's journey or Claudio's span of life. But the notion of defeated purpose is required if we are to get the flavour of Angelo's contempt. He's interrupting a course of life thought of as a meaningful journey. 'That's as far as *he* is going.' The actor would do well to stress 'his'.

I now come to passages in two tragedies in which, if we take 'pilgrimage' to mean just the passing of years or the journey of life rather than life as a commitment to a known and desired end, we impoverish not just the passage but the play as a whole.

When Othello tells the Senate how he won Desdemona, he explains that she was not able to hear the whole of what he rather dismissively calls the 'traveller's history' of his adventures abroad in the service of Venice while he was relating it to her father.[7] So he 'found good means'

> To draw from her a prayer of earnest heart
> That I would all my pilgrimage dilate,
> Whereof by parcels she had something heard . . .
>
> (1.3.152–4)

As we have seen, the word for a journey to a shrine to obtain favours ('pilgrimage') has to share the primary meaning of the Latin '*peregrinus*' from which it comes, that is, a traveller lodging in alien territory. Both these senses may be in Othello's mind as he uses the word 'pilgrimage': his wanderings overseas and the sense of his life as a journey with a purpose and a goal.

---

[7] This is to take the Folio reading. The Quarto gives the much weaker 'travels' history'.

In view of the hostility to Othello which reached its nadir in F. R. Leavis's characterisation of him as a weak person bolstering himself by self-dramatisation and boastful self-presentation, and so disguising his 'obtuse and brutal egotism',[8] it is difficult to persuade an actor to try to show in these early scenes the assurance, self-confidence and humour which are so soon to be destroyed. Othello's confidence in himself and his relationship with Desdemona allows him to speak of what is serious in a tone of amusement which may remind us of Romeo's tone in the passage I discussed above. 'Keep up your bright swords, for the dew will rust them' (1.2.59). He laughs at his would-be attackers with their drawn swords – such a pity to risk rusting those nice blades. This lightness of tone pervades the famous speech to the Senate, supposed to be a prime example of Othello's solemn boasting. The speech is his answer to the accusation that he had won Desdemona's affection by wicked charms. He won her by telling her the story of his life and adventures – a traveller's tale, he calls it. It was a wonder to him that his account had such an effect on her, but this narrative was all the witchcraft he had used.

> She loved me for the dangers I had passed,
> And I loved her that she did pity them.

Dark things are insinuated here by editors: that Othello does not understand her love, or his own. He might be permitted some reticence here; to share the view in Donne's poem that ''Twere profanation of our joys / To tell the laity our love'.[9] The lightness of his tone in this bland conclusion conceals what is not for public display.

A lightness of tone which risks self-disparagement may also be present in Othello's use of the word 'pilgrimage' for his adventures. He may not really mean that they were part of a planned progression. But if he was being ironical in suggesting such a high estimate of his career, he spoke an unintended truth. For Othello *was* a pilgrim. To what shrine was he travelling? Success certainly. 'The plumèd troops and the big wars / That makes ambition virtue' (3.3.349–50). But

[8] F. R. Leavis, 'Diabolic Intellect and the Noble Hero', in his *The Common Pursuit* (1952; Harmondsworth, Middlesex: Penguin Books, 1962), pp. 136–59.
[9] John Donne, 'A Valediction: forbidding mourning'.

there is more to it than that. The journey to the shrine of military success is a journey from afar by a member of an alien race. Whether as a Moor he was (in Shakespeare's understanding) a 'tawny moor' or a black-a-moor, he was an alien in Venice. Roderigo calls him 'an extravagant and wheeling stranger / Of here and everywhere' (1.1.136–7). This precisely nails him as, in Venetian eyes, a *peregrinus* in the basic Latin sense: a wandering foreigner who does not 'belong'. Othello saw himself with different eyes: 'I fetch my life and being / From men of royal siege' (1.2.21–2). He has committed himself to acceptance and leadership in a civilisation and culture not his own. That which is to cancel his racial difference, dissolve the pigmentation problem so to speak, is a love-marriage to a white European woman of high social standing. The award of leadership follows the marriage immediately, when he is summoned by the Senate and commissioned to confront the Turks at Cyprus.

It is often pointed out that, in his speech in his own defence to the Senate, Othello speaks as if he were not an African but a European who has ventured into mysterious unknown territory. This is particularly the case in his reference to cannibals and 'men whose heads / Do grow beneath their shoulders' (1.3.143–5). Both these peoples figure in Ralegh's *Discoverie of Guiana*, published in 1596, and, as the stock symbols of European expectations of exotic regions, they show Othello's immersion in the thought-habits of his host culture.

The play shows the impossibility of that absorption into Venetian culture which was Othello's true pilgrimage. He may have used the word lightly and ironically in his speech to the Senate, but at the deepest level it faithfully renders his conception of himself and his aspiration. The word lends a special poignancy to his utterance when he looks at the dead body of the wife he has murdered, knows that she was innocent, and knows that he has lost her and everything else.

> Here is my journey's end, here is my butt
> And very sea-mark of my utmost sail.
> (5.2.267–8)[10]

---

[10] The full implication of this couplet is the subject of Chapter 4 of my book *Sea-Mark* (Liverpool: Liverpool University Press, 1997).

Finally, *King Lear*. In the very last scene of the play, Edgar, disguised, has defeated his half-brother Edmund in single combat. He reveals his identity, and in answer to Albany's question tells his story, adding the news of how Gloucester died to what the audience already knows. There are two slightly different versions of his speech. Here is the Quarto version of 1608 (with modernised spelling). Edgar explains how, as Poor Tom, he met his newly blinded father, and

> became his guide,
> Led him, begged for him, saved him from despair;
> Never (O father) revealed myself unto him
> Until some half-hour past, when I was armed.
> Not sure, though hoping of this good success,
> I asked his blessing, and from first to last
> Told him my pilgrimage; but his flawed heart –
> Alack, too weak the conflict to support,
> 'Twixt two extremes of passion, joy and grief,
> Burst smilingly.

The Folio has two different readings: 'O fault' for 'O father' in the third line, and in the seventh line 'our pilgrimage' for 'my pilgrimage'. It is difficult to know what Edgar might mean in saying that he told his father 'our pilgrimage'. If it is a joint pilgrimage, why does he need to tell it to him? R. A. Foakes, in his Arden edition of 1997, is one of the few editors who, accepting the Folio reading, provides an explanation. 'Pilgrimage', he writes, means 'course of life, all that had happened', and he refers to the same 'neutral sense' in the passage of *Othello* we have just been discussing. It has been my contention that this neutral sense is not actually to be found in Shakespeare's plays and poems, and certainly not in the *Othello* passage. To accept the Folio reading (as I once did)[11] is to weaken the passage and the play. A pilgrimage is a journey undertaken to fulfil a particular purpose, and this passage is Edgar's declaration that in his extraordinary fluctuation of roles his mission has been less to protect himself than to save or punish others according to their deserts.

---

[11] In an edition of 1975 for 'The Macmillan Shakespeare'; *mea culpa*.

Illustration 2. 'Visionary' Head of Edgar in *King Lear*, by George Romney.
Fitzwilliam Museum, Cambridge.

It is initially to preserve himself that he declares the alienation
which had become the prerequisite of the pilgrim. As a lunatic beggar,
Poor Tom, he will 'take the basest and most poorest shape / That
ever penury, in contempt of man, / Brought near to beast' (2.3.7–9).
When he is discovered in his hovel by the Fool and Lear in the storm,
his nakedness and penury bring the king to his understanding of 'unac-
commodated man'. Edgar's role is the man of sin pursued by the foul
fiend. 'Keep thy foot out of brothels . . . and defy the foul fiend' is Poor
Tom's advice to all. As he joins the king and his thin retinue in the
hovel at the end of the scene (3.4), he suddenly creates the extraordinary image of the medieval pilgrim-knight whom he is to become in
the play's final scene.

> Child Rowland to the dark tower came,[12]
> His word was still, 'Fie, foh, and fum,
> I smell the blood of a British man.'

---

[12] This is the Folio reading. The Quarto reads: 'to the darke towne come'.

The British man in the dark tower whom Edgar pursues is the half-brother Edmund who has defamed, expelled and dispossessed him. But first he meets his blinded father. The 'Old Man' leading Gloucester says, 'Alack sir, you cannot see your way!', to which Gloucester replies, 'I have no way' – purposing to reach Dover cliff with the help of the 'naked fellow', there to end his life. 'Poor Tom shall lead thee', says Edgar (4.1). He now has a double mission: to save his father and to punish Edmund. His determination in both objectives is as frightening as his self-righteousness. When, in his ultimate 'semblance' (5.3.188), he stands over the brother he has mortally wounded, and is at this moment prepared to 'exchange charity' with him, he proclaims that their father has already been punished for his sin in begetting the bastard Edmund. 'The dark and vicious place where thee he got / Cost him his eyes.' So, as he recounts, his mission has been to save his father from despair, and from the further sin of suicide. He must have explained to Gloucester the deception on Dover cliff, and why he perpetrated it. The two-fold mission, to punish the son and redeem the father, is similar to what Hamlet conceives as his own mission – to punish Claudius and redeem Gertrude. Edgar's sense of his mission is entirely self-generated, but it is most certainly his pilgrimage and no-one else's. He accepts the responsibility with the words 'my pilgrimage', the pilgrimage which he manages to explain to his father before he dies. The reading of the Quarto must be right, and that of the Folio wrong.

Pilgrims and pilgrimage are not to the fore in Shakespeare's plays and poems. The two most prominent references to historical pilgrimage are, first, the episode of Simpcox in *2 Henry VI*, rehearsing a well-worn example of the fraudulent miracles which, reformists believed, sustained the whole culture of pilgrimage. Secondly, Helena's purported pilgrimage to the tomb of St James, which is anything but realistic. The one incident in the plays which could be called a true pilgrimage occurs in a late romance of dubious status, *Pericles, Prince of Tyre*.

All the same, 'pilgrims' and 'pilgrimage' are words of power and importance in Shakespeare. The practice of pilgrimage had been obliterated in England almost thirty years before Shakespeare was born, and the abbeys and priories which maintained the shrines had been closed down. That Shakespeare, whether through upbringing or inclination, felt the presence of the old faith and was moved by its destruction seems undeniable, in spite of what look like his sturdy Protestant attitudes to friars and the confessional.

> That time of year thou mayst in me behold,
> When yellow leaves, or none, or few, do hang
> Upon those boughs which shake against the cold,
> Bare ruined choirs, where late the sweet birds sang.[13]

This celebrated similitude creates a universal sadness as it unites the ageing of a person with the dying of the year, and the dying of the year with the upheaval of historical change. It is scarcely conceivable that in 'bare ruined choirs' Shakespeare was not referring to the monasteries of England, desolate and often roofless since the 1530s. In his book *Hamlet in Purgatory*, Stephen Greenblatt convincingly argues that Shakespeare's imagination needed the lost Catholic doctrine of Purgatory to voice what is essential to his tragedy, the communion of the living and the dead – Prince Hamlet and his father.[14] Purgatory and pilgrimage were closely allied, since the purpose of a great many pilgrimages was to obtain for the contrite and penitent pilgrim an indulgence which would lessen by quantified amounts the pains of Purgatory.

Whatever Shakespeare's religious leanings, pilgrimage, like Purgatory, was an attractive imaginative concept. Its theological justification had declined to near-extinction under decades of vociferous and menacing scepticism. Yet it remained for the playwright a focus of worship and power, an *idea* of devotion. Otherwise, for Romeo to call Juliet 'this holy shrine' is absurd. And if this is the case, then Helena's business-like pursuit of the reluctant Bertram in *All's Well*, assisted by her counterfeit pilgrimage to the curiously dislocated shrine of St Jaques le Grand, sets up a rivalry between counterfeit and true pilgrimages

---

[13] Sonnet 73; 'ruined' is the accepted emendation of the Quarto's 'rn'wd'.
[14] Stephen Greenblatt, *Hamlet in Purgatory* (Princeton and Oxford: Princeton University Press, 2001), Chapter 5.

in which the residual sanctity of the true exposes the sterility of the false.

Even though the evidence of *Pericles*, *Romeo and Juliet* and *All's Well that Ends Well* suggests that actual pilgrimage, pilgrimage on the ground, had an appeal for Shakespeare as an image of spiritual access, the word had a greater importance as an image for a fierce dedication neither specifically religious nor specifically secular. The word is used to convey a commitment which fits the Hegelian view of the tragic hero as one who identifies himself with the realisation of his objective to bring into being a world of more exalted values than prevails: a world of absolutes and authenticity. This mission is doomed from the start.

The evidence for the use of pilgrimage to express the tragic mission is slight and fragile. The main pointer is the inspired identification of Ophelia's song in her madness, which sees Hamlet as the 'true love' who has abandoned his mistress to become a pilgrim. Ophelia is not aware, as the audience of the play is aware, that Hamlet has been tearing himself apart in questioning and redrafting the commission of his ghostly father, because he knows to the depth of his soul that the future of Denmark depends on the shape of his obedience. Her insight that Hamlet's extraordinary treatment of her does not mean that he is deranged but that he has consciously committed his life to a new goal is a wild and true leap. It is a leap which in identifying Hamlet as a pilgrim also redefines the metaphor of pilgrimage as a search, perhaps fruitless, for a hidden divinity. Ophelia's Hamlet, pursuing possibility with failure in his scope,[15] with the ruggedness of his mental journey and the flickering perception of its destination, carries into pilgrimage a tragic quality not easily observable elsewhere.

The attempted fulfilment of Othello, the Moor of Venice, as military leader and wedded lover, is a less complex and wide-ranging pilgrimage than Hamlet's. It is in the mysterious, scarcely comprehensible self-imposed mission driving Edgar in *King Lear* that we find the confirming force of the Shakespearian metaphor. In exile, self-degradation and assumed madness, he cleanses the understanding of

---

[15] Compare Robert Browning, 'Childe Roland to the Dark Tower Came', stanza 4.

the infected by a blend of punishment and redemption which he thinks is justified *sub specie aeternitatis*. Hamlet's efforts to redirect the world lead to disaster, while Edgar's seem to triumph. But it is a curious fact that in the earlier Quarto text of *King Lear*, following the deaths of his father, of Cordelia and of Lear himself, Edgar appears to be in no state of mind to accept Albany's offer of a share in controlling 'the gored state' and so to continue his endeavour to 'cleanse the foul body of th'infected world'.[16]

Shakespeare's tragedies hover in their own Purgatory, a state of indecision between the faint possibility and the extreme unlikelihood of divine concern for and intervention in human affairs. An image of the tragic hero as a pilgrim hopefully making his way among the shattered shrines of past certainties reinforces that view.

---

[16] Jaques's words in *As You Like It*, 2.7.60. At the end of both texts of *Lear*, Albany suggests that 'you twain', seemingly Kent and Edgar, 'rule in this kingdom, and the gored state sustain'. Kent declines. In the earlier Quarto, Edgar makes no reply, and Albany speaks the concluding four lines beginning 'The weight of this sad time we must obey'. In the Folio these final lines are ascribed to Edgar, who thereby seems to accept Albany's offer of government.

CHAPTER 4

Motion and spirit

The Passionate man's Pilgrimage,
supposed to be written by
one at the point of death.

Give me my Scallop shell of quiet,
My staffe of Faith to walke upon,
My Scrip of Joy, Immortall diet,
My bottle of salvation:
My Gowne of Glory, hopes true gage,   5
And thus Ile take my pilgrimage.

Blood must be my bodies balmer,
No other balme will there be given,
Whilst my soule like a white palmer
Travels to the land of heaven,   10
Over the silver mountaines
Where spring the Nectar fountaines:
And there Ile kisse
The Bowle of blisse,
And drinke my eternal fill   15
On every milken hill.
My soule will be a drie before,
But after it, will nere thirst more.

And by the happie blisfull way
More peacefull Pilgrims I shall see,   20
That have shooke off their gownes of clay,
And goe appareld fresh like mee.
Ile bring them first
To slake their thirst,
And then to tast those Nectar suckets   25
At the cleare wells

Where sweetnes dwells,
Drawne up by Saints in Christall buckets.

And when our bottles and all we
Are fild with immortalitie,   30
Then the holy paths weele travell
Strewde with Rubies thicke as gravell,
Seelings of Diamonds, Saphire floores,
High walles of Corall and Pearle Bowres.

From thence to heavens Bribeles hall,   35
Where no corrupted voyces brall,
Nor forg'd accusers bought and sold,
No cause deferd, nor vaine spent Jorney,
For there Christ is the Kings Atturney,
Who pleades for all without degrees,   40
And he hath Angells, but no fees.

When the grand twelve million Jury
Of our sinnes and sinful fury
Gainst our soules blacke verdicts give,
Christ pleades his death, and then we live.   45
Be thou my speaker taintles pleader,
Unblotted Lawyer, true proceeder:
Thou movest salvation even for almes:
Not with a bribed Lawyers palmes.

And this is my eternall plea   50
To him that made Heaven, Earth and Sea,
Seeing my flesh must die so soone,
And want a head to dine next noone,
Just at the stroke when my vaines start and spread
Set on my soule an everlasting head.   55
Then am I readie like a palmer fit,
To tread those blest paths which before I writ.

This beautiful, haunting work is easily the most important pilgrimage poem of its time. I have never thought that it had anything to do with Sir Walter Ralegh, to whom it has been attributed since the seventeenth century. It was first published in 1604, as an addendum to a long dull poem by 'An. Sc.' (Anthony Scoloker) called *Daiphantus*.[1] No-one

---

[1] The transcript above is edited from the Bodleian copy of the original.

seems to have commented on the poem or copied it until after 1625, when a manuscript version was made, headed 'Verses made by Sir Walter Raleigh the night before hee was beheaded'. This legend was refined by the historian Henry Spelman in a copy made before 1641: 'Verses written by Sr Walter Raleigh in the gatehouse att west[minste]r the evening before he died'.[2] Ralegh had been executed in 1618. But the poem had been in print since 1604, so could not have been written the night before he died. The original attribution was incorrect. Once the romantic association of the poem with Ralegh had been made, however, it was hard to give it up. Ralegh had been sentenced to death in November 1603, but the sentence was suspended during his long incarceration in the Tower and in the period when he was permitted to make his second Guiana voyage. So it was argued that the poem belonged to the time of the original sentence. Yet there is not a shred of evidence to connect the poem with Ralegh except the enthusiastic and untenable idea of the copyist, years after Ralegh's death, that he wrote it the night before he died. I have never seen anything in the poem that speaks of Ralegh's mind, art or devotion. The poem must be allowed to speak for itself, and not be a mouthpiece for a famous historical figure.[3]

The question arises, however: is this a Catholic or a Protestant poem? In a long article written a number of years ago[4] I pointed out that, although the poem did not declare itself with any certainty one way or the other, I was swayed by lines 7–8, 'Blood must be my bodies balmer, / No other balme will there be given.' I still think this must mean the denial on the scaffold of extreme unction, the anointing of a person at the point of death by balm or chrism. The word 'viaticum', used for the last rites expected by a Catholic, was in fact a metaphor,

[2] See Michael Rudick (ed.), *The Poems of Sir Walter Ralegh: A Historical Edition* (Tempe, Ariz.: Arizona Center for Medieval and Renaissance Studies, with Renaissance English Text Society, 1999), pp. lxx–lxxii, 130, 176–7.

[3] When I was working on my 1974 essay on this topic at the University of Essex (see next note), we had Robert Lowell as a visitor in my department, and he would growl at me 'Can't think why you're trying to take the man's best poem from him.' But Ralegh does not need the poem.

[4] 'Who Wrote *The Passionate Man's Pilgrimage*?', *English Literary Renaissance* 4 (Winter 1974), 83–97.

with the literal meaning of provisions for a journey – such a journey as the poem is about to describe. I also said that this poem, 'supposed to be written by one at the point of death', was not necessarily the work of a martyr, but might have been composed by a Catholic recusant as a spiritual exercise in contemplation of the faith and death of such men as Edmund Campion, Henry Walpole or Robert Southwell.

A remarkable feature of our poem is that the pilgrimage it describes takes place *after* death. Normally the Christian metaphoric pilgrimage concluded with death. Here as an example is Robert Herrick's poem, from *Hesperides* (1648).

> Here down my wearyed limbs Ile lay;
> My Pilgrims staffe; my weed of gray:
> My Palmers hat; my Scallops shell;
> My Crosse; my Cord; and all farewell.
> For having now my journey done,
> (Just at the setting of the Sun)
> Here I have found a Chamber fit,
> (God and good friends be thankt for it)
> Where if I can a lodger be
> A little while from Tramplers free;
> At my up-rising next, I shall,
> If not requite, yet thank ye all.
> Meane while, the *Holy-Rood* hence fright
> The fouler Fiend, and evill Spright,
> From scaring you or yours this night.[5]

Donne's great sonnet, which I quote next, dates from earlier in the century, and is even more important for us since it not only ends life's pilgrimage with death but also envisions the period between death and judgement (which is the subject of 'The Passionate Man's Pilgrimage') as a flight to heaven.

> This is my play's last scene, here heavens appoint
> My pilgrimages last mile; and my race
> Idly, yet quickly runne, hath this last pace,
> My spans last inch, my minutes last point,

[5] Robert Herrick, *Hesperides*, in *Poems*, ed. L. C. Martin (London: Oxford University Press, 1965), p. 123.

And gluttonous death will instantly unjoynt
My body, and soule, and I shall sleepe a space,
But my ever-waking part shall see that face,
Whose feare already shakes my every joynt:
Then, as my soule, to heaven her first seate, takes flight,
And earth-borne body in the earth shall dwell,
So, fall my sinnes, that all may have their right,
To where they are bred, and would presse me, to hell.
Impute me righteous, thus purg'd of evill,
For thus I leave the world, the flesh, and devill.[6]

Our poem begins with the dressing of the pilgrim for the pilgrimage which is to begin at the moment when, with his body blood-stained and 'unaneled' on the scaffold, his soul will depart for heaven. If the poem is a devotional exercise, a poet imagines himself to be a prisoner awaiting execution, and has that prisoner imagining the progress of his soul to judgement as a pilgrimage. His life's journey is over. His vestments, the equipment that he needs, are his faith, which, giving him his hope of salvation, is sufficient to fill him with joy as he contemplates the quiet of death, when the 'corrupted voices' (line 36) of his accusers fall silent, and he begins his promised share in the divine glory.

The blood which is to stain his body will take the place of the balm which should anoint it, and as it is the blood of a true believer killed for his faith it serves as the sacrament which is denied him. So begins the extraordinary journey, doubly imagined. What actually happened to the soul after death before entry to the full bliss of heaven was the subject of fierce debate. It wearied Calvin, who thought the argument futile, 'bien frivole et sotte'.[7] If our poem was indeed written by a Catholic it is strange that there is no hint of the purifying fires of Purgatory, but Greenblatt's quotations from *The Vision of Tondal*, written by an Irish monk in the twelfth century and circulating for centuries afterwards, show clearly that Catholics were permitted a vision of the souls of the faithful, as they waited, in 'a state of being

---

[6] Number 3 of the Holy Sonnets, in John Donne, *The Divine Poems*, ed. Helen Gardner (Oxford: Clarendon Press, 1952), p. 7 (punctuation altered).

[7] *Ibid.*, p. 116. Helen Gardner gives a full account of these bewildering speculations, and Donne's changing views, in pp. xliii–xliv and 114–17.

very close to the joys of Paradise', in 'a fragrant, flowery meadow . . . resting by the fountain of life'.[8] The imagery of the fantastic pilgrimage is loosely biblical, chiefly from Revelation and the Song of Solomon, for the clear water of life, for the fountains and for much of the jewel imagery, though rubies, sapphire, coral and pearl appear in Job 28. The 'milken hill' of line 16 seems to derive from Joel 3:18: 'the hills shall flow with milk'. But the configurations are the poet's own, as is the sense of the sheer happiness of release from life, and of the fellowship of the pilgrimage. The pilgrimage ends at the court of divine judgement, described as the sharpest possible antithesis to the corruption, lies and delays of earthly justice. Seemingly confident of a merciful outcome, the pilgrim comes back to the moment on earth that will precede the journey – his execution.

There are problems about 'The Passionate Man's Pilgrimage', beside the big problem of its authorship and occasion. Prosodically, its form is very unusual, with rapid changes in line length, rhyme-scheme and stanza structure. More difficult to explain is the co-presence of what seem like quite different styles. It is not easy to equate the quaint picture of the saints drawing up the water in crystal buckets, or the image of filling up the pilgrims and their bottles with immortality, with the majesty of the opening lines or the bitter wit of the ending ('want a head to dine next noon'). Yet the scheme of the poem as a whole is brilliant, and perhaps there is a conscious naïveté in the journey of the deliriously happy pilgrim.

There is a remarkable similarity, which can hardly be fortuitous, between 'The Passionate Man's Pilgrimage' and a poem by Emily Dickinson, written in the early 1860s.[9]

> The Doomed – regard the Sunrise
> With different Delight –
> Because – when next it burns abroad
> They doubt to witness it –

---

[8] Stephen Greenblatt, *Hamlet in Purgatory* (Princeton and Oxford: Princeton University Press, 2001), pp. 61–2; see also p. 73.

[9] Johnson 294; Franklin 298 (see Chapter Six, note 9). The earlier poem could have been found in Sir Egerton Brydges's *Poems of Sir Walter Raleigh*, 2nd edn (1814), entitled 'His Pilgrimage'.

> The Man – to die – tomorrow –
> Harks for the Meadow Bird –
> Because its Music stirs the Axe
> That clamors for his head –
>
> Joyful – to whom the Sunrise
> Precedes Enamored – Day –
> Joyful – for whom the Meadow Bird
> Has ought but Elegy!

To return to the seventeenth century, the posthumous pilgrimage of the 'passionate man' – the word 'passionate' referring to suffering and grief – places his poem in a distinctive position in poetry of the late sixteenth and earlier seventeenth centuries, apart from its other merits. Most pilgrimage poems of the period stress the feeling of exile of the *peregrini*, strangers and pilgrims, pilgrims in being strangers, found in the Epistles. They concentrate on the utter foreignness of the world's values and habits to the convinced Christian. Such alienation is the condition from which 'The Passionate Man's Pilgrimage' starts, inspiring its first line, 'Give me my scallop shell of quiet'. The poet – real or imagined victim – waits for the corrupt world literally to cut him off, brutally expelling him into the journey of joy. The pilgrimage of the conventional poem takes place among the 'corrupted voices' and jostling of Vanity Fair, and the pilgrim is much less certain than the passionate man of the way through. As in the beautiful motet of 1615 by John Amner, organist of Ely Cathedral:

> A Stranger heere, as all my fathers were
> That went before, I wander too and fro;
> From earth to heau'n is my pilgrimage,
> A tedious way for flesh and blood to go.
> O thou that art the way, pittie the blinde,
> And teach mee how I may thy dwelling finde.[10]

What is so succinctly expressed by Amner, the struggle of the Christian to find his true direction in an alien environment, was given a much longer treatment two decades later by Francis Quarles in his *Emblemes* of 1635, with an accompanying illustration showing the barefoot

---

[10] John Amner, *Sacred Hymnes* (1615), xxiii. For the first line, cf. Psalms 39:12.

pilgrim trying to make his way through a maze, guided by a distant angel who holds a line out to him. Here are five of the eight stanzas.

> Thus I, the object of the worlds disdaine,
>   With Pilgrim pace, surround the weary earth;
> I onely relish what the world counts vaine;
>   Her mirth's my griefe; her sullen Griefe, my mirth;
>   Her light, my darknesse; and her Truth my Error;
> Her freedome is my Jayle; and her delight my Terror.
>
> Fond earth! Proportion not my seeming love
>   To my long stay; let not my thoughts deceive thee;
> Thou art my Prison, and my Home's above;
>   My life's a Preparation but to leave thee:
>   Like one that seeks a doore, I walke about thee.
> With thee I cannot live; I cannot live without thee.
>
> The world's a Lab'rinth, whose anfractious wayes
>   Are all compos'd of Rubs and crook'd Meanders:
> No resting here; Hee's hurried back that stayes
>   A thought; And he that goes unguided, wanders:
>   Her way is dark, her path untrod, unev'n;
> So hard's the way from earth; so hard's the way to Heav'n.
>
> . . . .
>
> Where shall I seek a Guide? Where shall I meet
>   Some lucky hand to lead my trembling paces?
> What trusty Lanterne will direct my feet
>   To scape the danger of these dang'rous places?
>   What hopes have I to passe without a Guide?
> Where one gets safely through, a thousand fall beside.
>
> . . . .
>
> Great God, that art the flowing Spring of Light,
>   Enrich mine eyes with thy refulgent Ray:
> Thou art my Path; direct my steps aright;
>   I have no other Light, no other Way:
>   Ile trust my God, and him alone pursue;
> His Law shall be my Path; his heavnly Light my clue.[11]

---

[11] Francis Quarles, *Emblemes* (1635), Book 4, number ii. In the second line, 'surround' means 'travel round'; *OED*'s first citation (*v.* 4) is 1638; 'anfractious' (properly 'anfractuous') in line 13 means 'winding', 'circuitous'.

To the poem which follows this, Quarles appends a quotation from a sermon by St Augustine containing the following injunction: 'Always add, always walk, always proceed; neither stand still, nor go back, nor deviate.' But if we now look at the work of three major devotional poets, writing between (roughly) 1585 and 1655, we shall see that this demand for forward motion, which is the essence of the pilgrimage metaphor, does not appeal to any of them. The three are Robert Southwell, George Herbert and Henry Vaughan.

Southwell was an alien in his own homeland when in 1586 he returned to England from his education and training abroad as a Jesuit. It was as a hunted man that he wrote his poems, living in hiding in the face of a campaign of ferocious suppression. His pilgrim was Jesus Christ, the archetypal exile, who had chosen to 'sojourne with us in exile' and wear our clothes.

> This made him wander in our Pilgrim weede,
> And taste our tormentes, to relieve our neede.[12]

The title of this poem is 'At Home in Heaven'. It is not only Christ but, after the crucifixion, St Peter who is pilgrim as *peregrinus*, the exiled wanderer. 'St Peter's Complaint' is Southwell's longest and most substantial poem. A 'banishd wretch', by reason of his betrayal of Christ excluded from the 'spheres of love', 'I outcast from these worlds exiled rome', 'From lande of life, strayed pilgrim still I wander.'[13]

The image of journeying is rarely if ever used by Southwell to portray the life of a Christian. He knows of course the conventional metaphor, but it seems he has no time for its forward march.

> Life is a wandring course to doubtfull rest,
>   As oft a cursed ryse to damning leape,
> As happie race to winne a heavenly crest,
>   None being sure, what finall fruites to reape.[14]

Journeying in Southwell is always restless wandering; a sign of absence from God, a punishment even. As regards human fulfilment, images

---

[12] Robert Southwell, *The Poems*, ed. J. H. McDonald and N. P. Brown (Oxford: Clarendon Press, 1967), p. 56.
[13] *Ibid.*, p. 88.   [14] 'Life is but Losse', *ibid.*, p. 51.

of flight, of nestling, of stillness have all the power; the journeying of
the pilgrim has little or none.

> O happy soule that flies so hie,
>   As to attaine this sacred cave:
> Lord send me wings that I may flye,
>   And in this harbour quiet have.[15]

Flight, so important in Vaughan's verse, is not as it must seem to us
an alternative form of travel, but its opposite: an image of effortless
transition. Death frees the soul to make its flight: 'Come cruell death
why lingrest thou so long?'[16] It seems an ironic complaint, considering
the efficiency of Southwell's pursuer, Richard Topcliffe.

> Soare up my soule unto thy rest,
>   Cast off this loathsome loade:
> Long is the date of thy exile,
>   Too long thy strait abode.[17]

In Herbert as in Southwell, travel is away from God not towards
him; it is part of the ordained restlessness of which 'The Pulley'
speaks.[18] The cry 'I will abroad' in 'The Collar' is the cry of defiance,
of separation. It is in the context of the vanity of travel[19] that one ought
to read Herbert's most extended poem on Christian journeying, 'The
Pilgrimage',[20] which begins, 'I travell'd on, seeing the hill, where lay /
My expectation'. The Christian pursues his painful journey towards
his 'expectation', past desperation, pride, care and passion.

> At length I got unto the gladsome hill,
>   Where lay my hope,
> Where lay my heart; and climbing still,
>   When I had gain'd the brow and top,
> A lake of brackish waters on the ground
>   Was all I found.

---

[15] 'Man to the Wound in Christs side', *ibid.*, p. 73.
[16] 'Life is but Losse', *ibid.*, p. 51. [17] 'Seeke Flowers of Heaven', *ibid.*, p. 52.
[18] In *The Works of George Herbert*, ed. F. E. Hutchinson (1941; Oxford: Clarendon
Press, 1953), pp. 159–60.
[19] See especially the questioning of the riches available for sea-travellers in 'The Pearl'
and 'The Size'.
[20] Herbert, *Works*, ed. Hutchinson, pp. 141–2.

'Can both the way and end be tears?' he cries, but 'then perceiv'd / I was deceiv'd'.

> My hill was further: so I flung away,
>   Yet heard a crie
> Just as I went, *None goes that way*
> *And lives:* If that be all, said I,
> After so foul a journey death is fair,
>   And but a chair.

This poem does not so much discredit the metaphor of Christian life as a pilgrimage as question its adequacy and warn of the dangers of false 'expectation' which the metaphor may generate. It may in fact be asked if Herbert's pilgrim gets past the rock of pride. His determined and arduous efforts end in brackish waters and tears. None can be sure, Southwell had said, 'what finall fruites to reape'. The hill that's always 'further' is accessible only by dying, and you reach it not on your feet, but by being taken there, in 'a chair', that is to say, a litter, for, as the poem 'Mortification' says,

> A chair or litter shows the biere,
> Which shall convey him to the house of death.[21]

The ways by which men and women toil towards their expectation of grace, Herbert tells us in 'A Wreath', are 'crooked winding wayes' – like the lines of his own poetry.[22] What a Christian needs is not the contrivance of his own efforts, but simplicity.

> Give me simplicitie, that I may live,
> So live and like, that I may know, thy wayes.

Achieving simplicity is something for which the metaphor of journeying, even the journeying of pilgrimage, seems inappropriate.

I turn now to Henry Vaughan and the remarkable two volumes of *Silex Scintillans*, the spark struck from the flint (1650 and 1655).[23] It was once customary for good critics to say that the dominant theme

---

[21] *Ibid.*, p. 98.   [22] *Ibid.*, p. 185.
[23] There is a sensitive and sympathetic reading of Vaughan's poetry in Stevie Davies's *Henry Vaughan* (Bridgend, Mid Glamorgan: Seren; Poetry Wales Press, 1995).

of Vaughan's poetry was the pilgrimage. 'For Vaughan, life is . . . a pilgrimage to a known shrine, the journey into the Promised Land . . . Life may be a dark labyrinth, but Vaughan cannot lose his way.' This was Molly Mahood in 1950, and there are similar statements by Fredson Bowers in 1962 and Barbara Lewalski in 1979.[24] There is, however, a constant debate in Vaughan's poetry about the value of the metaphor of pilgrimage. In so much of his verse he is testing the power of images to convey something of the inexpressible Christian experience of union and bliss. The pilgrim's journey is almost always shown to be insufficient. As John N. Wall so rightly put it in his book *Transformations of the Word* (1988), speaking of Vaughan's poem 'Regeneration', the effect is 'to throw into doubt the whole notion of the religious life as a narrative of a journey with a goal'. 'Traditional language for situating and interpreting significant religious experience fails.'[25] Traditional language is of course inescapable, but it is always questioned. 'O for thy Center and mid-day!', writes Vaughan of what children instinctively understand, 'For sure that is the *narrow way*' ('Childe-hood', p. 521).[26]

In 'The Resolve' (p. 434), the speaker reprimands himself for his inaction and urges himself to run the traditional race. 'Call in thy *Powers*; run, and reach / Home with the light.'

> [T]here is
> An ancient way
> All strewed with flowres, and happiness
> And fresh as *May*;

[24] Molly Mahood, 'Vaughan: The Symphony of Nature', in her *Poetry and Humanism* (1950), reprinted in Alan Rudrum (ed.), *Essential Articles for the Study of Henry Vaughan* (Hamden, Conn.: Archon Books, 1987), pp. 40–2; Fredson Bowers, 'Henry Vaughan's Multiple Time Scheme', *Modern Language Quarterly* 23 (1962), reprinted in Rudrum (ed.), *Essential Articles*, pp. 91–2; Barbara Lewalski, *Protestant Poetics and the Seventeenth-Century Religious Lyric* (Princeton: Princeton University Press, 1979), esp. pp. 318–19, 331.

[25] J. N. Wall, *Transformations of the Word* (Athens: University of Georgia Press, 1988), pp. 307, 313.

[26] Page references are to the edition of Vaughan's *Works* by L. C. Martin (2nd edn; Oxford: Clarendon Press, 1957), from which the quotations are taken (punctuation sometimes altered).

> There turn, and turn no more; Let wits
>   Smile at fair eies,
>   Or lips; But who there weeping sits,
>   Hath got the *Prize*.

In the end the speaker repudiates his journey and returns to inaction. To turn into the right path is to cease travelling; to win the race is to sit and be still. The ending of the poem reflects Herbert's poem 'The Reprisall', whose first line it borrows, about the sinner overthrown 'in all vict'ries': 'Yet by confession will I come / Into thy conquest'.

Alternatively, Vaughan can suggest that the pilgrim's journey is an obsolete concept. With what seems to be a reference to the Epistle to the Hebrews, he argues that it was the lot of those who lived before the coming of Christ, and is not required under the new law ('Mans fall, and Recovery', pp. 411–12).

> This makes me span
> My fathers journeys, and in one faire step
> O're all their pilgrimage, and labours leap,
>   For God (made man,)
> Reduc'd th'Extent of works of faith; so made
> Of their *Red Sea*, a *Spring*; I wash, they wade.

The Christian in Vaughan's poetry is indeed a pilgrim, but pilgrim as exile, as in Southwell's verse. Being a Welshman estranged from his own people, an Anglican utterly opposed to the changes imposed on his church, living in seclusion by his beloved river Usk, Vaughan knew on his pulses the alienation of which he wrote.[27] Accepting for himself, we might say, the title of *'peregrinus'* as exile, he awards to all who ignore the salvation offered them the title of *'peregrini'* as wanderers. What title is to be awarded to those who, aware of themselves as exiles, truly understand the offered redemption and attempt to prepare themselves is the question his verse will try to decide. The fitness of the title 'pilgrim' is, as I have been indicating, debatable. To Vaughan it conveys too much the suggestion of reward for personal effort, too little the humility of patient stillness. Travel

---

[27] See for example, Christopher Hill, *Collected Essays*, vol. 1: *Writing and Revolution in Seventeenth Century England* (Brighton: Harvester, 1985), Chapter 9.

has in any case been already allocated to those who have not seen the light.

> He hath no root, nor to one place is ty'd,
>   But ever restless and Irregular
>   About this Earth doth run and ride,
>   He knows he hath a home, but scarce knows where.
>
> ('Man', p. 477)

Vaughan's great poetic 'discovery' was of the instinctive awareness in the child of the celestial bliss from which it has come and to which it may return. By this, Vaughan was able to make his fullest exploration of the Christian metaphor of pilgrimage. In 'Regeneration' (pp. 397–9), the child's early life is imaged as a journey of horror.

>   I straight perceiv'd my spring
>   Meere stage, and show,
>   My walke a monstrous mountain'd thing
>   Rough-cast with Rocks, and snow;
>   And as a Pilgrims Eye
>   Far from reliefe,
>   Measures the melancholy skye
>   Then drops, and rains for griefe,
>   So sigh'd I upwards still . . .

The pilgrim here refers both to the worldly person committed to his journey and the Christian who knows it is taking him away from his God. A phantasmagoria of shifting scenes follows: a surreal dream-sequence of emblematic visions presented to the 'restless Eye', none of which brings the speaker into the presence of Christ. The eye having failed, it is the turn of the ear, which hears 'a rushing wind'. Where is it coming from? Impossible to tell. 'It whisper'd; *Where I please*' (see John 3:8). It is not searching but being sought that brings one to Christ. The visitation of grace is unpredictable, incalculable. It will not be found by a journey, but by stillness and readiness.

In 'The Search' (pp. 405–7), the speaker greets the 'Pilgrim-Sunne'. 'All night have I / Spent in a roving Extasie / To find my Saviour.' He recounts his 'visits': to Bethlehem, to Gethsemane and to other places 'where my deare Lord did often tread' until (again) he hears a voice: 'Leave, leave, thy gadding thoughts; . . . Search well another world'; that is, the world within. This poem is usually taken to be about meditation and its insufficiency,[28] and so it is, but the meditations are metaphoric pilgrimage-journeys to the Holy Land and the poem is as much opposed to the real as to the imagined journeys. It is in 'Looking back' (p. 660) that we find the idea of the return to childhood vision as the true pilgrimage.

> Fair, shining *Mountains* of my pilgrimage
>   And flow'ry *Vales*, whose flow'rs were stars:
> The *days* and *nights* of my first, happy age;
>   An age without distast and warrs . . .

The idea of the pilgrimage-return is fully developed in the unmatchable poem 'The Retreate' (pp. 419–20).

> Happy those early dayes! When I
> Shin'd in my Angell-infancy.
> Before I understood this place
> Appointed for my second race,
> Or taught my soul to fancy ought
> But a white, Celestiall thought . . .

In this innocence, the visible world had borne 'some shadows of eternity'; and the speaker had felt through his 'fleshly dresse' 'bright *shootes* of everlastingnesse'.

> O how I long to travell back
> And tread again that ancient track!
> . . . .
> From whence th'Inlightned spirit sees
> That shady City of Palme trees;
> But (ah!) my soul with too much stay
> Is drunk, and staggers in the way.
> Some men a forward motion love,
> But I by backward steps would move,
> And when this dust falls to the urn
> In that state I came return.

---

[28] See L. L. Martz, *The Poetry of Meditation*, rev. edn (1950; New Haven and London: Yale University Press, 1962), pp. 86–90, and Lewalski, *Protestant Poetics*, p. 335.

The idea of pilgrimage as return is of great antiquity and indeed is implicit in the whole concept of heaven as the home of the spirit. As in the *Odyssey*, one's ultimate destination is where one starts from. In ancient Greece the religious festivals of Athens were seen as home-comings. Athenians re-established their identity in the sacred place of their birth.[29] In Vaughan the return is a kind of counter-pilgrimage, a pilgrimage of the mind to set against the dreary wandering of the daily course.

It is only in the light of the two kinds of pilgrimage that Vaughan's poem called 'The Pilgrimage' (p. 464–5) can be properly understood. The travellers are the wanderers of this world. They lodge in a 'Jacob-like' place,

> Where till the day restore the race
> They rest and dream homes of their own.

Quite unlike them in their contented rest is the speaker, unable to sleep. Exiled from what he knows to be his true home, he longs to receive, as Jacob received, a visitation from God, longs to receive the food that Elijah received (1 Kings 19) which enabled him to make his journey 'unto Horeb the mount of God'.

> So strengthen me, Lord, all the way,
> That I may travel to thy Mount.

So this is a pilgrimage within a pilgrimage. The inn is the world; the other travellers are unaware of where they are – benighted people. The speaker has the knowledge denied the others, but his role is to wait for the visitation which alone can, in due time, transport him to his home.

Certainly, therefore, there is journey imagery in Vaughan's concept of Christian experience, even though it is featured most strikingly as travelling *back*. All the same, the essence of Christian life, it seems to me, is expressed with greater power in other kinds of imagery. Entrance into the divine presence is most frequently portrayed by the

---

[29] See the early pages of S. Colman and J. Elsner, *Pilgrimage Past and Present* (London: British Museum Press, 1995), esp. pp. 10–15.

Hermetic image of flight, as in the bodiless assumption of 'Ascension-day' (pp. 481–2). In 'a love-sick souls exalted flight' ('Cock-crowing', pp. 488–9), time is collapsed into a momentary flash of transformation.

> Brush me with thy light, that I
> May shine unto a perfect day,
> And warme me at thy glorious Eye!

A particularly beautiful poem, 'The Seed growing secretly' (pp. 510–11), rejects the Miltonic appeal for virtue to show itself in the arena of public contest,[30] and finds the proper image of increasing holiness in the silent growth of the seed.

> What needs a Conscience, calm and bright
> Within it self, an outward test?
> Who breaks his glass to take more light,
> Makes way for storms into his rest.
>
> Then bless thy secret growth, nor catch
> At noise, but thrive unseen and dumb;
> Keep clean, bear fruit, earn life and watch
> Till the white winged Reapers come!

True pilgrimage, if it can be called pilgrimage, shows itself in Vaughan without muscularity as a vision of the soul waiting in quietness for its ultimate bonding, as in 'The Night' (p. 522), which seems to set the Song of Solomon ('it is the voice of my beloved that knocketh, saying Open to me') against St Matthew ('Seek, and ye shall find; knock, and it shall be opened unto you.')

> Gods silent, searching flight:
> When my Lords head is fill'd with dew, and all
> His locks are wet with the clear drops of night;
> His still, soft call . . .

---

[30] John Milton, *Areopagitica* (1644).

CHAPTER 5

Westward ho!

The great European movement to take ships beyond the Pillars of Hercules to explore and exploit the new world had an enormous impact on the word 'pilgrim'. Perhaps the most prominent extension was the use of the word for the founding fathers of the United States of America, particularly those who settled in New England in the seventeenth century, providing for the later nation an image of fore-sight, courage, endurance and rectitude as an essential element in its heritage. The role of three men in particular in the crucial christening of the Pilgrim Fathers is worth investigating: St Brendan, William Bradford and Samuel Purchas.[1]

Coming late to the carve-up of the new world, Elizabethan England sought to establish its right to the North American coast, from New-foundland as far south as was practicable. The right lay in the need to extend Christianity (in its purest form) across the Atlantic, and in the historical record of English involvement on the North American coast. St Brendan may seem an unlikely candidate either for exporting Protestantism or for exploring America, but his presence is significant. The life of this Irish saint is obscure.[2] He was probably born at the end of the fifth century and died around AD 575. His name is connected with the founding of various monastic establishments, especially Clonfert

---

[1] The link between Bradford and Purchas in the matter of American pilgrimage was made by John Seelye in *Prophetic Waters: The River in Early American Life and Literature* (New York: Oxford University Press, 1977).

[2] See J. J. O'Meara, *The Voyage of Saint Brendan: Journey to the Promised Land* (1976; Dublin: Dolmen Press, 1978); Eleanor Duckett, *The Wandering Saints* (London: Collins, 1959); Geoffrey Ashe (*et al.*), *The Quest for America* (London: Pall Mall, 1971); Peter Harbison, *Pilgrimage in Ireland* (London: Barrie and Jenkins, 1991).

in Co. Galway. The earliest legends make him a true *peregrinus*, one who wandered by sea to find an island of desire where he might most fittingly worship Christ. He is supposed to have visited St Columba in Iona. The later legend of his wanderings, gathering strength from the imposing body of *immrama*, Irish voyage narratives, is found in the Latin *Navigatio Sancti Brendani Abbatis*, well-known throughout Europe in the early Middle Ages, and thought to date from the late eighth or the ninth century.[3]

In the *Navigatio*, St Brendan hears from St Barrind of the island called the Promised Land of the Saints, where night does not fall nor day end, which God has prepared for 'those who come after us at the end of time'.[4] St Brendan resolves to seek this island. He builds a boat, ribbed with wood, covered with ox-hides and equipped with sail and oars, selects fourteen brothers from his community, and sets off on what turns out to be a seven-year pilgrimage. He encounters a whole series of magical islands. On some of them are communities of other Irish *peregrini*; one is an island of sheep; on another, uninhabited, they are miraculously fed; one turns out to be a whale; and one is the important Island of Birds. The birds are good angels who were caught up in the fall of Lucifer, and assume bodily shape every now and then. St Brendan and his monks are enabled to celebrate Easter here, and they receive good tidings of the Promised Land. Celebrations of the major Christian feasts on appropriate islands are an important feature of the voyage. All the time, although strenuous effort by sail and by oar is necessary, the ship is in the guiding hand of God, who wants to show the *peregrini* 'his varied secrets in the great ocean'[5] before he allows them to reach the Promised Land, which is concealed by a bank of fog. They are not permitted to stay here; St Brendan is told he is reaching the end of his days and must return home, taking what he can carry of the fruit and precious stones which abound on the island. The land, on which night never falls, 'for its light is Christ', is reserved for future times 'when persecution of the Christians shall have come'. So Brendan travels back to Ireland, and soon dies, as it was foretold.

[3] See Richard Sharpe, *Medieval Irish Saints' Lives* (Oxford: Clarendon Press, 1991), p. 17.
[4] O'Meara's translation, *Voyage of Saint Brendan*, pp. 4–5.   [5] *Ibid.*, p. 69.

The *Navigatio* is a brilliant work of imaginative literature. As an historical record its value is extremely questionable. Its doubtful standing in this respect, however, did not worry the learned John Dee (1527–1609). It was not only Dee's prodigious mathematical and astronomical knowledge, applied to the arts of navigation, which made him the adviser of every Elizabethan explorer, including Frobisher, Gilbert, Davis, Drake and Ralegh; it was his enthusiastic endorsement and encouragement of their aims in advancing the cause of extending the nascent English empire. In the late 1570s Dee prepared for Queen Elizabeth a document giving historical evidence of her title to oversea territories, and he included the voyages and discoveries of St Brendan as part of this.[6] In view of the imminent subjugation of what remained of an independent Ireland, the first fruits of English imperialism, the incorporation of an Irish abbot among the pioneers of English exploration might be excused. It is perhaps more important that the voyages of the abbot, whatever his nation, should be identified as exploration, and that the Promised Land he sought should assume the shape of the American continent. Dee's mentions of Brendan are casual but they effectively transform the Irish pilgrim, performing his *peregrinatio* for the closer worship of God, into the modern explorer and settler, justifying his appropriations with a religious excuse. Ernst Renan saw Brendan's expedition as 'cette combinaison du naturalisme celtique avec le spiritualisme chrétien'.[7] By 'naturalisme celtique' he meant this: 'Perhaps the profoundest instinct of the Celtic peoples is their desire to penetrate the unknown. With the sea before them, they wish to know what is beyond it. They dream of the promised land.'[8] Some modern writers have been convinced that St Brendan had actually reached America.[9] George Little, in *Brendan the Navigator* (Dublin, 1946) hailed his hero as 'Brendan the *conquistador*'

---

[6] See Ken MacMillan, 'John Dee's "Brytanici Imperii Limites"', *Huntington Library Quarterly* 64 (2001), 151–9, and O'Meara, *Voyage of Saint Brendan*, pp. xi–xii.

[7] Ernst Renan, 'La poésie des races Celtiques' (1913), quoted by O'Meara in *Voyage of Saint Brendan*, p. xi.

[8] As quoted by Shane Leslie, *Saint Patrick's Purgatory* (London: Burnes, Oates and Washbourne, 1932), p. xxiii.

[9] E.g., Denis O'Donoghue in *Brendaniana* (Dublin, 1895), p. 130.

(p. 139) and identified a great many of the islands in the *Navigatio* as real places on the American continent. 'It seems reasonably safe to hazard the surmise that Brendan and his crew landed near to the beach of modern Miami' (p. 147). Cooler research by Geoffrey Ashe believes that although the *immrama* do not prompt a theory of an Irish discovery of America, there is some historical truth in the fantasy of the *Navigatio*, and that 'it is arguable only, and far from proved' that the real Brendan had reached Newfoundland, Nova Scotia and the Atlantic seaboard of what became the United States.[10]

Most remarkable of the heirs of John Dee and Ernst Renan is Tim Severin. In his absorbing book of 1978, *The Brendan Voyage*,[11] he tells how, convinced that the *Navigatio* contained clues to the real voyages of St Brendan and other sea-going monks of 400 years earlier, he actually built a boat of wood and ox-hides and made a perilous voyage in 1976–7 from Ireland to Newfoundland by way of the Faeroes and Iceland. *The Brendan Voyage* is a scholarly book, yet its whole *raison d'être* is questionable. It depends, first, on the unhistorical apotheosis of exploration, implying that there could be no higher aim for a *peregrinus* than a voyage of discovery, and that their Promised Land must be America, and secondly, that one can 'vindicate' (p. 254) the *Navigatio* by showing it as the imaginative but muddied recension of actual voyages undertaken by St Brendan. That the *Navigatio* did indeed show knowledge of the sea-going experience of earlier *peregrini* is undoubted, and Severin has located and interpreted these fossils brilliantly, but that the *Navigatio* takes St Brendan to the new world is highly improbable.

It was without doubt Samuel Purchas who, in the early decades of the seventeenth century, most decisively identified pilgrims as explorers and thus by implication relocated the mythical adventures of St Brendan's search for the Promised Land of the Saints in the hard realities of colonialism, but it is to William Bradford, who more directly turned North American colonists into pilgrims, that I now turn.

[10] Geoffrey Ashe, *The Quest for America* (London: Pall Mall Press, 1971), p. 38. See also Ashe's prolonged investigation in *Land to the West* (London: Collins, 1962).
[11] Tim Severin, *The Brendan Voyage* (London: Hutchinson, 1978).

Bradford was born in Austerfield, south Yorkshire, in 1589, and as a boy became influenced by the 'separatists' who could not accept the practices of the established church and pursued their own form of worship.[12] Bradford joined a group of like-minded people at Scrooby, near his home, in the early years of the seventeenth century. The group was harried by the ecclesiastical authorities however, and the decision was taken to go overseas to Holland, where many other separatists had found greater freedom of worship. The group, perhaps as many as a hundred, were in the Netherlands, first at Amsterdam and then at Leyden, from 1609 to 1620. They never had a distinguishing name. They settled into their new country; they were well integrated, many became Dutch citizens and many were well-to-do. Bradford found occupation as a fustian worker, and married Dorothy May in 1613. But, for a number of reasons, they began to look for a place in the new world. There was strife in Holland over Arminianism, there was the constant problem of protecting the group's convictions from external influences, and there was the outbreak of the Thirty Years' War (in 1618).

The move to England and then to New England in the *Mayflower*, and the founding of the Plymouth settlement near Cape Cod, were described by Bradford in the history he later wrote, 'Of Plymouth Plantation'. He became the second Governor of the colony in 1621, and apart from a period of five years remained Governor until his death in 1656. He began writing his history as early as 1630, and completed it later, in 1646 and 1650. He movingly described the feeling of community and affection among the Leyden group, coming 'as near the primitive pattern of the first churches' as any of later times. The decision to uproot themselves was all the same neither easy nor happy; it meant the surrender of so much. The division in the minds of those who chose to go can be seen in the division of families: men leaving wives behind, couples leaving children behind – as William and Dorothy Bradford left behind their only son, John, who was

---

[12] This account owes much to Bradford Smith's biography, *Bradford of Plymouth* (Philadelphia and New York: J. B. Lippincott, 1951).

five years old. Bradford recorded the boarding in Holland of the *Speedwell*, their original ship, in the following famous words.

So they lefte the goodly and pleasante citie, which had been ther resting place near 12 years; but they knew they were pilgrimes, and looked not much on those things, but lift up their eyes to the heavens, their dearest cuntrie, and quieted their spirits.[13]

'They knew they were pilgrimes.' This is the crucial sentence that we shall be scrutinising; it was, of course, written years after the event. The separatists were never as a body referred to at that time as 'pilgrims'. Bradford also said that there was a missionary zeal among those most eager to go: the hope of 'laying some good foundation . . . for the propagating and advancing the gospel of the kingdom of Christ in those remote parts of the world . . . devoid of all civil inhabitants, where there are only savage and brutish men which range up and down little otherwise than the wild beasts of the same'.

The proposed destination of the group was Virginia. Agents of the Leyden group had been negotiating for a long time in London with the Virginia Company. It was proving impossible to gain for the Leyden group the religious freedom they required. But at last they got a patent for settling in Virginia. In the meantime, however, a second company had come on the scene, the Plymouth Virginia Company with territory in New England. The developer was Sir Fernando Gorges, and Captain John Smith was an advocate. The Cape Cod area had been reconnoitred, and the beach and harbour later to be used by the settlers had been explored and named 'New Plymouth'. Gorges was anxious to have settlers, and it is the confident opinion of Bradford Smith, the biographer of William Bradford, that the Leyden group intended to settle in New England even before they left Holland. This reverses the commonly held view that the

---

[13] In quoting from William Bradford I have normally used the edition *Of Plymouth Plantation 1620–1647*, ed. Samuel Eliot Morison (New York: Knopf, 1952). This gives modernised spelling, and I have occasionally, as here, used the spelling of the MS as given in *History of Plymouth Plantation 1620–1647* published for the Massachusetts Historical Society (Boston: Houghton Mifflin, 1912).

destination was Virginia and that the landing on Cape Cod was a kind of accident.

In Southampton the *Speedwell* was joined by the *Mayflower*, with many 'strangers' on board – other emigrants from England. They sailed on 5 August 1620, but the *Speedwell* leaked badly and proved quite unsuitable for the voyage. Eventually, the *Mayflower* left Plymouth (England) on her own on 6 September with 102 colonists, none of them gentry. After two months of stormy voyaging they reached Cape Cod and later moved west across the bay to disembark at the new Plymouth. Bradford wrote of their arrival as follows.

> What could they see but a hideous and desolate wilderness, full of wild beasts and wild men? . . . What could now sustain them but the spirit of God and his grace? May not and ought not the children of these fathers rightly say: Our fathers were Englishmen which came over this great ocean, and were ready to perish in this wilderness, but they cried unto the Lord, and he heard their voice, and looked on their adversitie, etc. . . . When they wandered in the desert and wilderness out of the way, and found no city to dwell in, both hungry and thirsty, their soul was overwhelmed in them. Let them confess before the Lord his loving kindness, and his wonderful works before the sons of men.[14]

Bradford gives two biblical references in the margin, to the Psalms (Psalm 107 is directly quoted) and to the 26th chapter of Deuteronomy, which tells of the Lord bringing the Israelites out of Egypt into a land flowing with milk and honey.

There can be little doubt that in writing of the Leyden group of separatists as pilgrims Bradford was influenced by the words of Robert Cushman, a senior member of the settlers. Cushman contributed two pieces to a remarkable publication generally known as 'Mourts relation' (thought to be by George Morton): *A Relation or Journall of the beginning and proceedings of the English Plantation setled at Plimouth in NEW ENGLAND*. This was sent back to England and published in London in 1622. Cushman contributed to this both a sermon on the danger of self-love, given in the new settlement in December 1621 (also published separately) and an afterpiece, 'Reasons and considerations touching the lawfulnesse of removing out of *England* into the

---

[14] This is transcribed from the Massachusetts Historical Society version (pp. 156–8), accepting S. E. Morison's modern spelling (pp. 62–3). See note 13 above.

parts of *America*.' The sermon, a powerful and lucid argument on the need for unselfishness and altruism in the circumstances in which they found themselves, ends with the wish that the settlers 'in brotherly love, and peace, may bee translated from this wandering wildernesse, into that joyfull and heavenly *Canaan*'.

In this conclusion to the sermon, Cushman accepts the implications of the pilgrimage metaphor in Hebrews, in which all earthly life is a temporary alienation from one's true home in the Promised Land of heaven, and rejects the physical 'promised land' as a 'wandering wildernesse'. And this is the burden of the afterpiece to 'Mourt's Relation' (signed 'R. C.'), which is entirely occupied with answering the question, why (if all earthly habitation is a hostile and temporary environment) have we come out here? In the past, Cushman says, God might have summoned our fathers to actual places and habitations but now 'there is no such calling to be expected'.

Neither is there any land or possession now, like unto the possession which the Jewes had in *Canaan*, being legally holy and appropriated unto a holy people the seed of *Abraham*, in which they dwelt securely, and had their daies prolonged, it being by an immediate voice said, that he (the Lord) gave it them as a land of rest after their wearie travels, and a type of *Eternall* rest in heaven, but now there is no land of that Sanctimonie, no land so appropriated; none typicall; much lesse any that can be said to be given of God to any nation as was *Canaan*, which they and their seed must dwell in, till God sendeth upon them sword or captivitie: but now we are in all places strangers and Pilgrims, travellers and sojourners, most properly, having no dwelling but in this earthen Tabernacle; our dwelling is but a wandering, and our abiding but as a fleeting, and in a word our home is nowhere but in the heavens: in that house not made with hands, whose maker and builder is God, and to which all ascend that love the comming of our Lord Jesus.

'We are in all places strangers and Pilgrims.' So why do we emigrate? 'To plant a rude wildernesse, to enlarge the honour and fame of our dread Soveraigne, but chiefly to displaie the efficacie and power of the Gospell.' 'We have here great peace, plentie of the Gospell, and many sweet delights and varietie of comforts.' As for the lawfulness of the enterprise, the original inhabitants have not made proper use of the land. 'It is lawfull now to take a land which none useth, and make use of it.' In addition, the original inhabitants have granted us suzerainty. The duty of converting the heathen is all-important, and there is no reason why, given voluntary conversion, all should not live at peace.

I am very much in debt to John Seelye for the attention he gave in his book *Prophetic Waters*[15] to Robert Cushman's contributions to 'Mourt's Relation', and particularly to the magnificent passage I have just quoted and its argument that there is no true pilgrimage except to heaven. But a difference in interpretation now arises. Seelye emphasised the radical and contentious nature of Cushman's epilogue, seeing it as an attempt to maintain the other-wordly definition of Canaan against Bradford, whom he lines up with the worldly Samuel Purchas, eager for the commercial exploitation of the new world. 'From *Purchas his Pilgrimes* to *Of Plymouth Plantation* is not merely an alliterative bridge' (p. 101). I see a very wide gulf between Purchas and Bradford. It has to be remembered that Cushman, writing at the close of the first year of the Plymouth settlement, was the first person to refer to the emigrants as pilgrims, and there is no doubt at all that he meant they were celestial pilgrims, who should not regard the land they had come to as the land promised them by God. When Bradford, beginning his history a decade later, said that his companions were heavy-hearted at leaving Leyden for the unknown, and wrote 'but they knew they were pilgrimes, and looked not much on those things', he can only have meant 'pilgrims' in the sense that Cushman used it, pilgrims on their way to a heavenly promised land, for whom all worldly abode, however congenial, was alien and temporary. What Bradford and his fellows wanted was what Cushman (after a year in the settlement) thought he had got, namely elbow-room in the new world to exercise and strengthen their faith.

It seems to me that Seelye imposed on the Leyden settlers the image stamped on them many years afterwards, as pilgrims to America who tamed the wilderness and established the commercial possibility of the United States. In his book he always called them what they never called themselves, the pilgrims. Yet if they thought of themselves in those early days as pilgrims they used the word as Cushman used it,

---

[15] See note 1.

as Bradford used it and as the Epistle to the Hebrews used it, as a metaphor for Christians who despised the world and saw themselves en route to a heavenly promised land. In later life Bradford wrote a 34-line elegy which began as follows.[16]

> From my yeares young in dayes of youth,
> God did make known to me his Truth,
> And call'd me from my Native place
> For to enjoy the Means of Grace.
> In *Wilderness* he did me guide,
> And in *strange Lands* for me provide.
> In *Fears* and *Wants*, through *Weal* and *Woe*,
> As *Pilgrim* past I to and fro:
> Oft left of them whom I did trust;
> How vain it is to rest on *Dust*!
> A man of *Sorrows* I have been,
> And many *Changes* I have seen.[17]

Of course it may be the case that as he looked back Bradford felt that his initial hopes for a new-world religious community had been to some extent betrayed, and also that the land they had come to from Leyden was a more tangible realisation of God's promise than it had at first seemed, but when he wrote the word 'pilgrim' in this poem, he used the term as he had used it to describe the emigrants of 1620, pilgrims to heaven.

It was the strange figure of Cotton Mather who, in the mid 1690s, conferred on the Plymouth settlers the legend of the territorial pilgrims. This was in his *Magnalia Christi Americana* ('the wonderful works of Christ in America').[18] Mather was the son of Increase Mather, and like his father he entered Harvard at the age of twelve. He is best known for the prominent part he played in the persecution of witches in New England, including those of Salem, though he objected to the procedures of the prosecution in the Salem trials. He was convinced that Satan had reigned among the heathen Indians, and that

---

[16] See Nathaniel Morton, *New Englands Memoriall* (Cambridge, 1669), p. 144.

[17] In the original, my italic and roman are reversed.

[18] Published in London in 1702. I have used the edition of Books One and Two by K. B. Murdock and E. W. Miller, *Magnalia Christi Americana* (Cambridge, Mass: Belknap Press of Harvard University Press, 1977).

his malevolence was still evident among the settlers. He was also convinced that North America had been concealed by God, and reserved for the coming of Christianity when it had been perfected by the Reformation. He read Bradford's *Of Plymouth Plantation* as the coming of 'a pilgrim people, a little Israel in the vast new Canaan of the Western hemisphere'. 'These good People were now *satisfy'd*, they had as plain a command of Heaven to attempt a Removal, as ever their Father *Abraham* had for his leaving the *Caldean* Territories.' 'They took their leave of the pleasant City, where they had been *Pilgrims* and *strangers* now for Eleven Years' (pp. 123–7). Mather picked up the term which Bradford followed Cushman in using, and transformed the celestial pilgrimage into a territorial pilgrimage. And in so doing, he transformed Bradford into a reincarnation of Moses.

The *Leader* of a people in a *Wilderness* had need be a *Moses*; and if a *Moses* had not led the People of *Plymouth-Colony*, when this worthy Person was their Governour, the People had never with so much Unanimity and Importunity still called *him* to lead them. (p. 207)

Mather's curious sentence indicates the requirement of his own mythology for a Moses figure to piece out the biblical analogy. It took a hundred years, however, for Mather's transformation of the Leyden pilgrims to be fully effected.[19] In 1793 the Rev. Chandler Robbins used Bradford's pilgrim reference in a sermon on Forefathers' Day and reinforced his words by two hymns, one of which had the line, 'Hail Pilgrim Fathers of our Race!' In December 1798, the 'Heirs of the Pilgrims' held a feast at Boston, and in 1819 the Pilgrim Society was founded.

The work of Samuel Purchas was well known to Cotton Mather, who recommended his record of early settlements in America.[20] Purchas's major works were *Purchas His Pilgrimage* (1613, with three later editions); *Purchas His Pilgrim* (1619); and *Purchas His Pilgrimes*, also entitled *Hakluytus Posthumus* in some copies (four volumes, 1625).

[19] See Albert Matthews, 'The Term Pilgrim Fathers', *Transactions of the Colonial Society of Massachusetts* 17 (1913–14), 293–393.
[20] Mather, *Magnalia*, ed. Murdock and Miller, p. 121.

This last was a huge collection of voyage narratives, many of them originally in the possession of Richard Hakluyt.

Purchas's use of the words 'pilgrim' and 'pilgrimage', which may seem obsessive, all-embracing and indiscriminate, was in fact a determined effort to push the idea of pilgrimage into a signification which looked old but was new. Born in 1577 at Thaxted in Essex, Purchas discovered while he was at Cambridge his 'travelling Genius, whereof (without travelling) he hath travelled ever since'.[21] He was ordained in 1601, and became vicar of Eastwood, Essex, in 1604. He added other livings to this, and in 1614 became rector of St Martin's, Ludgate. He was a prodigious reader, and he had a wide acquaintance among those connected with the sea: travellers, explorers, merchants and sailors. He met Hakluyt in 1614. Hakluyt died in 1616, and his great collection of unpublished voyage material came into the possession of Purchas, who used it in *Hakluytus Posthumus, or Purchas His Pilgrimes* in 1625. It is not known how Purchas acquired these manuscripts; they were not bequeathed to him, and there is no evidence that he bought them. Purchas personally presented a copy of *Pilgrimes* to James I shortly before his death, and was gratified to hear that the king had read *Pilgrimage* seven times. Purchas died in September 1626.

To go then to the first major work, *Purchas His Pilgrimage* of 1613, and congratulating James I on coping seven times with the tortuous verbosity of Purchas's prose (Thoreau called *Pilgrimes* 'an impassable swamp'[22]), we have to ask, why pilgrimage? The sub-title of the work explains that it is the first part of a vast structure (there was never a second part) giving 'Relations of the World and the Religions, observed in all ages and places discovered, from the Creation unto this Present'. This first part, specially concerned with 'Ancient Religions before the Flood', deals with Asia, Africa, and America. The work, he writes, is history clad in the garments of geography, and his colossal bibliography includes those who 'by their Navigations and Discoveries, have

---

[21] In discussing Purchas I constantly use the invaluable *Purchas Handbook*, edited by L. E. Pennington and published in London by the Hakluyt Society in 1997 (in two volumes), hereafter called *Handbook*; biographical details are from D. A. Ransome 'A Purchas Chronology', in *Handbook*, vol. I, pp. 329–80.

[22] *Handbook*, vol. I, p. 3.

made the world knowne to it selfe'. He tells his reader that 'I here bring *Religion* from *Paradise* to the *Arke*, and thence follow her round the World, and (for her sake) observe the World it selfe.' So the author himself is a pilgrim, 'this my *Pilgrimage*', but although he calls the book 'my first Voyage of Discoverie', it is only 'a second Pilgrimage' in that he is following the progress of the first pilgrim, Christ, whose footsteps have traversed the world.[23] Later editions, in which Purchas more modestly refers to himself as 'your poore Pilgrime' and his book as 'this tedious Pilgrimage', elaborate this layering of pilgrimage, in which both the author and the book qualify as pilgrims, following Christ who is the first pilgrim. Insofar as Purchas is a pilgrim in that he is a literary voyager, his voyage, and the term 'pilgrim', are sanctified in that his 'perambulation' follows the perambulation of Christ. This is the structure which explains Purchas's repetitive book-titles and honours his own writings.

Purchas His Pilgrimes of 1625 is explicit about the meaning of its title. Because the book is a collection of edited voyage narratives by a host of different writers, with commentary by the editor, the focus and emphasis of Purchas's philosophy of pilgrimage make a significant change of direction. Purchas tried to explain to the king the difference between the earlier work, the *Pilgrimage*, and the later, *Pilgrimes*, when he presented the later work to him.

These Brethren holding much resemblance in name, nature and feature, yet differ both in the object and subject: This [the *Pilgrimage*] being mine own in matter (though borrowed) and in forme of words and method: Whereas my *Pilgrims* are the Authors themselves, acting their owne parts in their owne words.[24]

Pilgrimes, Purchas further explained, was 'a full Voyage, and in a method of Voyages'. That is to say, it might, like his previous work, be metaphorically termed a voyage, but this time it was made up of the narratives of actual voyages. The importance of Purchas's remarks

[23] See the Dedication to the Archbishop of Canterbury.
[24] This reminiscence is from the Dedication of the 1626 edition of *Pilgrimage* to Charles I. It is reprinted, with Purchas's further efforts in clarification, in *Handbook*, vol. I, pp. 365–6.

is to show the all-important identification (always implicit) of real voyages by sea with the metaphoric journey of the writer, and the investment of those real voyages with the sanctity already granted to the writer's efforts. Both the writer and the navigator are pilgrims. The first charts Christianity, the second extends it.

The first two chapters of the first book of *Pilgrimes* are devoted to the task of the sanctification of voyages. Solomon provides a rock-like biblical blessing. In 1 Kings 9:26–8 and 2 Chronicles 9:21–4 it is recorded that Solomon made a navy of ships and sent them to Ophir, and they fetched gold for him thence, and Solomon passed all the kings of the earth in riches and wisdom. Solomon's riches, of course, may be understood in a tropical sense as the riches of Truth, a Truth to which we shall all return 'after our Navigation and earthly Pilgrimage ended'. Nevertheless, in a more material way of looking at things, Solomon may 'first by his example teach us the lawfulnesse of Navigation to remote Regions'. The second chapter, 'Mans life a Pilgrimage', widens the context of the holiness of 'peregrination'. Though Adam was 'turned out of Paradise to wander, a Pilgrime over the world', God 'added a world supercelestiall, where fallen regained Man might supply the roomes of fallen forlorne Angels'. To make this ascent possible, the greatest of all peregrinations took place, 'when the *word was made flesh* and (leaving his Fathers house) *dwelt amongst* us'. The Ascension was the next major peregrination, but even before that Christ's earthly journeys were 'sufficient to yeelde a large Volumne of Voyages'. The journeys of the Apostles continue the story of divine peregrinations. At this point Purchas goes into lyrical praise of modern navigation, which, along with printing, had made possible the dissemination of true religion, 'that Christ may bee salvation to the ends of the Earth, and all Nations may serve him'.

In the preliminary 'To the Reader', Purchas had already put in a Baconian claim that the value of a history of voyages and discovery was the revelation of God's world. His pilgrims, he wrote, 'minister individuall and sensible materials (as it were with Stones, Brickes and Mortar) to those universall Speculators for their Theoricall structures'. Wisdom being the science of things divine and human, his concern is with natural things, notwithstanding his position as 'a professed

Divine'; his concern is 'the Workes of God in the Creatures', and the travellers whose works he will reproduce are the 'Pilgrime-Guides' enabling others to 'travell to and over the most uncouth Countries of the World'.

Purchas's claim for a religious base to voyaging has been denounced as hypocrisy, most curtly by Francis Jennings in 1975: 'a system of ideas designed for a conqueror's needs'.[25] It is true that Purchas was an ardent imperialist, particularly as regards English settlement in North America. The question of how far his belief in the value of territorial acquisition abroad was balanced by his belief in the need to spread Christianity is best judged from 'Virginias Verger: Or a Discourse shewing the benefits which may grow to this Kingdome from American English Plantations, and specially those of Virginia and Summer Ilands'. This discourse is Purchas's own, and it appears as Chapter 20 of Book 9, in volume IV of *Pilgrimes*.[26] Purchas was writing shortly after the 1622 massacre of settlers by Indians and the vengeance policy of Edward Waterhouse, whose account of the massacre Purchas had printed in his Chapter 14. His message is one of mercy and the need for collaboration, while recognising, as Christians, 'that all things are ours, and wee Christs, and Christ Gods; without thoughts of invasion and usurpation'. The scope of the Virginian plantation, he writes, is not 'to make Savages and wild, degenerate men of Christians, but Christians of those Savage, wild, degenerate men; to whom preaching must needs be vaine, if it begins with publike Latrocinie [violent plundering]'.

Purchas establishes the right of the English to settle in Virginia (without 'invasion and usurpation') with familiar arguments. The land was not properly inhabited, the English were the first to discover Virginia (he passes over the claims of 'King Malgo' and 'Saint Brandon'), the land was voluntarily surrendered to them. Above all is the need for 'Christian Plantations', 'to plant Christianity, to produce and multiply Christians'. 'So good a Countrey', he goes on, 'so bad people,

---

[25] Francis Jennings, *The Invasion of America* (Chapel Hill: University of North Carolina Press, 1975), p. 81. See also Seelye, *Prophetic Waters*, Chapter 4.

[26] In the indispensable MacLehose reprint of *Purchas His Pilgrimes* (Glasgow, 1905–7), this is vol. XIX, pp. 218ff.

having little of Humanitie but shape, ignorant of Civilitie, of Arts, of Religion; more brutish than the beasts they hunt . . . captivated also to Satans tyranny in foolish pieties, mad impieties, wicked idlenesse, busie and bloudy wickednesse: hence have wee fit objects of zeale and pitie, to deliver from the power of darknesse.' Murderers must be rooted out, but mercy should be shown to those 'capable of Christian Faith'. The return for all this effort is prodigious. 'All the rich endowments of Virginia . . . are wages for all this worke: God in wise-dome having enriched the Savage Countries, that those riches might be attractives for Christian suters, which there may sowe spirituals and reape temporals'. Admittedly there is no gold or silver, but who knows what 'further Discovery of parts adjoyning' may not reveal?

Purchas now becomes dithyrambic about the prospects of the yield from Virginia; he has pages of expectations, including 'Wal-nuts in three sorts'. He keeps coming back to the massacre of the colonists, and to the harshness necessary for the murderers and the clemency to be shown to the rest. The terms he uses make discrimination hard to understand. The situation requires, he writes, that 'servile natures be servily used: that future dangers be prevented by the extirpation of the more dangerous, and commodities also raised out of the servileness and serviceablenesse of the rest'. This astonishing sentence appears to use 'servile' in two senses, but in both the indigenous people of Virginia as a whole are regarded as slaves. One group of these people behave as brutishly as you would expect slaves to behave, and they must be extirpated; the other group are not dangerous, but, as they belong to a slave-class, they will be useful (even as Christians) to work for colonists in producing 'commodities'.

It is unfair to call Purchas a cynical hypocrite; he probably believed in all sincerity in what he wrote. But that does not make it the less dreadful. The religious justification for colonialism given in 'Virginia's Verger' is perfunctory. The work is fundamentally a patriotic call for occupation and conquest. His understanding of Christianity seems extremely limited, and his conception of spreading it to expropriated 'natives' extremely distasteful. Those who make his oversea empire possible he christens pilgrims. This is not the terminology of Cushman or Bradford. Purchas's vociferous claims have little to add to the idea of pilgrimage. Indeed, one might say that he plays a big part in the softening of the word which currently afflicts it. His use of the word to describe authorship is flawed because despite his huge book-list his ideas are routine and full of prejudice. The idea of the explorer as pilgrim is much more interesting, but he so dilutes it in combining it with imperialist acquisition that he makes it very vulnerable.

Reading *Heart of Darkness*, written two and three-quarter centuries later (1899), one wonders if Conrad had been reading *Purchas His Pilgrimes* (which has a fair amount on the Congo). It seems unlikely. Yet his great work seems almost a dialogue with Samuel Purchas. (Read Belgium for England and Africa for America.) Conrad's pilgrims, or rather Marlow's pilgrims, appear on the banks of the Congo, waiting for Marlow to repair the sunken river-boat he has inherited, which is to take them further into the interior.

White men with long staves in their hands appeared languidly from amongst the buildings . . . They wandered here and there, with their absurd long staves in their hands, like a lot of faithless pilgrims bewitched inside a rotten fence. The word 'ivory' rang in the air, was whispered, was sighed. You would think they were praying to it. A taint of imbecile rapacity blew through it all like a whiff from some corpse. (pp. 72, 76)[27]

Marlow, the narrator of his own story, has engaged himself with a continental country – obviously Belgium – trading in the Congo. 'They were going to run an over-sea empire, and make no end of coin by trade' (p. 55). His journey in the French steamer down the African coast 'was like a weary pilgrimage amongst hints for nightmares' (p. 62). The nightmares are explained later, but Marlow's feeling of the unreality of it all is stressed. A 'momentary contact with reality' comes when he sees a boat paddled by energetic 'black fellows'. Unlike the colonists, 'they wanted no excuse for being there' (p. 61).

The 'pilgrims' he finds when he eventually reaches his stricken steamer are an indefinite bunch. Their identity as pilgrims is confirmed by each having his staff, a useless staff for faithless pilgrims. They are

[27] Quotations and page references to *Heart of Darkness* are from the Dent Collected Works Edition of 1946 (reprinted 1961), though the text is over-punctuated in comparison with that in the Norton edition, ed. Robert Kimbrough (1963; New York: Norton, 1988).

adventurers, and like true pilgrims they are expectant. 'They were all waiting – all the sixteen or twenty pilgrims of them – for something' (p. 77). All their activity, or inactivity, seemed unreal to Marlow, as unreal as 'the philanthropic pretence of the whole concern'. 'The only real feeling was a desire to get appointed to a trading-post where ivory was to be had, so that they could earn percentages' (p. 78). Thus they do not have the independence of the true explorers, such as the members of the Eldorado Exploring Company, who disappear without trace into 'the patient wilderness', though their aims are much the same as the aims of these 'sordid buccaneers': 'to tear treasure out of the bowels of the land was their desire, with no more moral purpose at the back of it than there is in burglars breaking into a safe' (p. 87).

In the long, slow journey up-river towards Kurtz's station, 'deeper and deeper into the heart of darkness', the pilgrims are particularised only in one of their band, 'a little fat man with sandy hair and red whiskers, who wore side-spring boots, and pink pyjamas tucked into his socks' (pp. 95, 102). Considering themselves superior to workmen and to black people, they have nothing to do with running the vessel, but keep their Winchesters at the ready when there is fear of an attack, and fire them wildly into the bush when the attack comes. But the steamer is now level with Kurtz's station and the rest of the story belongs to Marlow and Kurtz.

Conrad places his pilgrims as sordid adventurers, mere hangers-on and subsidiaries in the enterprise which makes the whole Congo world so incomprehensible and unreal to Marlow, and this placing is a significant, derisive demotion, a riposte, as it were, to the nobility of Purchas's pilgrims. Early in his narrative, Marlow is guardedly prepared to grant that those who plan oversea empires might have an ideal in mind.

The conquest of the earth, which mostly means the taking it away from those who have a different complexion or slightly flatter noses than ourselves, is not a pretty thing when you look into it too much. What redeems it is the idea only. An idea at the back of it; not a sentimental pretence but an idea; and an unselfish belief in the idea – something you can set up, and bow down before, and offer a sacrifice to . . . (pp. 50–1)

When Marlow is in the last stages of his voyage up-river, in those pages in which Conrad creates one of the most compelling of all journey narratives in English literature, he feels that the travellers are 'cut off from the comprehension of our surroundings', 'wanderers on a prehistoric earth . . . that wore the aspect of an unknown planet' (pp. 95–6). When that incredible cry of lament reaches them, followed by the storm of arrows from the banks, Marlow shares with one of the pilgrims the thought that Kurtz must be dead. He surprises himself with 'a sense of extreme disappointment'; 'I couldn't have felt more of lonely desolation somehow, had I been robbed of a belief or had missed my destiny in life' (pp. 113–14). He realises that his great desire had been to hear Kurtz *talk*, to hear the voice of this man whose extraordinary qualities had been constantly, and often jeeringly, recounted to him since his arrival; the 'emissary of pity, and science, and progress, and devil knows what else' (p. 79). 'Each station', he was reported to have said, 'should be like a beacon on the road towards better things, a centre for trade of course, but also for humanizing, improving, instructing' (p. 91). And this was the strangest thing: that besides possessing such high ideals, Kurtz was sending down-river more ivory than any other agent. To hear this gifted man talk, Marlow realised, had become, unknown to himself, his consuming need. And now, he thinks, he is dead.

He is wrong, of course. But as he narrates his story years after the event, after he has found Kurtz alive and has indeed heard him talk, it is more than interesting that he tells his listeners that *at this earlier time* his consuming desire was to experience the 'ability to talk' that everyone spoke of, Kurtz's 'gift of expression', whichever way it went, either 'the pulsating stream of light or the deceitful flow from the heart of an impenetrable darkness' (pp. 113–14). It is the desire for explanation that makes Marlow's voyage to Kurtz the great pilgrimage never described as such by Conrad, a pilgrimage which disgraces the journey to expected riches undertaken by those whom his story names as pilgrims. As the pilgrim approached his shrine he was prepared for an explanation of great light or great darkness, so long as it was an explanation. What Marlow eventually found, when the dying Kurtz began to talk indeed, was a 'hollow sham'. 'No eloquence could have been so withering to one's belief in mankind as his final burst of sincerity' (p. 145). The 'eloquence', that Marlow expected was shown in the report which Kurtz had prepared for the Society for the Suppression of Savage Customs – 'a beautiful piece of writing', proclaiming, with 'the unbounded power of eloquence', how the civilised races could exert a limitless power of good on the 'savages' – concluded with the unsteady scrawl, 'Exterminate all the brutes!' So Kurtz went on talking to Marlow. His voice 'rang deep to the very last'. It 'survived his strength to hide in the magnificent folds of eloquence the barren darkness of his heart' (p. 147). Marlow was able to see into the darkness, the darkness which led to Kurtz's final cry of 'The horror! The horror!', into the 'intense and hopeless despair' behind his story of his last days, with their utter cruelty and barbarism, and submission without restraint to every temptation. What Marlow finds at the end of his pilgrimage (which is never announced as such) is the final sincerity of Kurtz's last cry, 'The horror!' Marlow says, 'After all, this was the expression of some sort of belief . . . It was an affirmation, a moral victory paid for by innumerable defeats . . . But it was a victory. That is why I have remained loyal to Kurtz to the last' (p. 151).

It is strange that on Marlow's approach to Kurtz's station he finds it shrouded in fog. 'When the sun rose there was a white fog, very warm and clammy, and more blinding than the night' (p. 101). In that admirable fiction, the *Navigatio* of St Brendan, the boat draws near to the Promised Land, and 'as the evening drew on, a great fog enveloped them, so that one of them could hardly see another. The steward, however, said to Saint Brendan: . . . "That fog encircles the island for which you have been searching for seven years."'[28] In what I regard as the finest of T. S. Eliot's pilgrim poems, *Marina*, the transmuted Pericles reaches the 'granite islands' and hears the 'woodthrush calling through the fog'. At any rate, I think it can be argued that in *Heart of Darkness*, in the story of Marlow's approach to Kurtz's station,

---

[28] O'Meara, *Voyage of Saint Brendan*, p. 67.

Conrad redeemed the idea of pilgrimage from its materialist association with colonial enterprise which Mather and Purchas encouraged
(despite the religious colouring they gave it), and, even in the appar-
ent negativity of what Marlow found, restored to the idea something
of the spiritual dignity the word had for Cushman, and, originally,
Bradford.

CHAPTER 6

'Least Figure – on the Road –'

In this chapter I am looking at the use made of the pilgrimage metaphor in the poetry of two women, both born in 1830, Christina Rossetti in London and Emily Dickinson in Amherst, Massachusetts – each of them spending the whole of a seemingly quiet life in her place of birth. As children, both of these poets were saturated in the scriptures which provided so much of the imagery and language of their later poetry. Christina Rossetti was brought up in the high Anglican church, and remained in it; Emily Dickinson was brought up in the traditional Congregational church of New England, and she questioned its beliefs all her life. Neither of them married. The output of both poets was prodigious. Emily Dickinson is now rated among the foremost American poets, and her work has generated a great volume of commentary [1]; Christina Rossetti's work, apart from *Goblin Market*, is still underestimated, mainly because of the limitations of its range and its pervading mournfulness.

To begin with Christina Rossetti, here is a simple poem, 'Heaven', which accepts without question the time-honoured metaphor of heaven as the country towards which every Christian pilgrim strives.

> What is heaven? 'Tis a country
> Far away from mortal ken;
> 'Tis a land, where, by God's bounty,
> After death live righteous men.

---

[1] The complexities of the text and its transmission, and the history of the reception of the poems, are described in the early chapters of *The Cambridge Companion to Emily Dickinson*, ed. Wendy Martin (Cambridge: Cambridge University Press, 2002).

> That that blest land I may enter,
>   Is my humble, earnest cry;
> Lord! admit me to Thy presence,
>   Lord! admit me, or I die.
> (p. 649)[2]

This poem, which was never published, was written when Christina Rossetti was all of twelve years old. One of the best-known of her adult poems, 'Up-Hill', written when she was twenty-eight, and included in her first collection, *Goblin Market* (1862), is also a pilgrimage poem and may seem as uncomplicated as the juvenile poem above.

> Does the road wind up-hill all the way?
>   Yes, to the very end.
> Will the day's journey take the whole long day?
>   From morn to night, my friend.   (p. 59)

The poem concentrates on the traditional pilgrims' inn, where the travellers to heaven rest and prepare themselves for the remainder of the journey.

> Will there be beds for me and all who seek?
>   Yea, beds for all who come.

This is a poem of peace and welcome. It is only in the context of Christina Rossetti's other pilgrimage poems that one notices that there is nothing at all about the ultimate destination of the pilgrims. The inn symbolises death, and the emphasis of the poem is wholly on the weariness of life, and the longing for the peace of death.

The pilgrim's journey, the fatigue of which is movingly sketched in the last poem, is easily and often described as the race which the Bible tells us we must all run (Hebrews 12:1), and it is in this association that an unexpected distaste for the journey metaphor makes its appearance, in 'After this the judgment', composed in 1856. The speaker feels herself inadequate in face of the eagerness of her confident and competitive 'fellow-pilgrims'.

---

[2] Page numbers of poems by Christina Rossetti quoted refer to *The Complete Poems*, ed. R. W. Crump and Betty S. Flowers (Harmondsworth, Middlesex: Penguin Books, 2001).

> As eager homeward traveller to the goal,
>   Or steadfast seeker on an unsearched main,
> Or martyr panting for an aureole,
>   My fellow-pilgrims pass me, and attain
> That hidden mansion of perpetual peace
>   Where keen desire and hope dwell far from pain:
> That gate stands open of perennial ease;
>   I view the glory till I partly long,
> Yet lack the fire of love which quickens these.
>
> (p. 178)

She beseeches a 'passing Angel' to speed her, but as she addresses the 'Love of God', needing its assistance 'thro' the dry desert of life', the image of the race to heaven is forgotten, to be replaced by the extraordinary intensity of the speaker's longing to be enfolded by Christ's love as an end in itself, especially before 'the Great White Throne' of judgement, when she will stand, 'all creation's gazing stocks / Exposed and comfortless on every side'.[3]

> Brood over me with yearnings of a dove;
>   Be Husband, Brother, closest Friend to me;
> Love me as very mother loves her son,
>   Her sucking firstborn fondled on her knee . . .

To attain the 'love of love', which is Christ's own love, is the ultimate aim of the suppliant, and, in this poem, it makes ridiculous the effort of the martyr panting for his halo.

The fervour with which Christina Rossetti portrays the love of Christ – always a mutual love – as something which surmounts and obliterates every other aim and need in life is a distinguishing feature of her verse, and it shapes the nature of her pilgrimage poems. This fervour, which must draw strength from the loss of human love, so frequently lamented in her verse,[4] dominates 'I will arise' (p. 326). In this poem the concept of the journey of life as a race, scorned in the earlier poem, is quite happily accepted.

---

[3] This striking image of isolation and accusation is repeated in 'Memory' (p. 142): 'to face the naked truth, / I stood alone – I faced the truth alone, / Stripped bare of self-regard'.

[4] E.g., 'Remember' (p. 31), 'Memory' (p. 141).

Weary and weak, – accept my weariness;
　　Weary and weak, and downcast in my soul,
With hope growing less and less,
　　And with the goal
Distant and dim, – accept my sore distress.
I thought to reach the goal so long ago,
　　At outset of the race I dreamed of rest,
Not knowing what now I know
　　Of breathless haste,
　　Of long-drawn straining effort across the waste.

One only thing I knew, Thy love of me;
　　One only thing I know, Thy sacred same
Love of me full and free,
　　A craving flame
Of selfless love of me which burns in Thee.
How can I think of Thee, and yet grow chill:
　　Of Thee, and yet grow cold and nigh to death?
Re-energize my will,
　　Rebuild my faith;
　　I will arise and run, Thou giving me breath.

I will arise, repenting and in pain;
　　I will arise, and smite upon my breast
And turn to Thee again;
　　Thou choosest best,
Lead me along the road Thou makest plain.

The idea in this poem of the pilgrimage of life as a wearisome journey, a pointless race, given meaning by the love of Christ, is worth comparing with an earlier very beautiful poem, 'They desire a better country' (p. 189). The refrain, 'Follow me here, rise up, and follow here', is based on Christ's words to Matthew. But the speaker is not really 'following'. 'As the dry desert lengthens out its sand', she is aware of being accompanied.

　　And who is this that veiled doth walk with thee?
　　　　Lo, this is Love that walketh at my right;
　　One exile holds us both . . .

Invoking the journey to Emmaus, the pilgrim goes along her journey *with* Christ –

> Till for one moment golden city walls
> Rise looming on us, golden walls of home . . .

These shifts and changes in the pilgrimage poems may seem slight. They are important because they show that the ubiquitous journey imagery is only a background to be used and exploited for what really matters. This is very clear in what I have already touched on, the neglect of the culmination of the journey, the 'better country' of heaven. In competition with the depiction of all-consuming divine love, the conventional imagery of heaven as destination can lose its lustre.

> Lord, hast thou so loved us, and will not we
> Love thee with heart and mind and strength and soul,
> Desiring Thee beyond our glorious goal,
> Beyond the heaven of heavens desiring Thee?   (p. 408)

'Beyond the heaven of heavens': it is a striking concept. But certainly beyond the heaven which is normally pictured. These lines come from the central section of one of Christina Rossetti's many three-part poems, 'Because He first loved us'. Christ's parable (Luke 5) of the shepherd who rightly goes after the one strayed sheep, leaving the ninety-nine who have not strayed to look after themselves, is used to make a contrast between (once again) those confident Christians, 'Souls in green pastures of the watered land', and those who, like the speaker, are struggling to keep going: 'Faint pilgrim souls wayfaring thro' the sand'. 'Kind Lord, renew Thy quest / After new wanderers.' The bounty of being gathered up, like the strayed lamb, borne on Christ's shoulders and caressed by Him, is what makes descriptions of 'the golden city walls' of heaven something of an embarrassment.

Christ will follow those who follow Christ (or try to) 'beyond the heaven of heavens'. That there can be something perfunctory about Christina's sketches of the expected heaven is clearly shown in the poem 'Beautiful for situation' (p. 491). The first stanza describes heaven in orthodox imagery: angels with palm-branches, agate windows, pearl gates and so on. Then, with a huge increase in poetic power, we revert to the known reality of the journey towards this tame imagined destination.

> Lord, by what inconceivable dim road
>   Thou leadest man on footsore pilgrimage!
>   Weariness is his rest from stage to stage,
> Brief halting-places are his sole abode.

Here, as so often, the journey-imagery is actually strengthened when it portrays not the race to the goal but the suffering of the wayfarer.

> How tenfold inconceivable the goal,
>   His goal of hope deferred, his promised peace . . .

But then, suddenly, in the last three lines of the poem, we are asked to see the unhappy wanderer 'sitting down at ease . . . refreshed in soul' in the routinely described heaven of the first stanza. This phrase, 'hope deferred', is a constant with Christina Rossetti. It comes from Proverbs (13:12), 'Hope deferred maketh the heart sick: but when the desire cometh, it is a tree of life.' Christina Rossetti herself called attention to the second half of this proverb,[5] but she paid little regard to it in the poems. Not only is the hope of the pilgrim constantly deferred, but it is too often hope for the wrong things, and it is, I believe, the vain expectations of a Bunyanesque heaven which make Christina Rossetti's portrayal of the bright pavilions so often pallid.

> Who would wish back the Saints upon our rough
>   Wearisome road?
> . . . .
> I would not fetch one back to hope with me
>   A hope deferred,
>   To taste a cup that slips
>   From thirsting lips   (p. 517)[6]

In 'Whither the Tribes go up' (p. 506), the known harshness of life's journey is set against the questionable possibilities of the destination. Christina Rossetti uses the word 'set' in three distinct senses to help her show the grimness of a Christian's commitment to the unknown.

[5] See B. S. Flowers in Rossetti, *Complete Poems*, pp. xl–xli.
[6] From 'The end is not yet'.

> Our face is set like flint against our trouble
> . . . .
>
> Our sails are set to cross the tossing river,
>   Our face is set to reach Jerusalem.
> . . . .
>
> Marvel of marvels, if I myself shall behold
> With mine own eyes my King in His city of gold
> . . . .
>
> Cold it is, my beloved, since your funeral bell was tolled:
> Cold it is, O my King, how cold alone on the wold.

Hope for the wrong things, hope for realisations encouraged by the metaphor of pilgrimage and the paradisal images of the Epistles, only increases the burdens of the journey. What is to take the place of hope? Obviously, love. A kind of warfare between love and hope develops. There is a little poem of 1885 which interestingly extends the quotation from Hebrews which she had already used – 'They desire a better country' – with the word 'now': 'Now they desire a better country'. ('My first roundel', she wrote.[7])

> Love said nay, while Hope kept saying
>   All his sweetest say.
> Hope so keen to start a-maying! –
>   Love said nay.
>
> Love was bent to watch and pray:
> Long the watching, long the praying:
>   Hope grew drowsy, pale and grey.
>
> Hope in dreams set off a-straying,
>   All his dream-world flushed by May:
> While unslumbering, praying, weighing,
>   Love said nay.   (p. 521)

In another late poem, 'One of the Soldiers with a Spear pierced his Side' (p. 530), Hope is given a burial, not in the earth but in the silent soul; 'It lived once, it is dead. / Brief was the day of its power.' In its place is love. Though love is full of sorrows, 'where love is, all

---

[7] Rossetti, *Complete Poems*, p. 1056.

perfection / Is stored'. But at the very end of the poem – at the very end of life – hope re-appears: 'Lo, the Hope we buried with sighs / Alive in Death's eyes!' It is a curious and moving resurrection and reconciliation. Hope has been a disturbance and a distraction, its ends ever 'deferred'. But what is the love which has replaced it – love for the divine, love from the divine? At the end of life, it is, once again, hope. No doubt Christina Rossetti was suggesting that this new hope was something very different from the hope of earlier days, which tore at the heart with its perpetual disappointments, but inevitably she brings into the new hope, so soon to be realised in eternal life, the characteristics of the old: the possibility that it would never be realised.

> Our heaven must be within ourselves,
>   Our home and heaven the work of faith
> All thro' this race of life which shelves
>   Downward to death.
>
>   (p. 523)

Christina Rossetti wrote these lines in 1854, when she was twenty-four. (She saved them and much later added two more stanzas.[8]) She began as she ends. Her commitment to Christianity is never in doubt. Yet the variety of forms in which she rehearsed the pilgrimage metaphor shows that a commitment which never lessened never hardened into confident certainty.

Emily Dickinson's unique style makes any explanatory sorting of her work a reductive denial of what the poems actually 'say'. The words and images which cascade into her poems find their places in disconnected phrases unanchored by grammar, in surrealist yokings and perpetual inconsequence. Expectations are always defeated. To make order and sense of single poems is to rewrite them and to take the life out of them. Almost every poem shakes up and challenges the affirmations and assurances that criticism wants poems to provide. To make order and sense of a segment of the work is even more frustrating, since it soon becomes clear that the poems are so interrelated that there

---

[8] *Ibid.*, p. 1057.

are no separate and distinct segments, as though in the hundreds of poems, unpublished, which Emily Dickinson left behind her at her death, she had really been composing one huge single work. Lift one poem out of the pile and try to 'explain' it and you find yourself lifting all the others out. So, in making the attempt to 'lift out' those poems of Emily Dickinson that are concerned with the structure of the basic Christian pilgrimage metaphor, I acknowledge not only the impossibility of paraphrasing individual poems, but that the issue in question involves Dickinson's treatment of Christian theology and her attitude to death; that is to say, almost the whole of her poetry.

There is a good deal of humility, or mock humility, in Emily Dickinson's comparatively few direct references to pilgrim and pilgrimage. In 'Deprived of other Banquet' (773),[9] the poet says that her 'scant nutrition' has grown 'sumptuous enough for me', and compares herself to a robin (a very British robin).

> A Robin's famine able –
> Red Pilgrim, He and I –
> A Berry from our table
> Reserve – for charity –

The robin, like the sparrow, has learned how to subsist on a few crumbs. In 'Victory comes late' (690) we're told that the 'Eagle's Golden Breakfast' is too much for him, and the poem ends:

> God keep His Oath to Sparrows –
> Who of little Love – know how to starve –

Like the sparrow and the robin, Emily Dickinson has learned how to subsist on crumbs, crumbs of faith, and her consolation is that those with a bigger supply of food may find it 'strangles' them as it does the eagle.

The pilgrim's journey, undertaken on such meagre rations, is a constant in the poetry as it is in Christina Rossetti's.

---

[9] I take the numbers of poems from T. H. Johnson's one-volume edition, prepared from his three-volume edition of 1955 (Harvard University Press). R. W. Franklin's three-volume edition of 1998 (also published by Harvard University Press) improves on Johnson's work in its access to MS sources, and on p. 124 I list his corresponding numbers for the quoted poems (using his one-volume edition of 1999).

No Man can compass a Despair —
As round a Goalless Road
No faster than a Mile at once
The Traveller proceed —   (477)

From Blank to Blank —
A Threadless Way
I pushed Mechanic feet —
To stop — or perish — or advance —
Alike indifferent —   (761)

Both 'anguish' and 'agony' are the strong words which Dickinson uses,[10] as well as 'despair', to describe what Rossetti calls the weariness of the pilgrim condition. Ordinarily the journey fizzles out in the nightmare experience of the feet refusing to obey (550, 1664), but once, superbly, we get as far as the pilgrims' inn,[11] to the great surprise of the poet.

What Inn is this
Where for the night
Peculiar Traveller comes?
Who is the Landlord?
Where the maids?
Behold, what curious rooms!
No ruddy fires upon the hearth —
No brimming Tankards flow —
Necromancer! Landlord!
Who are these below?   (115)

The 'peculiar' traveller is of course the Christian (e.g. 1 Peter 2:9). The traveller suddenly realises that the people in the inn are all dead. He, or she, summons the landlord — as a necromancer. Much force in that word! He's a conjurer, calling up the dead, and exploiting them in the interests of his narrative. In that word Emily Dickinson questions not only the iconography of the pilgrimage, but its truth. Is death truly the final staging-post of our long journey to Paradise, the 'other country' of the metaphor? Or is this just a story, no more true than a conjuring trick?

---

[10] E.g., 193, 241.   [11] Compare the pilgrims' inn in Rossetti's 'Up-Hill' (see p. 107).

Emily Dickinson was preoccupied by death: her own death and the death of others. Her poems are filled with death. It is death which constantly aborts her pilgrim's journey. Death becomes the huge barrier beyond which lie the icons of Christian theology, a barrier beyond which Dickinson's intellect and imagination refused to go. Was death the end?

> I cross till I am weary
> A Mountain – in my mind –
> More Mountains – then a Sea –
> More Seas – And then
> A Desert – find –
> . . . .
> At last – the Grace in sight –
> I shout unto my feet –
> I offer them the Whole of Heaven
> The instant that we meet –
>
> They strive – and yet delay –
> They perish – Do we die –
> Or is this Death's Experiment –
> Reversed – in Victory?   (550)

In that saddest of the journey poems, 'I did not reach Thee / But my feet slip nearer every day' (1664), enigmatic Death again ends the pilgrimage.

> We step like Plush,
> We stand like snow,
> The waters murmur new.
> Three rivers and the Hill are passed –
> Two deserts and the sea!
> Now Death usurps my Premium
> And gets the look at Thee.

('Premium' here means 'prize'.) In both these last two poems it is only Death that knows what's to come – if anything. Elsewhere, Dickinson writes, speaking of death and almost certainly thinking of Hamlet's 'no traveller returns',

> Once to achieve, annuls the power
> Once to communicate.   (922)

In this matter of what lies after death Emily Dickinson seems to hover over every possibility. It is perhaps as much a question of language as belief. In the sardonic poem I quoted in my first chapter (p. 17), the image of the dazzling new dawn to express the awakening from death into immortality appears ludicrous.

> Will there really be a "Morning"?
> Is there such a thing as "Day"?
> Could I see it from the mountains
> If I were as tall as they?
>
> Has it feet like Water lilies?
> Has it feathers like a Bird?
> Is it brought from famous countries
> Of which I have never heard?
>
> Oh some Scholar! Oh some Sailor!
> Oh some Wise Man from the skies!
> Please to tell a little Pilgrim
> Where the place called "Morning" lies!
>
> (101)

This poem was rewritten years later as a derisive comic squib.

> Not knowing when the Dawn will come,
> I open every door,
> Or has it Feathers, like a Bird,
> Or Billows, like a Shore –   (1619)

Even the phrase 'going to heaven' is (in an early poem, 79) an embarrassing cliché. The yearning for what might lie behind these clichés is often balanced against the embarrassment of the clichés themselves.

> I shall know why – when Time is over –
> And I have ceased to wonder why –
> Christ will explain each separate anguish
> In the fair schoolroom of the sky –
>
> He will tell me what "Peter" promised –
> And I – for wonder at his woe –
> I shall forget the drop of Anguish
> That scalds me now – that scalds me now!
>
> (193)

The reality of that last line is unnerving, and it highlights the fantasy of Christ as a schoolmaster explaining the dogmas of the church to departed souls.

At times the iconography is polluted by the preoccupations and prejudices of those who use it (234).

> You're right – "the way *is* narrow" –
> And "difficult the Gate" –
> And "few there be" – Correct again –
> That "enter in – thereat" –
>
> '*Tis* Costly – So are *purples*!
> 'Tis just the price of *Breath* –
> With but the "Discount" of the *Grave* –
> Termed by the *Brokers* – "*Death*"!
>
> And after *that* – there's Heaven –
> The *Good* Man's – "*Dividend*" –
> And *Bad* Men – "go to Jail" –
> I guess –

'We pray – to Heaven – / We prate – of Heaven' (489). This is the problem. One stanza of this poem beautifully sums up the problems of belief created by confident eschatological metaphors.

> Is Heaven a Place – a Sky – a Tree?
> Location's narrow way is for Ourselves –
> Unto the Dead
> There's no Geography –

The church, of course, cannot live without 'geography'. But 'Priests – adjust the Symbols – / When Sacrament – is done – ' with the casualness of women folding away their summer gowns (342). The poet scans the skies 'with a suspicious Air', like a child who has been 'swindled' before (476). Is a poet, then, unable to create for herself the symbols of what lies beyond death? She has 'known a Heaven' – which suddenly disappeared, 'like a Tent' when a 'Show' has moved on (243). Heaven is 'what I cannot reach!' (239). A poet's heaven is 'a Brittle Heaven' (680):

> It is too difficult a Grace –
> To justify the Dream –
> (569)

Yet if the poet's moment of vision, which Dickinson calls 'Our Best Moment', could only last, "Twould supersede the Heaven' which we are asked to believe in. Alas, this 'Grant of the Divine' withdraws as quickly as it comes –

> Withdraws – and leaves the dazzled Soul
> In her unfurnished Rooms   (393)

Creating a new mythology is hardly a practical proposal. There is a strange beginning to an alternative pilgrimage in 'Our journey had advanced' (615), the meaning of which is much disputed.[12]

> Our journey had advanced –
> Our feet were almost come
> To that odd Fork in Being's Road –
> Eternity – by Term –
>
> Our pace took sudden awe –
> Our feet – reluctant – led –
> Before – were Cities – but Between –
> The Forest of the Dead –
>
> Retreat – was out of Hope –
> Behind – a Sealed Route –
> Eternity's White Flag – Before –
> And God – at every Gate –

But in the end this poem shows as much bafflement about the afterlife as others. It seems to be an attack on the calvinism of Dickinson's youth. The final line brings in the note of despair, with God as a sentinel denying entrance 'at every gate' to those not of the elect, to the reprobates who form 'the Forest of the Dead'. I assume that Dickinson did not believe in the doctrine of election, and that her poem is pointing out that Bunyan's celestial city of 'pure Gold' is available only for those who, accepting Bunyan's theology, believe themselves chosen. The 'despair' of the poem, for one who does *not* accept it, is not so much at being refused entrance as at being refused knowledge.

---

[12] See David Porter, *Dickinson: The Modern Idiom* (Cambridge, Mass.: Harvard University Press, 1981), pp. 279–80.

If 'Our journey had advanced' wrestles with the narrowness of calvinism, what do we say of the poem which brings back that fundamental element in the pilgrimage story, so long buried in abuse, the shrine? It is prayer at the shrine that for Catholicism provides the access to the knowledge the poet has been seeking. And here is a poem in which the speaker is a nun communing with the Madonna (918).

> Only a Shrine, but Mine –
> I made the Taper shine –
> Madonna dim, to whom all Feet may come,
> Regard a Nun –
>
> Thou knowest every Woe –
> Needless to tell thee – so –
> But can'st thou do
> The Grace next to it – heal?
> That looks a harder skill to us –
> Still – just as easy, if it be thy Will
> To thee – Grant me –
> Thou knowest, though, so Why tell thee?

In *The Passion of Emily Dickinson*,[13] Judith Farr goes quite deeply into the presence of Catholic ideas and practices in calvinist New England in Emily Dickinson's time, including those of the Dickinsons' eight Irish servants. We have to remember that Susan Dickinson, Emily's close friend and collaborator over many years, had actually pondered becoming a Catholic.[14] Of course, this is a comic sort of poem, taking a Latimer-like pleasure in pointing to the absurdity of the idea of saintly intercession, especially via a statue, since God knows all the secrets and desires of each human heart. At the same time we should treasure this Protestant shrine. It may mock the need for the Madonna, but it does not mock prayer as an access to knowledge which can heal.[15]

---

[13] Judith Farr, *The Passion of Emily Dickinson* (Cambridge, Mass.: Harvard University Press, 1992), pp. 35–8.

[14] See Martha Nell Smith, 'Susan and Emily Dickinson: Their Lives, in Letters', in *Cambridge Companion to Emily Dickinson*, ed. Martin, p. 70.

[15] See further the very interesting article by Ursula Brumm, 'The Virgin Mary among American Puritans: A Difficult Relation', *Amerikastudien/American Studies* 47 (Heidelberg, 2002), 449–68, esp. 454–5.

In a number of poems Dickinson seems prepared, as a matter of convenience, to allow a credence to the conventional images of the last stages of the pilgrim's journey.

> Better an ignis fatuus
> Than no illume at all –
>   (1551)

The danger of discrediting the traditional icons is that such questioning may go too far and make 'the Gods – a lie' (428). The value of accepting them is that 'the broken creatures' of our scepticism may be transfigured, '– mended –', and come to represent truth. It is a perilous stratagem! Once 'those Jasper gates / Blazed open – suddenly', but the Saviour's face within turned away from her (256). She can see the value in images which she often derides, such as the Morning of the new life, which might 'shatter me with Dawn!' (323). But it is hard for her to keep a straight face. There can be something impish in the poet's unsuccessful attempts to embrace convention. 'Forever at His side to walk', she proclaims, as Christina Rossetti had proclaimed, and goes on, 'The smaller of the two!' (246). She talks of her 'slow idolatry' (765) and it is indeed slow. Her ridicule of conventional ideas and images is irrepressible, but it is less than her fear that, having dismantled the images, there should be nothing there. Of the blankness of the phrase in Genesis (5:24) that Enoch 'was not', she says 'The Unpretension stuns –' (1342). Perhaps, she kindly says, comprehension was less in those days because 'They wore no Lexicons –'.[16] But where is Emily Dickinson to look for 'comprehension'? A famous early poem (338, about 1862) begins emphatically 'I know that He exists.' With her usual mischievousness, Dickinson suggests that the reason 'He has hid his rare life' is that He is playing hide and seek. But supposing He *really* wasn't there –

> Would not the fun
> Look too expensive!
> Would not the jest –
> Have crawled too far!

---

[16] There is a weaker MS version: 'They knew no Lexicons'.

Those are exclamation marks, not question marks. But whose fun, and whose jest, is it? The 'unpretension' of the poem's knowledge, or absence of knowledge, could hardly be greater, and I think it makes greater also the horror of not finding God.

I said earlier that to provide order in a segment of Emily Dickinson's poetry was to falsify the power of the individual poems. Her enormous poetic output is not the sum of its parts. The unique qualities of her verse are in the very hesitations and contradictions which lie there in each poem as the coruscation of words 'settles down' between those enigmatic dashes. Affirmations do not lie within individual poems or in groups of poems. Summing up Emily Dickinson on the metaphor of pilgrimage is not a possibility. I end, therefore, with her own pilgrimage poem (400), the very best she wrote, I think, and written quite early on (about 1862), in which, breathless and incoherent, she bribes some ragged child with untold wealth to go and tell God that in spite of all disbelief, in spite of all vain beliefs, she has in the end joined the pilgrim train.

A Tongue – to tell Him I am true!
Its fee – to be of Gold –
Had Nature – in Her monstrous House
A single Ragged Child –

To earn a Mine – would run
That Interdicted Way,
And tell Him – Charge thee speak it plain –
That so far – Truth is true?

And answer What I do –
Beginning with the Day
That Night – begun –
Nay – Midnight – 'twas –
Since Midnight – happened – say –

If once more – Pardon – Boy –
The Magnitude thou may
Enlarge my Message – If too vast
Another Lad – help thee –

Thy Pay – in Diamonds – be –
And His – in solid Gold –
Say Rubies – if He hesitate –
My Message – must be told –

Say – last I said – was This –
That when the Hills – come down –
And hold no higher than the Plain –
My Bond – have just begun –

And when the Heavens – disband –
And Deity conclude –
Then – look for me. Be sure you say –
Least Figure – on the Road –

It would be a disgrace to argue that this poem 'says' that the speaker, having questioned orthodox belief all her life, sees herself at the ending of Time (when the hills come down), when all the 'geography' of apostolic imagery has been erased (when the heavens disband), at last sees Truth, and belatedly acknowledges it. The sheer comedy of the poem undermines such sentimentality: the comedy of bribing the messenger, and getting another lad to help if the message is too vast or too late. This is the self-mockery in which Dickinson delights. And yet! It is often in such self-mockery that depth and seriousness inhere, as with her image of herself as a starving robin or sparrow, subsisting on crumbs. One of Dickinson's most famous lines is 'I dwell in Possibility' (657). She was speaking of the power of poetic imagination to conceive a paradise, as against what 'prose' had to offer. In my reading, this conception proves not to be possible. As Shelley wrote, 'the deep truth is imageless'.[17] What seems to me truer about dwelling in possibility is that in all the large corpus of her poems, within the comedy, the questioning and the mockery, which sabotage accepted creeds, there remains intact the *possibility* 'that He exists'. It is towards such a 'possibility' that the panting speaker runs, sending ahead of her, along the pilgrims' road, the ragged child, 'to tell Him I am true!' A comic figure of course.

[17] Percy Bysshe Shelley, *Prometheus Unbound* (1820), 2.4.116.

CORRESPONDENCIES

The following table lists the numbers of Emily Dickinson's poems cited, first as in Johnson's edition and then as in Franklin's edition (see footnote 9).

Johnson	Franklin
79	215
101	148
115	100
193	215
234	249
239	310
243	257
246	264
256	316
323	14
338	365
342	374
393	560
400	673
428	386
476	711
477	714
489	476
550	666
569	533
615	453
657	466
680	724
690	195
761	484
765	488
773	872
918	981
922	938
1342	1277
1551	1581
1619	1647
1664	1708

CHAPTER 7

Journey of the magus

In the development of T. S. Eliot's poetry between 1919 and 1942, the pilgrim's journey is one of the most potent images, though it is largely undeclared and though it undergoes major transformation. The first journey to ponder must be the unfulfilled pilgrimage of section v of *The Waste Land* (1922), but it is worth pausing on a possible 'beginning' in 'Mr. Eliot's Sunday Morning Service', published in *Poems* (1919). In an imaginary painting (by a 'painter of the Umbrian school') of the baptism of Christ, 'the wilderness is cracked and brown'. This line looks forward from John the Baptist's wilderness to the arid journey in the desert in *The Waste Land*. The intense longing for water of the travellers in that later passage may influence our reading of the next two lines in this earlier, largely comic poem, with its jokey vocabulary.

> But through the water pale and thin
> Still shine the unoffending feet . . .
>
> (p. 54)[1]

These lines do no honour to Christ, but they do not dishonour him. His frailty and innocence provide a purity which is overlaid in the rest of the painting. The painter has given him a 'nimbus', a halo, and placed above him (as to be expected from the gospel account) God the Father and the Dove (or holy spirit). It looks as though we are momentarily in Gerontion's 'juvescence of the year' when Christ came, and at the same time, as in 'Gerontion', we are also in that later era when the True Church is 'wrapt in the old miasmal mist', as the neighbouring poem, 'The Hippopotamus', describes it. The

---

[1] Numbered references are to the relevant pages of *T. S. Eliot: The Complete Poems and Plays* (London: Faber and Faber, 1969).

'unoffending feet' scarcely belong to Christ the tiger, but I am moved by this detail of the holy feet seen through the shallow water at the Jordan's edge. If the poem looks back to 'Gerontion' and forward to *The Waste Land*, where 'sweat is dry and feet are in the sand', then surely those feet in the water have something to do with the hallucinatory figure who glides, 'wrapt in a brown mantle', by the side of the two exhausted travellers approaching the Chapel Perilous. The purpose of the earlier satirical poem may well be to mock the desiccation of the contemporary Christian church, but it cannot do that without, as in so many of Eliot's poems in this 'pre-conversion' period, conferring a glimmer of sanctity on that which has supposedly become corrupted.

To the pilgrims' journey then. After the fourth stanza we have left the Umbrian painting and may be back with the stained-glass of the first stanza, so that the 'sable presbyters' who approach 'the avenue of penitence' may be kin to the 'sapient sutlers of the Lord' (the hangers-on who make money out of the church). The stratagem of the poem is the same as that in *The Waste Land*, to tarnish some ancient lustre by means of a derisive accompaniment, so that approaching the 'penitential gates' (sustained by seraphim and surrounded by 'the souls of the devout') are not only the sombre presbyters but also the pimply altar-boys, 'clutching piaculative pence'. Before we reach Sweeney shifting his buttocks in the bath we have to pass the sexless bees, reminding us of the castrated Origen in the second stanza, and hence of the church's infertility.[2] Yet, in the light of what Eliot was later to write, none of this derision destroys the force of 'the avenue of penitence' which old and young are here approaching. Obviously the buttocks in the water in the final stanza, brutally strong, contrast with the unoffending feet, 'pale and thin', in the fourth stanza. Why are we told, in the last two lines of the poem, that 'The masters of the subtle schools / Are controversial, polymath'? It must be that these masters, presumably 'of the Umbrian school', foresaw the degradation Eliot describes, from the vulnerable holy feet in the Jordan to Sweeney's

---

[2] Cf. Robert Crawford, *The Savage and the City in the Work of T. S. Eliot* (Oxford: Clarendon Press, 1987), pp. 116–20.

muscular hams in the bath. If that is correct, then, as Gerontion said –

> Think at last
> We have not reached conclusion, when I
> Stiffen in a rented house.   (p. 38)

In later poems, Sweeney's bath water will not be the only water remaining to us. Mr Eliot will be attending a quite different Sunday morning service, in which there will be a much less mocking perspective on the approach to 'the avenue of penitence'.

In section v of *The Waste Land* Jesus Christ is a forceful if subliminal presence. The section begins with the agony in the garden, the seizure, and the crucifixion, and then follows the outstanding desert journey of those trying to find their way out of the waste land towards the Chapel Perilous and the life-giving water. It is a journey which vies with the horror of Childe Roland's journey in Browning's poem – which Eliot much admired.[3] One of the weary travellers is confused by a third figure who seems to walk beside his companion.

> There is always another one walking beside you
> Gliding wrapt in a brown mantle, hooded . . .
>   (p. 73)

We hardly need Eliot's note that this section of the poem uses the journey to Emmaus as a theme, and because of the Emmaus theme it is now in order to call the travellers to the chapel pilgrims. Gregory the Great (c. AD 540–604) had made a firm association between St Luke's account of the Emmaus journey and the idea of pilgrimage.[4] In Luke's gospel (24:13–31), two disciples, Cleopas and one unnamed, are making their way to Emmaus, a few miles north of Jerusalem, immediately after the crucifixion and the extraordinary news of the women concerning the empty tomb. A third person,

---

[3] See Ronald Bush, *T. S. Eliot: A Study in Character and Style* (New York and Oxford: Oxford University Press, 1983), pp. 74 and 90.

[4] See F. C. Gardiner, *The Pilgrimage of Desire: A Study of Theme and Genre in Medieval Literature* (Leiden: E. J. Brill, 1971), p. 20. My account of the pilgrim-plays is based on Gardiner's book.

Jesus himself, whom they do not recognise, joins them and questions them about the recent events. When they come to the village they persuade their unknown companion to join them, 'though he would have gone further'. At meat, 'he took bread, and blessed it, and brake, and gave to them. And their eyes were opened, and they knew him; and he vanished out of their sight.' Throughout medieval Europe this episode became the subject of the 'pilgrim-plays'; the version in the Towneley cycle is called *Peregrini*. The two disciples are dressed as pilgrims, and they recognise and salute their mysterious companion as a fellow-pilgrim (he may indeed be dressed as a pilgrim). The sense of fellowship, as exiles and pilgrims, enters a wholly new dimension when the pilgrim-Christ reveals himself and his heavenly destination.

In *The Waste Land*, Christ does not reveal himself. The chapel is reached, but it is empty, a ruin; 'grass is singing / Over the tumbled graves'. There is no water. Voices sing 'out of empty cisterns and exhausted wells'. But there is 'a damp gust / Bringing rain', and, as Europe collapses, there is a cry – from someone – 'Shall I at least set my lands in order?'

The speaker in 'The Hollow Men' (1925) is even more clearly on the verge of a commitment which the society around him refuses, or cannot reach. The epigraph of the poem is from Conrad's *Heart of Darkness*, 'Mistah Kurtz – he dead', the message delivered by the manager's boy 'in a tone of scathing contempt'. Marlow had been prepared to admit, as we saw in Chapter Five (p. 104), that Kurtz's dying exclamation, 'The horror! The horror!', had been a kind of affirmation, a 'final burst of sincerity', a 'moral victory' indeed, though it was 'paid for by innumerable defeats, by abominable terrors, by abominable satisfactions'. Marlow's acknowledgement is not the kind of thing the poet is looking for in the kingdom of the hollow men. Kurtz belongs to that kingdom of death, though, as one of the 'lost violent souls', he is an exception among the quiet meaningless lives which we are familiar with from *The Waste Land*. And what the hollow men – and women – require is something very different from the blackness which Kurtz and thence Marlow perceive at the end of the tunnel.

We grope together
And avoid speech
Gathered on this beach of the tumid river.

(p. 85)

There is an odd resemblance here to Conrad's Congo, on the banks of
which his pilgrims were waiting and waiting for the boat which was
to take them to their enrichment. These hollow people are pilgrims
too, with a difference. With the poet, they have had intimations of
'death's other kingdom' where sightless eyes will truly 'see'. The role
of pilgrim for these more hopeful inhabitants of the waste land is
struck by three successive images of the ruins of stone shrines and
fanes. There is a sudden vision of 'sunlight on a broken column' in
line 23. Much more clearly, the two stanzas of section II show the
hollow people attempting to worship.

This is the dead land
This is cactus land
Here the stone images
Are raised, here they receive
The supplication of a dead man's hand
Under the twinkle of a fading star.

Is it like this
In death's other kingdom
Waking alone
At the hour when we are
Trembling with tenderness
Lips that would kiss
Form prayers to broken stone.

(p. 84)

These prayers to broken stone betoken the lack of both sexual and
spiritual fulfilment. There is no response to these prayers because the
prayers are broken like the shrines at which the supplicants worship.
Towards the end of the poem we hear what is presumably one of
the 'voices . . . in the wind's singing' giving us one phrase from the
Lord's prayer, *For Thine is the Kingdom*. These are marginal voices
on the page. Within the poem, the speakers, those who try to pray
at broken shrines, can manage only the beginning even of this one
phrase.

> For Thine is
> Life is
> For Thine is the
>   (p. 86)

And the poem concludes with other voices chanting '*This is the way the world ends*'; the 'whimper' which betokens the end may be, as was suggested many years ago, the whimper of the newly born Christ-child.

In 1927 Eliot was formally received into the Church of England. The exhausted pilgrim, the ruined chapel, the broken shrine, the uncompleted prayer, the haunting presence of a shadowy Christ – all these undergo a sea-change as the new imagery of conversion takes over.

The first major poem of Eliot's conversion is, appropriately enough, about the Nativity, and it is his most overt pilgrimage poem, *The Journey of the Magi*, published in 1927. But there is a puzzle. After the ache and pain of the journeying to the empty chapel in *The Waste Land*, and the unfulfilled longing of those who pray at the shrines in 'The Hollow Men', this poem, written in the fruition of belief, is strangely empty of belief. Eliot has gone to Lancelot Andrewes's nativity sermon of 1622 and brilliantly eviscerated it, taking from it more or less word for word his first five lines and then wholly ignoring the burden of what Andrewes had to say, except for that emphatic 'Set down this', applied to a predicate very different from that of Andrewes. Lancelot Andrewes's sermon, for all the wire-drawn angularity of the style, is a most moving account of what makes a true pilgrimage. First, there is the extraordinary act of faith among these faraway wise men in recognising that star, then the harrowing journey following it (used by Eliot), then the search for the new-born king, and then, above all, the act of worship, the offering of themselves and what belonged to them. It is the first and last of these which Eliot excludes. The first, the mysterious awakening of faith. 'How came you to believe?' asks Andrewes,[5] and he tries to answer his own question. In the poem we have only the 'voices' in the magi's ears saying 'That this was all folly.' It is when we come to Bethlehem that the divergence is really

---

[5] *Lancelot Andrewes: Sermons*, ed. G. M. Story (Oxford: Clarendon Press, 1967), p. 104.

important. Andrewes makes much of the Vulgate's *ubi est?*, turning the magi's enquiry for the place into the search by all who have faith for the true presence of Christ. 'If you misse of that, you misse of Him.'[6] And finally, having found him, the fulfilment of the whole purpose of the pilgrimage, the worship. The wise men 'are come to worship him'. Andrewes makes the falling down of the wise men but a small part of their worship, which is their offering of what they hold precious. 'If all come from Him, all to returne to Him: If He sent all, to be worshipped with all.'[7]

Eliot's wise man, remembering in old age that seemingly preposterous commitment to the cold and hazardous journey, says only this of the arrival, the finding of the new-born king, and the worship.

> So we continued
> And arrived at evening, not a moment too soon
> Finding the place; it was (you may say) satisfactory.
> (p. 103)

This renowned understatement is, to say the least, disappointing. It is of course the old man speaking. 'All this was a long time ago', and, of course, 'I would do it again.' But his plaintive question is, 'Were we led all that way for / Birth or Death?'

> this Birth was
> Hard and bitter agony for us, like Death, our death.
> We returned to our places, these Kingdoms,
> But no longer at ease here, in the old dispensation,
> With an alien people clutching their gods.
> I should be glad of another death.   (p. 104)

Eliot emphasizes the wrench, the dislocation and the pain which inevitably follow conversion, and this alienation becomes the centre of the poem. The old magus shows no sense at all of the exaltation which *Ash Wednesday* suggests is the privilege of separation. The more one thinks about the poem the less possible it is to treat the joyless recollections of the old man as Eliot's celebration of his choice of Christ. The absence of any reference to a lifetime of service in worship, which

---

[6] *Ibid.*, p. 112.   [7] *Ibid.*, p. 116.

is the main point of Andrewes's sermon, is seen to be a careful dramatic point, like the casualness given to the finding of the Christ-child. The last words of the old magus, 'I should be glad of another death', replicate almost exactly the words of the Sibyl of Cumae placed as an epigraph to *The Waste Land*, ἀποθανεῖν θέλω [I wish I were dead]. It is a question whether Eliot's gloomy magus achieved enough by his journey and his conversion.

The difference between *The Journey of the Magi* and Eliot's defiantly autobiographical conversion-poem, *Ash Wednesday*, published in 1930, could not be greater. Here is a convert who rejoices in his conversion, and who wholly rejects the image of a journey to represent his new state. 'Because I do not hope to turn again', 'Because these wings are no longer wings to fly', 'Teach us to sit still.' The renunciation of new directions, of purposeful search for recognisable gains, is paradoxically joyful. 'I rejoice that things are as they are.'

> End of the endless
> Journey to no end
> (p. 92)

This new state puts an end to Madame Sosostris's vision of 'crowds of people, walking round in a ring' in *The Waste Land*, and Harry's of 'many creatures moving / Without direction' in *The Family Reunion*. The 'lady' who recurs throughout the poem in various guises, 'lady of silences', 'silent sister', 'veiled sister', seems to be the spirit of a shrine, an intermediary who prays 'for those who walk in darkness', and in the final section the supplicant asks for the gift of the wise passiveness which replaces fruitless journeying.

> Blessèd sister, holy mother, spirit of the fountain, spirit of the garden,
> Suffer us not to mock ourselves with falsehood
> Teach us to care and not to care
> Teach us to sit still
> Even among these rocks,
> Our peace in His will . . .   (p. 98)

It might be thought, from *The Journey of the Magi* and *Ash Wednesday*, that the image of the journey to betoken spiritual advance had exhausted itself. Yet the pilgrim's journey had enormous value in *The*

Waste Land, and it returns with great potency in another supreme poem, *Marina* (1930).

In 1928 George Wilson Knight sent to Faber and Gwyer, the publishing firm which Eliot had joined in 1925, the typescript of a book called *Thaisa*, a pioneering work on Shakespeare's last plays.[8] Eliot may or may not have seen this; the rejection note was signed by Richard de la Mare. Next year Wilson Knight found a minor publisher (E. J. Burrow) willing to publish a shortened version of his book, now called *Myth and Miracle.*[9] *Thaisa* was a pioneer work, particularly concerned with the 'theophanies' in Shakespeare's late plays, with much to say about *Pericles, Prince of Tyre*, in which the hero is miraculously reunited with his daughter, Marina, whom he thought dead, and then, during a pilgrimage to Ephesus, reunited with his wife Thaisa, also believed to be dead.[10] Eliot's poem *Marina* is deeply indebted to Knight's work, and it is only fitting that Eliot should have sent Knight a signed copy of his poem, possibly as an acknowledgement of his firm's earlier discouragement.

Marina has an epigraph from Seneca's play *Hercules Furens* (line 1138): 'Quis hic locus, quae regio, quae mundi plaga?' [What place is this, what region, what part of the world?]. Hercules, driven mad by Juno, has in his frenzy killed his wife and his children. He awakens into sanity and finds, to his utter despair, what he has done. 'I intend', said Eliot, 'a criss-cross between Pericles finding alive, and Hercules finding dead – the two extremes of the recognition scene.'[11]

The poem opens with an invocation of the New England shore.[12]

[8] See Philip Edwards, 'Wilson Knight and Shakespeare's Last Plays', in *Shakespeare's Universe: Renaissance Ideas and Conventions*, ed. J. M. Mucciolo (Aldershot: Scolar Press, 1995), pp. 258–67.
[9] Republished as part of Knight's *The Crown of Life* by Oxford University Press in 1947.
[10] As described at the start of Chapter Three.
[11] See F. R. Leavis, in *T. S. Eliot . . . A Casebook*, ed. B. C. Southam (London: Macmillan, 1978), p. 224; and Bush, *T. S. Eliot*, p. 167.
[12] Lyndall Gordon says this is not Massachusetts but Casco Bay, Maine; the destination of the young Eliot's most ambitious sailing ventures. Gordon, *T. S. Eliot: An Imperfect Life* (London: Vintage, 1999), p. 240.

What seas what shores what grey rocks and what islands
What water lapping the bow
And scent of pine and the woodthrush singing through the fog
What images return
O my daughter   (p. 109)

The scene and the daughter are images in the poet's mind. In *Pericles*, the hero, having heard that his daughter, like his wife, is dead, sinks into total apathy, refusing communication with anyone. His aides have brought his ship into harbour at Mytilene. The governor suggests that an extraordinary young woman he has rescued from a brothel may be able to help the suffering prince. So Marina is brought aboard the ship, and, very slowly, father and daughter recognise each other. In *Marina*, Eliot writes on behalf of Pericles, but in identifying with him he brings him into his own life, and transforms both the voyage and Marina. There is no Mytilene in the poem, no Ephesus; and Eliot had no daughter. The New England coast, which Eliot loved, takes the place of Shakespeare's Aegean. If at the time of writing *Marina* Eliot was committed to a life in England, the transatlantic New England with which he was proud to associate his ancestry remained strongly in his imagination, evoking both the happiness of holidays in the past, and the entire myth of the land promised to the seventeenth-century pilgrims – 'a better country, that is, a heavenly'.

The coastal fog may be real enough, but I have mentioned before the frequency with which the visionary Promised Land is concealed by mist or fog. The song of the woodthrush will bring to mind thrushes elsewhere in the poetry. There is the hermit-thrush in section v of *The Waste Land* (with a note by Eliot), famous for its sweetness of song, and, in context, its 'water-dripping song' evoking the long-sought life-giving refreshment. There is 'the walker, the water-thrush' in the short poem 'Cape Ann'.[13] There is also 'the deception of the thrush' in the first section of *Burnt Norton*; the bird leads the way into the opportunities 'which we did not take' – the garden and the laughter of the children hidden behind the leaves, laughter which is explicitly

---

[13] The three thrushes are clearly described and photographed in the *National Audubon Society Field Guide to North American Birds, Eastern Region* (New York: A. A. Knopf, 1998), pp. 634–5, 680.

present later in *Marina*. *Burnt Norton*, like the rest of *Four Quartets*, explores the possibility of possessing again in more meaningful form the moments of happiness, past or missed, when 'the pool was filled with water out of sunlight'. Each of these thrushes invites entrance to spiritual enlightenment.

The poem now changes style dramatically. The deadly sins of wrath, pride, sloth and lust are summoned (e.g., 'those who glitter with the glory of the humming-bird') and each of them means death. But all these have become 'unsubstantial' for the speaker, quietened by the returning images of pine, 'and the woodsong fog' – 'By this grace dissolved in place'. It is generally assumed that 'this grace' refers to Eliot's conversion and its rewards. Grace dissolves the sins as it intensifies the 'place': that is to say, what is signified in the coastal imagery of the opening lines, which I take to be a life beyond and out of time. At this crucial moment, the poem evokes the face of Marina, growing clearer to Pericles, 'more distant than stars and nearer than the eye', and *also* the 'Whispers and small laughter between leaves' which so poignantly symbolise the presence of children who do not exist and never did exist, in *Burnt Norton* and elsewhere. It must be clear why Eliot uses the 'criss-cross' of the recognition scenes in both Shakespeare's *Pericles* and Seneca's *Hercules Furens*. Pericles awakes to find his child alive; Hercules awakes to find he has no children. Eliot places himself between the two, fusing the joy of the one with the despair of the other, accepting both presence and absence by suggesting a kind of alternative for the human child.

It was Wilson Knight's contention that Shakespeare was able to convey his glimpses of immortality and eternity by means of the rather naïve dramatic structures and incidents of his last plays, especially the coming-to-life of the supposedly dead. Eliot, needing symbols to portray his own vision of life beyond time, reworks the being of Marina to conform to his own childlessness.

Eliot's biggest change from Shakespeare's story is not only his New England shore but the boat which reaches it, 'Bowsprit cracked with ice and paint cracked with heat'. 'I made this', Eliot's speaker exclaims, though now the rigging is weak 'and the canvas rotten'.

> Made this unknowing, half conscious, unknown, my own.
> The garboard strake leaks, the seams need caulking.
> This form, this face, this life . . .   (p. 110)

It seems that the making of the boat is becoming confused in the speaker's mind with the idea of the daughter whose image is growing clearer to his sight. The commonplace language of the play (as preserved in the extant text) is transfigured at this point by the waking prince's cry to Marina, 'Thou that beget'st him that did thee beget'. The daughter whom he begot now brings *him* to life. The poem continues,

> This form, this face, this life
> Living to live in a world of time beyond me; let me
> Resign my life for this life, my speech for that unspoken,
> The awakened, lips parted, the hope, the new ships.
>   (p. 110)

It was an essential part of Wilson Knight's thesis about *Pericles* that the daughter Marina symbolised art. Marina is 'as it were, art incarnate'. She is 'all but art personified. She is that to which all art aspires, which it seeks to express.'[14] She is, according to Knight, both the energy of artistic creation and its product.[15] I am convinced that this major proposal of Knight's is inherent in Eliot's words about the battered and leaking boat making for the New England shore, and in the vision of what he has made and what will replace him. He has made that boat, which is his own verse, and with it he has completed the journey to the granite shore where eternity begins. What has now been granted to him is the vision of what his art has begotten. It must be that 'this life / Living to live in a world of time beyond me' is an extension of his own art; 'the hope, the new ships' must be a future poetry influenced by his own. The poem ends with a significant rewording of its opening.

> What seas what shores what granite islands towards my timbers
> And woodthrush calling through the fog
> My daughter.   (p. 110)

---

[14] Knight, *Myth and Miracle*, in his *The Crown of Life*, pp. 62, 64.
[15] See Edwards, 'Wilson Knight and Shakespeare's Last Plays', pp. 264–6.

The woodthrush is now not merely singing but calling, and, most significantly, the poet is not bringing to mind the image of a dead child ('O my daughter!'), but celebrating her living presence, 'My daughter!'. Eliot speaks for Pericles and for himself. Hercules and his despair are banished. Accepting from Wilson Knight the concept of Marina as a symbol of art and its power, Eliot sees renewal in the continuance of his art and belief in the hands of others.

Marina is a pilgrimage poem because the boat of the *peregrinus* reaches the mist-concealed islands which symbolise, as they did for St Brendan, the Promised Land reserved for faithful believers. The poem painfully lacks, however, the culmination of the pilgrimage in *Pericles* the play, when the reunited Pericles and Marina travel to Ephesus to discover the lost wife and mother, Thaisa.

Although its hero's tomb was the centre of pilgrimage in England for several hundred years, *Murder in the Cathedral* (1935) has rather little to say about pilgrims and pilgrimage, and what it does say is equivocal. The Fourth Tempter offers Thomas the prospect of 'glory after death'.

> Think, Thomas, think of enemies dismayed,
> Creeping in penance, frightened of a shade;
> Think of pilgrims, standing in line
> Before the glittering jewelled shrine,
> From generation to generation
> Bending the knee in supplication,
> Think of the miracles, by God's grace,
> And think of your enemies, in another place.
>
> (p. 254)

Thomas replies shortly that he has thought of these things. The Tempter, who is voicing the Archbishop's own thoughts and desires, reminds him that he has also seen forward to the pillage of the Reformation, knowing –

> That the shrine shall be pillaged, and the gold spent,
> The jewels gone for light ladies' ornament,
> The sanctuary broken, and its stores
> Swept into the laps of parasites and whores.
>
> (p. 254)

The Tempter knows that Thomas can foresee and accept both the vanity of the shrine and the humiliation of its destruction in view of the 'eternal grandeur' of the martyr's place in heaven, 'dwelling forever in presence of God'. But Thomas feels himself able to resist the 'greatest treason' of this last temptation, 'to do the right deed for the wrong reason', and in his Christmas Morning sermon foresees his martyrdom as the suffering of one 'who has become the instrument of God, and who no longer desires anything for himself, not even the glory of being a martyr' (p. 261).

In their final chorus, the Women of Canterbury thank God for 'the blood of Thy martyrs and saints', which —

> Shall enrich the earth, shall create the holy places.
> For wherever a saint has dwelt, wherever a martyr has given his
>   blood for the blood of Christ,
> There is holy ground, and the sanctity shall not depart from it
> Though armies trample over it, though sightseers come with
>   guide-books looking over it;
>   . . . .
> From such ground springs that which forever renews the earth
> Though it is forever denied.   (p. 281–2)

So, although both jewelled shrines and the pilgrims who visit them receive short shrift, there is a very strong defence of the idea of holy ground and the holy place, sanctified by martyrdom. The position of the 'genuine' pilgrim is implied only. Some part of the earth is enriched and renewed by the blood of martyrs and saints, and presumably the traditional belief is upheld that worship at the site enables the pilgrim to share in that renewal and enrichment.

It is a question how far this testimony of the Women of Canterbury is upheld in the remarkable brief poem 'Usk' which Eliot wrote in 1935, the year in which he also wrote *Burnt Norton*. Both poems derive from the visit Eliot made to Chipping Campden in the Cotswolds. In July, Frank Morley picked him up from there and took him on a ten-day tour of Wales. The tour included the little town of Usk in Monmouthshire, and the poem 'Usk' was privately printed in

October.[16] The poem (of eleven lines) was later included as number III of 'Landscapes' in the *Collected Poems*.

> Do not suddenly break the branch, or
> Hope to find
> The white hart behind the white well.
>
> (p. 140)

The first half of this poem is a series of light-hearted injunctions not to seek magic formulae for obtaining insight, power and favour. The branch is presumably the sacred bough (which gave Frazer the title of his renowned book) which had to be broken off to obtain kingship, and may also be the bough Aeneas had to pluck to enter the underworld. I wonder if Eliot recalled as well the admonition of Piers in his mock-pilgrimage in *Piers Plowman*: 'Look thou break no boughs there.'[17] The third line, for all its sense of mystery, seems to be a joke. Beside the church at Llangybi near Usk there is an ancient holy well, with whitewashed stone work, a few yards from the prominent White Hart Inn. A visit here might have suggested the medieval quest which Eliot invents.[18]

> Lift your eyes
> Where the roads dip and where the roads rise
> Seek only there
> Where the grey light meets the green air
> The hermit's chapel, the pilgrim's prayer.
>
> (p. 140)

The poem becomes more serious. Resist old enchantments, lift your eyes from the well and look about you. According to Mrs Eliot, her husband used to say that 'an understanding of "Usk" depends partly on the immediate evocation of the scenery in *The Mabinogion*'.[19] I find this

---

[16] See Lyndall Gordon, *Eliot's New Life* (Oxford: Oxford University Press, 1988), pp. 161–2.

[17] William Langland, *The Vision of Piers Plowman: A Critical Edition of the B-Text*, ed. A. V. C. Schmidt, Everyman edn (London: Dent, 1995), Passus v, line 575.

[18] See my note, 'Where Eliot Dipped In', *Times Literary Supplement*, 23 May 2003.

[19] See Nancy Duvall Hargrove, *Landscape and Scenery in the Poetry of T. S. Eliot* (Jackson: University Press of Missouri, 1978), p. 121.

comment baffling. The chief 'scenery' in the poem is in the wonderful line, 'Where the grey light meets the green air', which suggests the Monmouthshire countryside more than it does *The Mabinogion*.

If there was a holy well (dedicated to St Cybi, a Cornish saint), there were pilgrims. It is not now possible to locate a hermit's cell either in Llangybi or in Usk, but there may well have been one in either place. Eliot quite clearly associates the devotion of the pilgrim at the well and of the hermit in his cell with the misguidedness of the questers after the 'old enchantments' which were supposed to lead to spiritual experience and enlightenment. Eliot repeats, in this very lovely poem, what so many writers had been saying from the dawn of Christianity, that the discovery of Christ was not confined to special locations. It is fitting that he should call his poem 'Usk', the name not only of the little town but of the river which runs through it, the river which Henry Vaughan loved. He celebrates, as Vaughan did, not the shrines or the journeys thereto, but the open countryside, 'where the roads dip and where the roads rise', as holy ground.

In this poem, therefore, Eliot once again disparages the value of the pilgrim's journey and his prayer at the shrine he has travelled to, and once again he restores it, in his play *The Family Reunion*.

The Family Reunion was first staged in March 1939. Eliot had struggled with the play for years, and revisions continued right through rehearsals. Now, in the twenty-first century, it may still seem a work better suited to the stage than to the reader, though the times have gone when its risky blend of 'natural' and 'poetic' language was popular and acceptable in the theatre. The present-day reader is bound to be uncomfortable with the perilous moments when both the action and the dialogue teeter on the brink of absurdity. It's unfortunate, because the dialogue of the 'ordinary' people is often excellent, and some of the more rarefied passages contain brilliant anticipations of *Four Quartets*. So far as the action is concerned, some of the awkwardness is inherent in translating the basic pilgrimage metaphor into terms of real life, the awkwardness besetting *Pilgrim's Progress*. For *The Family Reunion* is Eliot's *Pilgrim's Progress*. The final speech affirms that this is indeed a pilgrimage play, but, since it is spoken as Agatha and Mary process round a birthday cake, it shows only too well the embarrassing difficulty of locating pilgrimage within daily events. Here are Agatha's concluding words.

> This way the pilgrimage
> Of expiation
> Round and round the circle
> Completing the charm
> So the knot be unknotted
> The crossed be uncrossed
> The crooked be made straight
> And the curse be ended
> By intercession
> By pilgrimage
> By those who depart
> In several directions
> For their own redemption
> And that of the departed –
>   May they rest in peace
>   (p. 350)

The characters all take their places on a kind of graph of spiritual awareness. There are the wholly obtuse: Ivy, Violet, Gerald and Charles, though their conviction that there is no world except their own everyday world is sabotaged by Charles's glimmering of understanding at the very end (pp. 345, 349). Both Agatha the aunt and Mary the young cousin are in a state of awareness denied to the others and are the instruments for bringing Harry to his conversion. They, like Downing the chauffeur, are able to see the Eumenides who pursue Harry. But they continue to live 'in the neutral territory between two worlds' (p. 343); Agatha calls the ordinariness of the life which they have chosen 'the enchantment under which we suffer' (p. 333). Amy, the Dowager Lady Monchensey, has a special place on the graph. The centre of the play is her determination to hand over to her son Harry responsibility for the house and the estate she has guarded since her husband left her. The house, Wishwood, becomes a symbol of the life of denial which Harry comes to see as the trap laid for him. But Amy has made a conscious choice in her way of life. She has shut out the voices which her husband must have heard when he fell in love with his wife's sister, Agatha, and has committed herself to the existence which she wishes Harry to enter when he takes command at Wishwood.

The course which Harry follows from the world we all know to the world which few understand is the subject of the play. He is an alien in his first world, and is constantly travelling – 'I have spent many years in useless travel.' His emphasis, like that of Bunyan's Christian, is on escape. Escape initially from a world of people he loathes, all of them travelling too – 'many creatures moving / Without direction . . . In flickering intervals of light and darkness' (p. 294). And then escape from the action he took, or thinks he took, to free himself by killing his wife at sea, the action which brought the Furies to pursue him. Now he has come to Wishwood for the family reunion hoping for some haven of rest and security in the home of his boyhood, but in his conversation with Mary, the first of his liberators, he knows that 'the instinct to return to the point of departure' is 'all folly', and the appearance of the Eumenides at the window confirms his words (pp. 308, 311).

Mary's banal line, 'What you need to alter is something inside you' (p. 308), begins the process of cleansing and enlightenment which is completed by Agatha's revelation that his father, in love with Agatha, had wanted to kill *his* wife when she was pregnant with Harry. Agatha had protected the unborn son as a sort of messianic being who might free the family from its unhappiness.

> It is possible that you have not known what sin
> You shall expiate, or whose, or why. It is certain
> That the knowledge of it must precede the expiation.
> It is possible that sin may strain and struggle
> In its dark instinctive birth, to come to consciousness
> And so find expurgation. It is possible
> You are the consciousness of your unhappy family,
> Its bird sent flying through the purgatorial flame.
> Indeed it is possible. You may learn hereafter,
> Moving alone through flames of ice, chosen
> To resolve the enchantment under which we suffer.
>
> (p. 333)

So now Harry has to begin his journeying again. Having travelled to Wishwood in the futile journey of escape, he must now leave Wishwood in the journey of true pilgrimage. And it is here that the strain of translating the metaphor of Christian pilgrimage into terms of real life shows itself. Where is Harry physically to go on this spiritual journey? The Furies have been his pursuers, but now (as in Aeschylus) they are friendly beings, and he must follow them. The play is now filled with the symbolism of pilgrimage. Agatha, the sedentary head of a woman's college, can speak, quite properly, of 'a lifetime's march' to the moment of illumination, 'across a whole Thibet of broken stones / That lie, fang up' (p. 332). Of Harry's new-found state, and his future course of life, she can say, quite properly, that he 'has crossed the frontier', that 'you have a long journey', and that 'in a world of fugitives / The person taking an opposite direction / Will appear to run away' (pp. 342, 338). In the action of the play, beyond metaphor if not beyond symbolism, Harry has to leave Wishwood. Where, with his motor-car and his chauffeur, is he to go? The blending of metaphor and realism is going to break down somewhere. Harry protests he does not know where he is going. 'There is only one itinerary / And one destination' (p. 336). 'Where are you going?' asks Amy, a literalist. Harry replies in the language of the true *peregrinus*:

> I shall have to learn. That is still unsettled.
> I have not yet had the precise directions.
> Where does one go from a world of insanity?
> Somewhere on the other side of despair.
> To the worship in the desert, the thirst and deprivation,
> A stony sanctuary and a primitive altar,
> The heat of the sun and the icy vigil,
> A care over lives of humble people . . .   (p. 339)

It is not in the least surprising that his mother should say scornfully, 'Harry is going away – to become a missionary.' Her son is stung to reply, 'I never said that I was going to be a missionary' (p. 344). It is not different worlds that the two inhabit, but different plays. At least Eliot avoids the violent incongruity of the end he gave to Celia's desert pilgrimage in *The Cocktail Party* – 'she must have been crucified / Very near an ant hill' (p. 434) – but he seems to me to make an error of judgement veering in quite the opposite direction when he makes the chauffeur Downing rush back on stage because the *peregrinus* 'remembered . . . he left his cigarette-case on the table' (p. 346).

At this point the metaphor of the journey, as a symbol of the yet-unknown shape of a Christian life of repentance and service, is in ruins, and indeed there could be no better indication of its discard than the final moment of the play, when Agatha and Mary walk *'round and round the table, clockwise'* as Agatha recites 'This way the pilgrimage / Of expiation / Round and round the circle / Completing the charm'.

Movement is the essence of the pilgrimage metaphor. The journey of a pilgrim to a holy place becomes in the Epistle to the Hebrews an image of the life and death of the committed Christian, who moves from the alienation of life to the bliss of union in his or her true home. Antagonism to the metaphor, say in Langland or Vaughan, is chiefly to the idea of progression, of moving stage by stage to an ultimate union, which seems implicit in it. The relationship between human and divine, a relationship of love felt dimly in life and longed for after death, seems enfeebled by any comparison with earthly travel in time and space. Yet for a devotional poet even to hint at a transfiguration hoped for by many and actually experienced by a few is to demand a vocabulary of motion of some kind: not *here*, but *there*. It is one of the achievements of Eliot's *Four Quartets* that, building on and learning from the successes and failures of his use of the pilgrim-journey metaphor in earlier writings, Eliot contrives both to accept and deny the value of motion, distinguishing between movement without meaning and movement with meaning, and reconciling within a concept of Christian insight both movement and stillness.

It is a main task of the four poems to repudiate a concept of life as a slow accretion of experience, knowledge and wisdom, as a gradual attainment of understanding; a concept of life or history compartmentalised into past, present and future. This concept is imaged in the lyric which forms the first half of section II of *The Dry Salvages*.

> Where is there an end of it, the soundless wailing,
> The silent withering of autumnal flowers
> Dropping their petals and remaining motionless;
> Where is there an end to the drifting wreckage,
> The prayer of the bone on the beach, the unprayable
> Prayer at the calamitous annunciation?

There is no end, but addition; the trailing
Consequence of further days and hours,
While emotion takes to itself the emotionless
Years of living among the breakage
Of what was believed in as the most reliable –
And therefore the fittest for renunciation.

(DS II, 49–60)[20]

The image of the fruitless journey of life becomes a train journey or a sea-voyage in the succeeding section of the same poem.

You are not the same people who left that station
Or who will arrive at any terminus,
While the narrowing rails slide together behind you,
And on the deck of the drumming liner
Watching the furrow that widens behind you,
You shall not think 'the past is finished'
Or 'the future is before us'.   (DS III, 139–45)

The very shape of the poems which make up *Four Quartets* is part of the 'attack' on the belief in sequential movement. For each of the poems denies the value of narrative continuity. Each is an assembly of sub-poems, and there are sometimes quite violent differences of style in the different sections. The main subject of each poem, and of *Four Quartets* as a whole, is refracted through the different lenses of the constituent parts. That the end crowns the work – *finis coronat opus* – is a famous dictum in poetry; it does not apply to the scheme of *Four Quartets*.

What is advanced against the idea of progression through time and space is the idea of a person's life or the march of history as a series of timeless moments, with 'a lifetime burning in every moment' (EC V, 194).

                    to apprehend
The point of intersection of the timeless
With time, is an occupation for the saint –
                    (DS V, 200–2)

---

[20] In referring to passages in *Four Quartets*, I use the initials BN (*Burnt Norton*), EC (*East Coker*), DS (*The Dry Salvages*) and LG (*Little Gidding*), followed by the section number (I, II, III etc) and line numbers (though these are not given in the standard collected editions).

These moments of stillness, when the perspective of eternity collides with and transforms the limited perspective of time, are moments of insight which revolutionise the meaning of previous experience. 'Every moment is a new and shocking revaluation / Of all we have been' (EC II, 86–7). The ghost of the 'dead master' in *Little Gidding* speaks movingly of this revaluation as

> the rending pain of re-enactment
> Of all that you have done, and been; the shame
> Of motives late revealed, and the awareness
> Of things ill done and done to others' harm
> Which once you took for exercise of virtue.
>   (LG II, 138–42)

Obviously the achievement of these moments of 'sudden illumination' (DS II, 92), involving the whole reorientation of a human life, cannot be described without resorting to images of movement. Distinguishing valid movement from meaningless movement is accomplished in part by Eliot's basic device in *Four Quartets*: his use of the riddling paradox which identifies difference in sameness and sameness in difference, opposition in unity and unity in opposites. So, 'What might have been and what has been / Point to one end' in *Burnt Norton*; 'In my beginning is my end' and 'where you are is where you are not' in *East Coker*; in *The Dry Salvages* 'the way up is the way down, the way forward is the way back'. These all give us sameness in difference; for difference in sameness we have the dark in *East Coker* (III), which can be the darkness of the life of the unredeemed or the darkness of God; and in the great lyric in *Little Gidding* (IV) we are given 'the choice of pyre or pyre – / To be redeemed from fire by fire' (destructive fire or purgatorial fire).

As regards movement, we have the verbal paradoxes of a 'white light still and moving', and 'as a Chinese jar still / Moves perpetually in its stillness' (BN II, 73; V, 142–3). The most important passage showing the merging of these opposites is in *East Coker*, where the demand for a new kind of perception leads directly to an image of the desolate sea.

We must be still and still moving
Into another intensity
For a further union, a deeper communion
Through the dark cold and the empty desolation,
The wave cry, the wind cry, the vast waters
Of the petrel and the porpoise.   (EC v, 204–9)

Achieving a stillness which recognises the futility of the movement of time demands movement of a different order. A boat making its way to a landfall through difficult and dangerous northern waters is Eliot's constant symbol for the spiritual movement which invalidates temporal movement. It is there at the end of *Gerontion*, written in 1919.

Gull against the wind, in the windy straits
Of Belle Isle, or running on the Horn.
White feathers in the snow, the Gulf claims . . .
(p. 39)

And it is there, centrally, in the *Marina* of 1930, as we have seen, when the approach to grace is symbolised by the song of a woodthrush heard through the fog as a battered boat approaches a granite shore.[21] The shore in *Marina* is very obviously recalled in the beautiful sea-poetry of the first section of *The Dry Salvages*, and it is particularly interesting that the boat which makes the difficult landfall in the earlier poem, a boat built by the poet which has only just been able to perform its task – 'the rigging weak and the canvas rotten . . . The garboard strake leaks, the seams need caulking' – reappears in the second section of *The Dry Salvages* as 'a drifting boat with a slow leakage', an image of *meaningless* motion, soon to be part of 'the drifting wreckage' of an undirected life. The proximity of the two orders of motion, sanctified and unsanctified, is shown later in the poem, when the voyagers and seamen who 'will suffer the trial and judgement of the sea' are admonished to remember their 'real destination'(DS III, 162–5).

Explorers in the past were daring voyagers. For Eliot, 'old men ought to be explorers', for the kind of exploration which is important

---

[21] There are some excellent things about the symbolism of the New England coast in Lyndall Gordon's book, *T. S. Eliot: An Imperfect Life* (mentioned in note 12); see pp. 12, 240–1, 346, 356.

for him is towards that 'deeper communion' beyond the dark cold northern seas. In reference to an early version of the great passage from *East Coker* quoted above (EC v, 204–9), Helen Gardner made a curiously undeveloped claim that it showed the union of the forests of Indian hermits with 'the desert of the Christian hermits and the sea of the early Irish missionaries'.[22] Though the text she quotes does not really bear out her claim, I am sure she was right to say that the spirit of the old *peregrini* is to be found in Eliot's use of the sea-motif. These *peregrini* crossed the sea to deepen their service to Christ either as hermits or as missionaries. Their spirit lived on in the Leyden separatists, who looked across the ocean to America for a place to perfect their communal worship. There was a confusion about whether their 'better country' was in heaven or in New England, and, with the help of Purchas, New England was established as the Promised Land. In the late poetry of Eliot, who fancied his ancestral roots to be in New England, that granite shore, wreathed in fog, is restored to its status of a purely symbolic Promised Land: a goal for all those who seek to attain the stillness of understanding.

The first of the Quartets, *Burnt Norton*, has the following beautiful ending

> Desire itself is movement
> Not in itself desirable;
> Love itself is unmoving,
> Only the cause and end of movement,
> Timeless and undesiring
>
> . . .
>
> Sudden in a shaft of sunlight
> Even while the dust moves
> There rises the hidden laughter
> Of children in the foliage
> Quick now, here, now, always –
> Ridiculous the waste sad time
> Stretching before and after.
>   (BN v, 161–5, 169–75)

---

[22] Helen Gardner, *The Composition of 'Four Quartets'* (London and Boston: Faber and Faber, 1978), pp. 57, 113.

Here are the two kinds of movement whose confrontation is the chief subject of the Quartets, and the stillness which is their object. The last two lines recall the drift of the meaningless journeying into which most people are locked; the movement of desire is the alternative movement of those who have been able to make the transition of faith towards the ultimate stillness of love, here imaged in the familiar metaphor of the laughter of the children who do not exist in the world of time.

It is proper to call this second, sanctified movement pilgrimage. Its favoured image is a sea-voyage to a fog-bound rocky coast, an image which it shares with the story of St Brendan's voyages. It is not the only image of pilgrimage in *Four Quartets*. The last poem, *Little Gidding*, is centred on Nicholas Ferrar's Christian community in seventeenth-century Huntingdonshire. It was visited by Charles I in 1633, and he came there again in 1642, and then for a last time, alone with his chaplain, in 1646, on his way to give himself up to the Scots. In the king's journey to the manor-house we are asked to see the undirected journey as transformed into the sanctified journey of pilgrimage, 'now and in England' (LG 1, 35–9). It is understood that the king kneels and prays and then continues his journey to the scaffold. His prayer is taken as one of the timeless moments so often spoken of, and his consequent death a death in which we can share. 'We die with the dying ... We are born with the dead' (LG v, 228, 230).

> history is a pattern
> Of timeless moments. So, while the light fails
> On a winter's afternoon, in a secluded chapel
> History is now and England.   (LG v, 234–7)

The chapel which was empty and derelict at the end of *The Waste Land* is at this moment rebuilt and holds worshippers.

There follow those lines of *Four Quartets* which everyone knows.

> We shall not cease from exploration
> And the end of all our exploring
> Will be to arrive where we started
> And know the place for the first time.
>   (LG v, 239–42)

We have seen how Purchas hijacked the term 'pilgrim' to include those intrepid voyagers whose promised lands were the undiscovered countries they proposed to acquire and exploit. For Eliot the undiscovered country is a spiritual appetence in every person, and exploration is a very different form of pilgrimage: the movement to uncover and respond to that appetence.

CHAPTER 8

Lough Derg

In Ireland, pilgrimage has remained as an important element in social
and religious life throughout the centuries, in spite of strenuous efforts
by the Protestant overlords to extinguish it.[1] Communal processions
to holy wells, which continued until modern times, suggest that pilgrimage itself was pre-Christian; 'Europe has nothing older than our
pilgrimages', said Yeats.[2] Pilgrimage in Ireland differed from that in
England not only because it survived the Reformation. The ascetic
dedication of the *peregrini*, who wandered to achieve solitary communion or to establish devotional communities or to bring Christ to
heathens, was always recognised as a particularly Irish endeavour. In
later times the severe penitential rituals of Irish pilgrimages give them
a special colouring. Obviously, penance has always been fundamental
in Christian pilgrimage. Without a conviction of sin and the desire in
some measure to absolve and purge that sin, few pilgrims would have
started on their journey. Apart from voluntary penance there was the
very widespread use of pilgrimage as a punishment for crime.[3] But
whether the pilgrimage was voluntary or enjoined, it was the whole
venture, especially an arduous and difficult journey and the time it
took, that constituted the penance. The rite of communion which was
the centre and purpose of the journey was more a matter of contrition
and blessing than of suffering. But in Irish pilgrimage suffering seems
to be at the centre of the rite of communion. This is certainly the case

[1] See Peter Harbison, *Pilgrimage in Ireland: The Monuments and the People* (London:
Barrie and Jenkins, 1991), esp. Chapter 23.
[2] W. B. Yeats, *Explorations* (London: Macmillan, 1962), p. 267.
[3] See Jonathan Sumption, 'The Penitential Pilgrimage', Chapter 7 of his *Pilgrimage*
(Totowa, N.J.: Rowman and Littlefield, 1975; London: Faber and Faber, 2002).

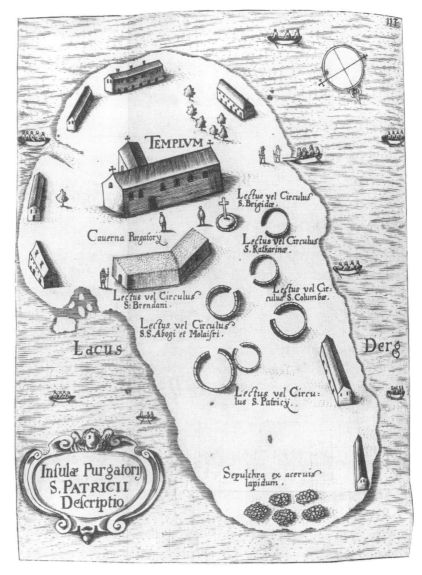

Illustration 3. Lough Derg, by Thomas Carve. *Lyra sive anacephaleosis hibernica,*
1666. Trinity College, Dublin.

in pilgrimage to Station Island in Lough Derg, which, with Croagh Patrick, is one of the most famous and most frequented of Ireland's holy sites.

Lough Derg in Donegal – there is also a much larger Lough Derg on the Shannon, to the south – is just outside the border drawn in 1922 to separate Northern Ireland from the Irish Free State. Legend has it that on one of its islands, either Saints' Island or Station Island, Christ appeared to St Patrick and showed him a cave that was the entrance to Purgatory. He said that anyone who had the courage to enter that cave and hold out for a day and a night would be purged of his sins and would witness both the torments of the damned and the joys of the blessed. Many of those who entered, it was said, never came out alive, but the twelfth-century manuscript by 'H. of Saltrey', an English monk, *Tractatus de Purgatorio sancti Patricii*, related the extraordinary underground adventures of Knight Owein, who went into the cave, endured the assaults of the devils and witnessed the glory of Paradise, and came out alive.[4] The legend was known all over Europe. It is supposed to have influenced Dante's *Inferno*. Ariosto mentioned the 'straunge tales' of St Patrick's 'solitarie cave' in *Orlando Furioso*.[5] Calderòn wrote *El Purgatorio de San Patricio* in 1634. Robert Southey's 'St Patrick's Purgatory' was first published in 1798, with an amplified version in 1801.

The pilgrimage to the holy site of St Patrick's cave has been centred on Station Island from time immemorial, despite uncertainty about whether earliest references refer to Station Island or to Saints' Island. Two major religious interventions have destroyed what remained of any cave. (There is now no cave on either island.) The first intervention came from Pope Alexander VI, who ordered the closure of the cave because of complaints that it was not producing spiritual visions. The second intervention was Protestant. In 1632, the Lords Justices and Council deplored 'the frequent and public resort of people in great

---

[4] See J.-M. Picard and Y. de Pontfarcy, *Saint Patrick's Purgatory: A Twelfth-Century Tale of a Journey to the Other World* (Dublin: Four Courts Press, 1985). For later English versions, see Stephen Greenblatt, *Hamlet in Purgatory* (Princeton and Oxford: Princeton University Press, 2001), pp. 75–82.

[5] Book 10, Stanza 78 (Sir John Harington's translation of 1591).

numbers to that place or Island called St Patricks Purgatory, there performing superstitious ceremonies, pilgrimages and offerings', and the landowner was ordered to 'pull down and utterly demolish that monster of fame called Saint Patrick's Purgatory, with Saint Patrick's Bed and all the vaults, cells and other houses and buildings; and to have all the other superstitious stones and materials cast in the Lough, and that he should suffer the superstitious Chapel in the Island to be pulled down to the ground and no boat to be there nor pilgrimage used nor frequented'.[6] It proved quite impossible to extirpate the pilgrimage, however, which continued throughout the penal days. In modern times there has been much rebuilding, and it is possible that the circles of stones which are thought to be the remains of ancient monastic cells, and which every pilgrim must traverse barefoot, have been restored. However, each year, in June, July and August, several thousand pilgrims arrive to perform 'this most ancient and most rigorous of penitential purges'.[7]

The present pilgrimage, which adheres to the traditional form, takes three days. The pilgrim arrives fasting and is taken by boat to the island. Fasting begins on the morning of arrival and continues until midnight on the third day, the day of departure. One exiguous 'Lough Derg meal' a day is provided.[8] On arrival the pilgrim removes his or her shoes and begins to perform the stations, which are the main exercises of the pilgrimage, involving circuits of the 'beds', the stony foundations of the ancient cells, the recital of prayers, and, at St Brigid's Cross, the renunciation, 'with arms fully outstretched', of the World, the Flesh and the Devil.[9] At 10 p.m. on the first night the Vigil begins in the Basilica. This, 'the chief penitential exercise of the Pilgrimage involves each pilgrim staying completely and continuously awake for 24 hours'. The second day begins with confession,

[6] Shane Leslie, *Saint Patrick's Purgatory* (London: Burnes, Oates and Washbourne, 1932), p. 78.
[7] Catherine Byron, *Out of Step: Pursuing Seamus Heaney to Purgatory* (Bristol: Loxwood Stoneleigh, 1992), p. 16.
[8] Of the many accounts of the pilgrimage, the most detailed is perhaps that of Catherine Byron (see previous note).
[9] From the leaflet given to the pilgrims on arrival.

here called 'the sacrament of reconciliation' and continues the performance of the stations. Sleep is possible in the dormitories on the second night. On the third day there is Mass and blessing and the final stations.

Every account tells in its own way how exhausting this routine proves to be: of the deprivation of food and sleep, the long night in the chapel, the physical pain of completing the stations barefoot. Forty-eight hours of prayer and self-inflicted suffering are endured in commemoration of St Patrick, with whatever hope each pilgrim brings to the performance of the ritual. The saint who is commemorated is the saint who was given by Christ a vision of Purgatory, with its penalties and its rewards. The three-day ritual at Lough Derg reminds us of the centrality of the doctrine of Purgatory to the entire practice of Christian pilgrimage. The link is indissoluble. If there were no intermediate state for the souls of the dead before the final judgement to pain or to bliss there would have been no flocking to Walsingham, to Canterbury, to Compostela to pray for intercession to abbreviate and alleviate the suffering of Purgatory and hasten the entry to eternal bliss of the souls of those who had gone before and the souls of those still to die. Of course there is still meaning in pilgrimage for those who do not accept the doctrine of Purgatory, as there is meaning in it for those who do not accept the idea of the immortality of the soul, but historically that is not the case. And it was not the theology of Purgatory alone that condemned pilgrimage in the Reformation, but the widespread abuses which followed in its train, particularly the belief that an intercession which would shorten the torments of the souls of the departed or the torments still to be inflicted on one's own soul could be purchased with hard cash.

The ritual of Lough Derg is an anticipation of Purgatory, and a preparation for it. It is there to accept penance, and to deepen it by depriving the pilgrims of comfort and pleasure, and so bring them to a new consciousness of the meaning of their lives, past and future. Renunciation is real. Therefore both confession and absolution may have more meaning. Ideally the pilgrim, a changed person, is the more ready to meet the challenge of the ultimate judgement after death.

For the writer in post-Reformation England pilgrimage was no more than a metaphor. For the writer in Ireland in the nineteenth and twentieth centuries it was a reality, and its reflection in literature has been on the spiritual value of something widely practised.

Thomas Moore's poem 'I wish I was by that dim lake', one of his *Irish Melodies*, published in 1824, does not specifically mention the pilgrimage, but it treats Lough Derg itself as a simulacrum of Purgatory, a place of gloom where the living may divest themselves of what supposedly has made life worthwhile.

> I wish I was by that dim Lake,
> Where sinful souls their farewell take
> Of this vain world, and half-way lie
> In death's cold shadow, ere they die.
> There, there, far from thee,
> Deceitful world, my home should be;
> Where, come what might of gloom and pain,
> False hope should ne'er deceive again.

It is William Carleton's story 'The Lough Derg Pilgrim', first published in 1828, which provides the first detailed literary account of the pilgrimage. This story, remarkable enough in itself, is remarkable also in offering a kind of template to later writers seeking to test the spiritual nourishment of the ritual. The ambiguities and contradictions of Carleton's life and writings are well known. His *Traits and Stories of the Irish Peasantry*[10] give a uniquely vivid picture of the Irish underclass in such stories as 'The Hedge School', 'Denis O'Shaughnessy Going to Maynooth', 'The Poor Scholar' and 'The Lough Derg Pilgrim'. But (it is held) he soured and sabotaged his insight into and knowledge of rural Catholicism when he changed his religion and wrote for a Protestant audience.[11] He was born in 1794, the youngest of the

[10] The first edition of Carleton's *Traits and Stories of the Irish Peasantry* was published in 5 vols. in Dublin, 1830–3. I have used the edition in 4 vols. edited by D. J. O'Donoghue (London: Dent; New York: Macmillan, 1896), and subsequent page numbers in the text refer to this edition.

[11] There is an excellent and sympathetic analysis of the Carleton enigma in Thomas Flanagan, *The Irish Novelists, 1800–1850* (New York: Columbia University Press, 1959).

fourteen children of Irish-speaking peasants in Co. Tyrone.[12] It was a time of destitution and eviction, and the youthful Carleton joined the Ribbonmen, a secret society of agrarian protest. He was, he says, 'designed for a priest', but going on the Lough Derg pilgrimage (1818?) changed the whole course of his subsequent life. He became a teacher, went to Dublin and married the niece of a Protestant schoolmaster. He had renounced his religion by the time that he met the Rev. Caesar Otway, who had founded and was editor of *The Christian Examiner and Church of Ireland Magazine*. Otway encouraged Carleton, and it was for the *Examiner* that Carleton wrote the first version of 'The Lough Derg Pilgrim' in 1828.

Carleton's story is an autobiographical fiction. It is impossible, when reading it, not to speculate on what Carleton's true feelings were when as a young man he made his pilgrimage, and what his true feelings were when as a man in his thirties he contrived a fictional account of that pilgrimage that would please the anti-Catholicism of his sponsor and his audience. For the story is full of incompatibilities. The narrator, Thomas Flanagan said, 'has two voices',[13] and those two voices are characteristic of the *Traits and Stories* as a whole. Carleton is at the same time full of respect and affection for the context of his poverty-stricken, Irish-speaking, rural Catholic childhood and scornful of its unsophisticated credulity. He himself said, 'Although I conscientiously left the church, neither my heart nor my affections were ever estranged from the Catholic people.'[14] Benedict Kiely rightly pointed out that Carleton's divided mind 'mirrored much of the contradiction and division' of the Ireland of his time.'[15] At the same time, the convert's virulent anti-Catholicism requires further explanation; there is something grossly facile and synthetic about it, wholly out of key with the sharpness and humour of most of the writing. Like

[12] Carleton's *Autobiography*, first edited by O'Donoghue in 1896, was twice reissued in the twentieth century, with a preface by Patrick Kavanagh (London: Macgibbon and Kee, 1968), and with a foreword by Benedict Kiely (Belfast: White Row Press, 1996).

[13] Flanagan, *The Irish Novelists*, p. 282.   [14] Carleton, *Autobiography* (1968), p. 92.

[15] Benedict Kiely, *Poor Scholar* (New York: Sheed and Ward, 1948; Dublin: Wolfhound Press, 1997), p. v.

everyone else Flanagan is rightly surprised at the venality of Carleton's pen. 'He cut his cloth to suit his odd assortment of employers, and had a chameleon ability to believe, for the moment, whatever he wrote.'[16] It seems to me that when Carleton gave up the faith of his boyhood, he was unable to replace it with anything else. What was firmly rooted in him gave way, and nothing else grew. In a shoulder-shrugging indifference to new creeds, his desire to please, and to make money, readily supplied the denunciations of superstition which his Protestant readership required.

In 'The Lough Derg Pilgrim', Carleton makes no secret of the indwelling scepticism of his youth, before which his Catholicism crumbled, the 'villainous curiosity' (p. 282) which made him delight in the scenery when he thought such levity was forbidden, and ruined 'the romance of devotion' when smoke from the prior's chimney 'brought me back to humanity', and 'the idea of roasting meat' drove out higher thoughts (p. 290). There seems little doubt that the Lough Derg pilgrimage had been something of a disillusionment for the young Carleton, but the violent oscillation in attitude, undercutting devotion at every point, and indeed the entire framing of the story, owe more to Caesar Otway and the readers of the *Christian Examiner* than to historical fact. The frame shows Carleton's genius for derisive comedy at its best. The hero is a brash, callow, vain, naïve young man clad in black, aspiring to become a priest. He meets two women pilgrims who minister to his vanity by assuming he is already a priest. We do not learn until the end of the story that these are Nell M'Collum and her accomplice, confidence tricksters who are performing the pilgrimage for its pickings. Nell asks her young priest to lead the prayers, and as the hero accepts the role, the pilgrimage is already a showground for impostors. The other pilgrims met en route are shown to be pretenders or doubters or bigots or charlatans of various sorts, but then (and who takes over the narration now?) among 'the flocks of gregarious babblers, I seldom failed to witness the outpouring of a contrite spirit'. One young woman, who 'evidently belonged to rather a better order of society' prayed in a corner of the lodging: 'her face told a tale

---

[16] Flanagan, *The Irish Novelists*, p. 257.

of sorrow, of deep, wasting, desolating sorrow'. Her suppressed sobs 'sufficiently proclaimed her sincerity'; 'I thought she appeared . . . woefully and pitiably alone' (pp. 286–7).

We have certainly lost (for the moment) the impudent young would-be priest who introduced the story. The approach to Lough Derg itself brings out a strange passage, beginning with a thought of seeing Rome for the first time – Childe Harold style. This is different. The poet seeing Rome was not 'submitted to the agency of a transcendental power'. 'My feelings on this occasion', says the narrator, 'with my thick-coming visions of immortality . . . almost lifted me from the mountain-path I was ascending, and brought me, as it were, into contact with the invisible world . . . In such a case the pilgrim stands . . . between life and death.' All the pilgrims began praying, and 'nothing broke a silence so solemn but a low, monotonous murmur of deep devotion' (pp. 288–9). Of course the narrator tells us that 'it was Superstition that placed him there', and this passage concludes with the mischievous thought of roast meat when the pilgrim sees the smoke curling from the prior's chimney. But that is the way 'The Lough Derg Pilgrim' is: devotion and irreverence juxtaposed, with a later layer of Protestant derision.

The most striking passage in 'The Lough Derg Pilgrim' relates to the night-long Vigil. As the hero makes his way to the chapel he is deeply impressed by the wild beauty of the stormy night, and this, with the loneliness and remoteness of the lake, 'joined to the feeling of deep devotion in which I was wrapped, had really a sublime effect upon me'. Of course, says Carleton quickly, the generality of people were blind to the beauty of the setting, and viewed it 'only through the medium of superstitious awe'. The scene in the chapel is wonderfully described, the faint candlelight, the crowd of kneeling pilgrims struggling to keep awake, and – above all – 'the deep, drowsy, hollow, hoarse, guttural, ceaseless, and monotonous hum which proceeded from about four hundred individuals half asleep and at prayer'. This hum had a hallucinatory effect. 'It still – still rung lowly and supernaturally on my ear . . . Human nature, even excited by the terrible suggestions of superstitious fear, was scarcely able to withstand it' (p. 295). It was at this point in the original version that Carleton spoke of 'that solemn, humble, and heartfelt sense of God's presence which Christian prayer demands'.[17] This sentence, which might have given an unfortunate impression of the power of a Catholic ritual, was carefully excised, and Carleton could go on with less trouble to the farcical side: the blow on the head from one of the minders to keep him awake, and the hero's contrivance to become a minder himself and return the blow with interest.

Later on the hero meets yet another confidence trickster who is working the pilgrims, and then, when he has left the island and is staying at an inn, he finds out the truth about the woman who had been his first companion – she makes away with his clothes during the night. The final irony is that when the hero indignantly tells this story to a priest, 'he laughed till the tears ran down his cheeks'. '"So," says he, "you have fallen foul of Nell M'Collum . . . Rest contented, you are not the first she has gulled – but beware the next time." "There is no danger of that," said I, with peculiar emphasis' (p. 304).

The priest's laughter completes for the hero the discrediting of the pilgrimage and his abandonment of the religion which sponsors it. But the reader has little difficulty, as he or she disentangles the threads of this story, in recognising that a more serious struggle has gone on than the one-sided contest displayed, between superstition and imposture on the one hand and emancipated good sense on the other. In spite of all the contempt and undercutting, there is a deep admiration for the genuine pilgrims, young and old, and even envy for the intensity of their experience. The young Carleton was challenging the experience, and he may well be right in saying that his rejection of what the pilgrimage offered changed his life. But, in repudiating it for Otway's readers, he made his victory altogether too easy, while his honesty, or his innocence, left behind clear traces of a respect he could not banish.

Over a hundred years later, the poet Patrick Kavanagh repeated Carleton's tussle with the Lough Derg pilgrimage. Kavanagh's background was not wholly dissimilar from Carleton's: he was one of the nine children of a cobbler and subsistence farmer in Inniskeen in Co.

[17] See *ibid.*, p. 283.

Monaghan (just south of the border with Northern Ireland).[18] He had almost no education, leaving school at thirteen to work on the farm, and his passion not only for poetry but to become a poet is unexplained. He was born in 1904, and it was not until 1939 that he freed himself from the drudgery of the farm (which was the source of his best poetry) and took himself to Dublin. Although he underwent no 'conversion' like Carleton's, his views on religion are uncertain and inconsistent. In 1945, when Cardinal McRory died, Kavanagh told Benedict Kiely, 'Now he knows what I always knew.' 'What's that?' Kiely asked. 'There's no God', answered Kavanagh. In 1967, 'his dying words, which he kept repeating, were "Oh God, I believe."'[19] His acceptance of the Catholic church is implied in his regular churchgoing in the forties and fifties, and in his curious long-term relationship with Archbishop John Charles McQuaid, who gave him signal help.[20] His questioning of the church and its beliefs nevertheless forms the substance of a good deal of his poetry.

Kavanagh made two visits to Lough Derg. He 'did' the pilgrimage in 1940 for the *Independent*, which printed his account of the Croagh Patrick pilgrimage, but rejected his report of Lough Derg as too contemptuous of the pilgrims, with its emphasis on 'the narrow primitive piety of the small huxter with the large family'.[21] His second pilgrimage was in June 1942, and his record of that is the long poem 'Lough Derg', written immediately afterwards. Probably Kavanagh made the pilgrimage and wrote the poem to clear his own mind about the magnetism of beliefs which he rejected, but he never published the poem. It was first printed by his brother Peter four years after Patrick's death, in *November Haggard* (1971).[22] The poem does indeed need a *miglior fabbro* to tidy it up and suppress its frequent weakness and self-indulgence, but, not unlike Ralegh's unruly masterpiece centuries earlier, 'The Ocean to Cynthia', it owes a lot of its strength to its untidiness, its jarring leaps and inconsistencies.

[18] Full details about Kavanagh's life and writings are in the biography by Antoinette Quinn, *Patrick Kavanagh* (Dublin: Gill and Macmillan, 2001).
[19] Both these stories from Quinn, *Patrick Kavanagh*, pp. 230, 462.
[20] See *ibid.*, p. 193, and Index, 'McQuaid'.   [21] *Ibid.*, pp. 132, 195–6.
[22] See note on p. 425 of Peter Kavanagh's edition of *The Complete Poems of Patrick Kavanagh* (New York: Kavanagh Hand Press, 1996).

Kavanagh's major long poem, *The Great Hunger* (1942), helpfully anticipates the difficult religious outlook of 'Lough Derg'. Derision tapers into compassion, irony into fellow-feeling, scorn into respect. The hero, Paddy Maguire, is scornful of the 'respectability' of his orthodox fellow farmers, and 'knelt beside a pillar where he could spit / Without being seen', wondering during the prayers whether he should 'cross-plough that turnip-ground'. Kavanagh sees the bleak awfulness of the condition of these small farmers and the vanity of their fond hopes, but he cannot deny to them their unconscious awareness of his own vision of God 'in the bits and pieces of Everyday', in the muck of the ditch as well as in the primroses of spring. 'Lough Derg' opens in a strong vein of contempt for those who come to the lake for the wrong reasons, 'petty mean people', the 'smug too-faithful', who 'push closed the doors that God holds open'. These are the selfish ones who offer up their comfort for their own gratification.

> That my son Joseph may pass the Intermediate
>   We beseech thee hear us.
> That my daughter Eileen may do well at her music
>   We beseech thee hear us.
> That her aunt may remember us in her will
>   We beseech thee hear us.[23]

There are sincere pilgrims too, but they are also locked in: not by their own small ambitions, but by what the church promises. As they make their renunciation of the World, the Flesh and the Devil, they are rejecting 'the music of Time's choir' (p. 48). Yet this music may come to them unawares during the punitive penance of the Lough Derg regimen.

> For here's the day of a poor soul freed
> To a marvellous beauty above its head.
> The Castleblaney grocer trapped in the moment's need
> Puts out a hand and writes what he cannot read,
> A wisdom astonished at every turn
> By some angel that writes in the oddest words.   (p. 47)

---

[23] Text from Patrick Kavanagh, *Selected Poems*, ed. Antoinette Quinn (London: Penguin Books, 1996), p. 61. Subsequent page numbers in the text refer to this edition.

Lough Derg is full of 'half-pilgrims'. Kavanagh is one himself, but he chooses 'Robert Fitzsimons' to symbolise the presence of those who cannot keep away from the pilgrimage, although they reject 'All truth for which St Patrick's Purgatory vouches'. Fitzsimons, who is a bit of a sermonising prig, sees Annie Meegan whose beauty is 'from the unconverted kingdom', and he is a lost man. 'He must have her.' And have her he apparently does. The 'unprotected gable / Of asceticism's granite castle' is easily breached. And Robert finds new life, and new day, as a poacher sees 'Primeval magic among the trees' (p. 55).

The argument (if it can be called an argument) is that through the severity of the Lough Derg penance, including the all-night vigil,

> the silver strands
> Of the individual sometimes show
> Through the fabric of prison anonymity.
>   (p. 49)

'Only God, the poet', and not the authority of the church, can discern the truth that a few people find in the ritual, and can construct 'a reasonable document' from the fire that is set alight (see pp. 56–7). 'O the boredom of Purgatory / Said the poet then.' But God is not bored by those who believe and are disillusioned. At the close of the fine prayer-sonnets towards the end of the poem, the supplicant says –

> I set my will in Communion and Confession
> But still the sore is dribbling – blood, and will
> In spite of penance, prayer and canticle.
>   (p. 63)

But, says the God-poet, Christ hears the 'poetry sweeping through' these voices of 'the meanly poor'. We have to take what comfort we can from that. Lough Derg has 'deeply . . . kept an ancient vow. / It knows the secret of pain.' Although there may be despair and disillusionment –

> the green tree
> Of humanity
> Was leafing again
> Forgiveness of sin.
>   (p. 64)

The poem ends with Fitzsimons being placed among those who 'had found the key to the lock / Of God's delight in disillusionment'. This must mean that people are disillusioned with the promises of the Lough Derg pilgrimage, but that God may be found in its exacting ritual. God (apparently) delights in the deception that He may be found at Lough Derg, but not where the church claims He is.

'Why Sorrow?', an unfinished long poem written over a number of years, reinforces the religious comment of 'Lough Derg'. It is about Father Mat, a priest who becomes aware that the true God is a pagan God, 'a different Deity', who is alive in the sun and the flowers of the garden. In fear at his discovery he goes on pilgrimage to Lough Derg. What he finds there was never written, though it may be imagined.

Among the many other appearances of the Lough Derg pilgrimage in Irish literature, Sean O'Faolain's well-known story 'Lovers of the Lake' stands out, though it may be thought rather soft-centred.[24] It is about a Dublin surgeon, Bobby, and Jenny, a childless married woman. They have had a sexual relationship for six years, and Bobby is astonished and annoyed when she asks him to drive her to Lough Derg so that she can do the pilgrimage. He has never known her to display her religious convictions and he is afraid she may be ending their relationship. 'All this penitential stuff is because of me, isn't it?', he says.

> To go off to an island, in the middle of a lake, in the mountains, with a lot of Crawthumpers of every age and sex, and no sex, and peel off your stockings and your shoes, and go limping about on your bare feet on a lot of hard stones, and kneel in the mud, psalming and beating your breast like a criminal, and drink nothing for three days but salt water . . . it's not like you. It's a side of you I've never known before.

Jenny is unable to explain. She protests that 'in an otherwise meaningless existence' all she has to hang on to 'is you, and God'. She is afraid

---

[24] In Sean O'Faolain, *The Stories* (London: Hart-Davis, 1958); Subsequent page numbers in the text refer to this edition. Benedict Kiely reprints the story in *The Penguin Book of Irish Short Stories* (London: Penguin Books, 1981).

of an incompatibility here, and it seems clear she is going to the island in the hope of help. (Her problem is of course intensified by the laws and morals of mid-twentieth-century Ireland: 'A husband I'm not in love with. And I can't marry you.')

So she goes to the island and commences the punishing routine. Then, in the darkness, she is astonished to find that Bobby has arrived. 'I've come to see just what it is that you believe in' (pp. 360–1). But she knows that his real reason was to be with her, because he loves her, and a wave of desire for him goes through her. She continues, and during the three days occasionally meets him. Eventually she feels she has 'received the island's gift . . . the sensation of the world's death'. 'In mutual generosity each recognises the other only as a form of soul; it is a brief, harsh Utopia of equality in nakedness' (p. 376). Later she feels that the island has broken down 'the barriers of self', and that for a short time both love and renunciation seem possible. 'Only when love desires nothing but renunciation, total surrender, does self surpass self' (p. 378). The lovers leave the island together, and as they break their fast Bobby says, 'Do you know what I'm thinking, Jenny? I'm thinking that I wouldn't mind going back there again next year. Maybe I might do it properly the next time?' (p. 384). They go back to the hotel but she says 'Not tonight!' (p. 385), and they go to their separate rooms.

It seems to me a great pity that O'Faolain does not relate what the priest said to Jenny during Confession. Her tortured feeling that she ought to give Bobby up, and her knowledge that she *couldn't* give him up, ought to receive some ecclesiastical comment. A troubled girl she meets gasps out: 'I found a lamb of a priest. A saint anointed! He was as gentle!' (p. 377). As things are, we have to try to make sense of Jenny's own vague feeling, which her penance has given her, that love and renunciation are not incompatible. What the pilgrimage seems to have given her is a sense of purification that does not deny her 'illicit' sexual relation with Bobby, and the story suggests, in Bobby's willingness to return, that there is some future in what she calls 'the island's gift'. The conclusion is vague, but pious.

According to Neil Corcoran, Seamus Heaney made the pilgrimage to Lough Derg three times in his youth.[25] The pilgrimage is central to Heaney's major publication *Station Island* (London: Faber and Faber, 1984). This volume is divided into three parts. Part One is a collection of personal poems, not very easy to penetrate, on the responsibilities of a poet and on the writer's divided self. Part Two, headed 'Station Island', is a dream sequence about the pilgrimage, in which the poet is visited by many ghosts from the past. Part Three is 'Sweeney Redivivus', and Heaney's note says that these poems are 'voiced for Sweeney', calling attention to *Sweeney Astray*, his 1983 translation of a medieval Irish poem.[26] 'I trust', says the author, 'that these glosses [that is, these newly contributed poems] can survive without the support system of the original story.' This is modest and unassuming, but misleading. The entire collection *Station Island* requires the closest attention to be given to 'the original story' – at least as it is translated by Heaney.

The Irish tale *Buile Suibhne*, partly in prose but mostly in verse, of uncertain date but possibly tenth century, is a wonderful and mysterious work telling the story of Sweeney, king of Dal-Arie in the seventh century, who for his outrageous conduct towards St Ronan was cursed to spend his life flying through the air, feathered like a bird, not only through his native Ulster, but throughout Ireland and the islands of the Irish Sea. The work was translated for the Irish Texts Society by J. G. O'Keeffe in 1913, and this bilingual edition, Heaney says, is the basis of his work in *Sweeney Astray*. Those of us who do not know Irish take O'Keeffe's fidelity to the original for granted: he seems a patient, cautious, scrupulous scholar. Heaney's fidelity to O'Keeffe is remarkable, but, subtly and stealthily – taking a hint from O'Keeffe and possibly another from the Irish, making explicit what is implied,

---

[25] Neil Corcoran, 'Writing a Bare Wire: Station Island', in *Seamus Heaney*, ed. Michael Allen (New York: St Martin's Press, 1997), pp. 107–27 (reprinted from Corcoran's *Seamus Heaney* (London: Faber and Faber, 1986)).

[26] *Sweeney Astray* was first published in Ireland by Field Day Theatre company (1983), and subsequently in London by Faber and Faber (1984); quotations are taken from the latter edition. Quotations from *Station Island* are from the Faber and Faber edition (1984).

using a synonym which changes the import, adding a word here and there, and above all creating his own poetry – Heaney transforms his original into a masterpiece carrying a meaning of its own, which is of the greatest significance not only for Heaney's own poetry but also for this book on pilgrimage.

Heaney twice calls the mad Sweeney a pilgrim when there is no hint of this from O'Keeffe. The first occasion is section 43, stanzas 5 and 6.[27]

> Fugitive, deserted, mocked
> by memories of my days as king,
> no longer called to head the troop
> when warriors are mustering,
>
> no longer the honoured guest
> at tables anywhere in Ireland,
> ranging like a mad pilgrim
> over rock-peaks on the mountain.

The second is in Moling's final lament, 85, stanza 5.

> Because Mad Sweeney was a pilgrim
> to the lip of every well
> and every green-banked, cress-topped stream,
> their water's his memorial.

What is the implication of these changes? I need first of all to give a fairly brutal summary of the story. Sweeney hears that St Ronan is marking out a church on his territory. In violent anger he attacks Ronan and flings his beautiful psalter into a pond, but is then pulled away to take part in the battle of Moira. The psalter is miraculously returned unharmed to Ronan, by an otter. Ronan utters a bitter curse against Sweeney, that he shall 'roam Ireland, mad and bare', but before this curse takes effect the battle of Moira commences, and Sweeney confronts Ronan once more and attacks him again, killing one of his men and just missing Ronan with his spear. Ronan intensifies his curse, banning Sweeney to madness among the trees and to die at last at spear-point. Sweeney undergoes a kind of convulsion and commences

---

[27] Reference numbers to quotations from *Sweeney Astray* henceforth relate to the marginal section numbers, and not to pages.

his life among the birds. For a year he roams, and then comes for a time to Glen Bolcain, a haven for madmen, where he reflects on the hardships of his new life and the terrible loss of his kingship and all that went with it. He resumes his aerial life, through cold, storm and hunger, but amongst the fine laments for the past and its contrast with the misery, fear and suffering of the present appears a new note of acceptance of his life of madness, especially in the severe beauty of Glen Bolcain. When his half-brother Lynchseachan tries to capture him and bring him back to normal life he resists with all the cunning of a madman. He revisits his wife, but resists her too. His acceptance of the hardship of his life is best shown in the long and beautiful hymn to the glory of the wild and its trees (40). After many adventures over many years, including his meeting with the English madman Alan, he begins to tire of his sufferings in the wild and thinks of settling himself among his people. Ronan vindictively curses him again, and the worst days of his madness follow, until he comes to earth (as it were) and meets the saintly Moling. He is killed at spear-point, as was foretold, in a farcical misadventure. He repents, and makes confession to Moling before he dies.

Within this story, so beautifully told in poems and lyrics as well as prose links, there is a simple pattern of explanation which is always present and is always inadequate. This pattern is one of crime and punishment. Sweeney sins in his violence against God's representative, Ronan, and he is terribly punished by his long years of suffering in the wilderness. He comes to accept his new life as a condign punishment for his crime, and in the end is reconciled to the church and its rites. The contrast between the rhythm of this meaning and the soaring possibilities of what the work *might* mean is the source of some suggestions made by Heaney in his Introduction (pp. v–vi), seeking to explain 'its double note of relish and penitence'. There is possibly 'a tension between the newly dominant Christian ethos and the older, recalcitrant Celtic temperament'. Or again, 'insofar as Sweeney is also a figure of the artist, displaced, guilty, assuaging himself by his utterance, it is possible to read the work as an aspect of the quarrel between free creative imagination and the constraints of religious, political, and domestic obligation'. Only in *King Lear*, in 'Edgar's jabbering masquerade as poor Tom', can Heaney find 'poetry as piercingly exposed to the beauties and severities of the natural world', and for the strange blend of suffering and the 'opposite moods of jubilation' he suggests 'the praise poetry of the early Irish hermits'. In his later prose collection *The Government of the Tongue* (1988), Heaney mentions Nora Chadwick among those who have helped him to appreciate that the beauty and abundance of nature was a source of poetic inspiration in the Celtic world.

Nora Chadwick's book, *The Age of the Saints in the Early Celtic Church* (mentioned in Chapter One), is enthusiastic about *Buile Suibhne*. She writes that the text which we have of the saga 'adheres throughout to the tradition' that Suibhne's flight from human society, his abandonment of his kingdom, and his wandering life were 'not the result of true madness, but of a deliberate way of life'. The word '*geilt*', applied to Suibhne, was often used of those who chose to live ascetic lives as hermits and recluses, and (oddly) some of them were warriors who became *geilt* in the heat of battle because of their horror at the slaughter. Early poetry associated with Sweeney is chiefly concerned with his relation with wild nature. 'It is clear that Suibhne is a recluse, and his oratory is the woodland.' In the original tradition, she suggests, 'Suibhne was a fanatical recluse and St Moling his *anmchara*, or "confessor". Both are practising the eremitical life, Suibhne's reflecting an extreme kind which soon passed out of practice everywhere, and was perhaps never firmly established in the West.'[28]

The ambiguity of *Buile Suibhne* as a story which at the same time records both a sin against God and its punishment and the deliberate choice of a penitential ascetic life may be more clearly seen in Heaney's rendering, with its rephrasings and interventions, than in O'Keeffe's more solidly literal version. At the same time, Heaney's introductory remark about a tension between 'a newly dominant Christian ethos' and the older Celtic temperament risks obscuring the vital point that *Sweeney Astray* is a contest between two forms of Christianity, one strongly Celtic, the faith and conduct of the old *peregrini*, and the

[28] Nora K. Chadwick, *The Age of the Saints in the Early Celtic Church* (London: Oxford University Press, 1963), pp. 105–8.

other feebly 'modern'. The contest is presented with great subtlety: a vision of discovering Christ in exile and deprivation continuously masquerades as the fulfilment of Ronan's curse. The littleness of Ronan's Christianity is obvious from the start. He is measuring out his church. He is the conformist, happy in his limitations, basking in his self-righteousness, proud of his beautiful psalter. Violated by the naked Sweeney's brute force, he returns anger for anger in his vitriolic curse. Sweeney, out of human society in the tree-tops, certainly lives the life of a madman, but this is, equally, *either* the curse of Ronan's God *or* a divine madness in service of a God who could never enter Ronan's imagination.

'God has exiled me from myself' (14). Heaney more than once uses the word 'exile' without authority from O'Keeffe, driving home, it would seem, his own link between Sweeney and Edgar of *King Lear* – 'Edgar I nothing am'. He often intensifies the original in emphasising the loneliness of the outcast, and leaves it open, as is the case with Edgar, whether this new identity is chosen or enforced.

If it is the case (as I think it always is) that Sweeney's freedom overrides his compulsion, it is not to be supposed that his free choice brings him much in the way of happiness. He has chosen to give up the honour, comfort, affluence and power of a king and to live alone in the wild – cold, wet and hungry. His great laments for what he has lost (e.g., 19, 21) are more moving, coming from one who has made the choice of his own free will, than as simple cries of deprivation. It is not surprising that 'At times I am afraid' (Heaney's words). He has made himself 'an outcast / for the way I sold my Christ'. Not Ronan's Christ but 'my Christ'; the personal pronoun is Heaney's. He has removed himself from human society, aware that it was corrupt and that he was corrupt in it, and now endures extreme privation in the hope that he can purge his sin and draw nearer to Christ. Little wonder that he is afraid. 'Christ ordained my bondage / and exhaustion' (32). The words 'penitence' and 'penitential' are both interventions by Heaney (23 and 45).

> O Christ, the loving and the sinless,
> hear my prayer, attend, O Christ,
> and let nothing separate us.
> Blend me forever in your sweetness.
>   (23)

Beside this conception of a purgatorial suffering for past sins which brings him nearer to Christ, Sweeney also continuously repents of his crime against Ronan. Perhaps this sin is included in the greater sense of himself as a sinner, but I take it as part of the extraordinary texture of alternative readings which this work presents.

Gradually Sweeney comes to love the rewards of his rigorous life. 'Cuckoos calling across water' are 'sweeter / than church bells that whinge and grind' (23).

> Keep me here, O Christ, far away
> from open ground and flat country.
> Let me suffer the cold of glens.
> I dread the cold of open plains.
>
> (58)

His half-brother Lynchseachan, who tries to capture him and bring him back to 'normality', recognises his devotion to his ascetic life.

> Woods and forests and wild deer –
> things like these delight you more
> than sleeping in your eastern dun
> on a bed of feather-down.   (36)

As often as he can, Sweeney goes back to his favourite Glen Bolcain, 'where all the madmen of Ireland used to assemble'. His happiness there is not available to those who have not endured and suffered and lost as he has. Twice Heaney inserts the word 'Eden' into Sweeney's lyrical description of the natural 'riches' of the glen. And indeed it seems clear that this beautiful early Irish nature poetry is symbolising a vision of Paradise, earned by purgatorial suffering. 'That dear glen', Glen Bolcain, is the centre of the work's great long hymn to the trees of Ireland, which is the peak of Sweeney's exaltation (40).

After many years, Sweeney feels 'a glimmer of reason' and thinks of returning to society. Ronan is appalled to hear of this and beseeches God not to relent in his vengeance. What follows now is quite terrible new suffering expressed as the possession of Sweeney by nightmare hallucinations of severed goat-bearded heads pursuing him, 'snapping and yelping, / whining and squealing' (64). Heaney inserts the words 'I return / to haunt myself . . . / I am the bare figure of pain' (67). It is as though real madness supervenes for a time on the metaphorical madness of ascetic exile, when Sweeney strives to readjust to 'normality'. He makes the effort again, and joins a religious community led by Moling. This saintly man immediately realises the superior insight of the 'holy fool', and is painfully aware of the insufficiency of his own ministration (75). Following the ironic stupidity of Sweeney's death-blow, and Sweeney's confession, acceptance of the eucharist, and his anointment, Moling honours his burial, saying that because of Sweeney he has learned to love Glen Bolcain. I find this way of putting his acknowledgement of Sweeney's dear-bought spiritual insight very moving, and I think Heaney's insertion of Moling's jest at this point is a deviation of frightening proportions.

> With holy viaticum
> I limed him for the Holy Ghost.
> (85)

There is no hint in O'Keeffe's translation of this conversion of Moling into a gleeful Lynchseachan, rubbing his hands at his cleverness in bringing Sweeney to normality. As I read this wonderful and subtle Irish work, Moling is in complete contrast with Ronan and the limitations of the latter's religious outlook. Sweeney has worked his way to an altogether exceptional awareness of Christ in his harsh experiences outside society, and Moling surely recognises and acknowledges an enlargement of his own sense of what Christianity may mean.

In his Introduction, Heaney speaks of the 'uneasy reconciliation set in St Moling's monastery'. For the poems which he had already written, and those he was still to write, for *Station Island*, it was perhaps necessary that *Buile Suibhne* should end with Sweeney being tricked and captured by orthodoxy, but it is Heaney's own wording of Sweeney's career that makes me see him as the archetypal *peregrinus*, the pilgrim alienating himself from the world to pursue a spiritual vision the world calls madness, and I don't see the ending as failure.

So, the question now is, how does Heaney, with his translation of *Sweeney Astray* behind him, see his own pilgrimage? And how does his answer relate to our final question, what meaningful remnants of pilgrimage, if any, remain to us?

Heaney published a particularly fine and famous poem, 'At the Water's Edge', in his *Field Work* in 1979. It is the third in a group called 'Triptych'.[29] The poet is visiting islands in Lough Erne in Co. Fermanagh, just within the border of Northern Ireland and therefore still part of Britain's 'United Kingdom'. On one island he sees 'carved monastic heads', on another the Caldragh Idol, a pagan 'sex-mouthed stone'; and among the ruins on a third he hears the noise of a British army helicopter.

> A hammer and a cracked jug full of cobwebs
> Lay on the windowsill. Everything in me
> Wanted to bow down, to offer up,
> To go barefoot, foetal and penitential,
>
> And pray at the water's edge.
> How we crept before we walked! I remembered
> The helicopter shadowing our march at Newry,
> The scared, irrevocable steps.

There is clear allusion here to the ritual of penance at the barefoot Lough Derg pilgrimage, with its instruction to pray 'at the water's edge'.[30] There is a remarkable juxtaposition of this extreme penance with the defiant march at Newry in 1972, in memory of the nationalists killed by British troops on Bloody Sunday in Derry the week before. We go back to the first stanza in which those carved monastic heads were 'crumbling like bread on water'. Chapter 11 of Ecclesiastes tells us of bread cast upon water that 'you shall find it after many days'. There is no doubt at all that what the poem is talking about is reclaiming Ireland's past and restoring it to those to whom it belongs. 'How we crept before we walked!' The 'irrevocable steps' of the Newry march are seen as the prelude to that restoration. But the prelude to *that* prelude, or at least its accompaniment, is the utter self-humiliation of pilgrimage.

Did that spirit last? Obviously no, if we look forward to the publication of *Station Island* in 1984, in which the value both of the armed struggle for independence and of the pilgrim's contrition are seriously

---

[29] Seamus Heaney, *Field Work* (London and Boston: Faber and Faber, 1979), p. 14.
[30] Byron, *Out of Step*, p. 258.

challenged. In the poems of Part One, which we are to take as preceding *Sweeney Astray*, we have repeated pictures of a divided self and an ironic view of the poet's own drift. In 'Remembering Malibu' (p. 30) a clear contrast is made between the ascetic dedication of the monks in their beehive huts on the Great Skellig island off Kerry, and what Brian Moore has found beside a 'wilder and colder' Pacific ocean, but it is not at all clear (to me at least) where in the end the poet's allegiance lies. There is much greater clarity in 'Sandstone Keepsake' (p. 20), which treats the political rather than the religious half of the equation. The poet is on the shore of the Inishowen peninsula, in the Republic but looking across the estuary of the River Foyle to a British army camp in Co. Londonderry. He has picked up a reddish stone, and, in his 'free state of image and allusion', imagines it might have come from 'hell's hot river' of Phlegethon, or might indeed have been 'the heart / that damned Guy de Montfort to the boiling flood'. Guy had been put in hell by Dante for a revenge killing on the English king's nephew, and, as the poem says, the heart of his victim was 'long venerated' in London. Meantime, the soldiers in their watchtower have been following the poet with their binoculars, but they drop him as 'not worth bothering about'; he was obviously 'not about to set times wrong or right'.

Donald Davie wrote that this last phrase 'alludes to a famous poem by Robert Frost'.[31] He presumably meant 'Acquainted with the Night', in which the speaker roams the back streets of a city by night and suddenly sees a 'luminary clock against the sky', which 'Proclaimed the time was neither wrong nor right'. Heaney's line also clearly points to Hamlet's remark at the end of the play's first act: 'The time is out of joint: O cursed spite, / That ever I was born to set it right.'[32] There is a world of difference between these two 'sources'. Frost's narrator finds a message that the received notions of right and wrong are all in question. Hamlet has no such doubt; he is talking of a mission to do

---

[31] Donald Davie, *Under Briggflats* (Chicago: University of Chicago Press, 1989), p. 247.

[32] As pointed out by M. R. Molino, *Questioning Tradition, Language and Myth: The Poetry of Seamus Heaney* (Washington, D.C.: Catholic University of America Press, 1994), p. 153.

battle with wrong and to establish right. Heaney, as we all know, was anxious and edgy about the accusation that he was not participating fully in the appalling conflict between Irish Catholic nationalism and Protestant 'loyalism'. It is only by seeing that he must have had in mind *both* the references attributed to him that we can define his ironic picture of himself as one of no consequence to the authorities. He could not be a killer, not only because of his temperament and profession (as a poet), but because he suspects that a simple right and wrong does not apply in the present conflict. He is not a killer, neither as uncertain a one as Hamlet, nor as vicious a one as Guy de Montfort, but, he writes, 'one of the venerators' (referring back to the 'long venerated' heart), always ready to lament the victim of a murderous struggle in which neither side is the sole possessor of right and wrong.

There is no doubt that as an Irish Catholic from the North Heaney's sympathies are for the political unity and cultural diversity of an independent Ireland, but there is precious little in the first section of *Station Island* to suggest, in the way 'At the Water's Edge' suggests, a commitment to a pilgrimage of political intent graced by religious dedication. With the last poem of the first section, 'The King of the Ditchbacks' (pp. 56–8),[33] the new element of *Sweeney Astray* enters. The first part of this three-part poem, Heaney said, was written a year or two before he thought of translating *Buile Suibhne*.

In retrospect, it seems as if Sweeney had already arrived and was presenting his visiting card: the 'trespasser' moving behind the hedges was simply biding his time. And, when his time came, I proceeded into the paths of absorption and 'migrant solitude' which the other two sections of the poem attempt to evoke.[34]

The second part of 'The King of the Ditchbacks' is full of promises. The poet casts himself as a young disciple who in translating the work about 'the trespasser' has created him, and created himself. 'He was depending on me as I hung out on the limb of a translated phrase like a youngster dared out on to an alder branch over the whirlpool.' *Sweeney Astray*, we are to understand, has become a self-fulfilment for

---

[33] I am told that in Ulster a ditchback is a raised wall or bank marking the edges of a field.

[34] Seamus Heaney, *Sweeney's Flight* (London: Faber and Faber, 1992), p. viii.

the poet, the creation of a second self, a 'dreamself'. In identifying himself with Sweeney, he felt 'as if I were coming into my own. I remembered I had been vested for this calling.' He has 'the sense of election'. This dreamself is admittedly 'a dissimulation': 'a rich young man // leaving everything he had / for a migrant solitude'. This last reference is to Matthew 19:16–22; it occurs again, more fully, at the end of the last poem in *Station Island*, 'On the Road', and is of the utmost importance.

So we move into the middle section of the book, the dream sequence of a pilgrimage to Lough Derg, with Suibhne, translated to Sweeney, to accompany us. (The poems are numbered I–XII.) The poet has gone back to Lough Derg at it seems everyone does – to test it out. His dead friend, Father Keenan, who lost his faith on a foreign mission, jeers at him for going back to a religion he had given up (IV). 'But all this you were clear of you walked into / over again. And the god has, as they say, withdrawn. // What are you doing, going through these motions?' Nearly everyone else jeers at him too. Sweeney, transformed into an old Sabbath-breaking gardener of Heaney's childhood with that name, tells the new pilgrim 'Stay clear of all processions!' (I). At the end, the ghost of James Joyce sniffs at his 'peasant pilgrimage', and tells him he won't discharge his obligation 'by any common rite' (XII). More than once, the ardour of faith impresses itself on the returning pilgrim as no more than an obsession of his childhood, his former life. This is particularly the case with the dream within a dream in poem X. In the pilgrim's hostel, a pot reminds him of a mug which stood on a shelf in his childhood. That mug had taken on a strange symbolic presence until, borrowed by actors to use as a loving cup, it was 'glamoured from this translation', a thing of glory, like Ronan's psalter returned by the otter 'miraculously unharmed'. 'The dazzle of the impossible suddenly / blazed across the threshold.' Both stories, the sanctity of the mug and the return of the psalter, are ridiculous. At the same time, the most moving part of the whole middle section is something from boyhood, the translation from St John of the Cross which the poet made as a school imposition (XI). I shall return later to the beautiful water imagery of this voice from the past.

How well I know that fountain, filling, running,
although it is the night.

That eternal fountain, hidden away,
I know its haven and its secrecy
although it is the night.

What Christianity has to offer does not here seem to be limited to
St Ronan. Yet the signals the reader is getting from the middle section
of *Station Island* as regards what church Catholicism has to offer the
poet are on the whole not good. Carleton's ghost, finding no value in
the pilgrimage, does not in any case believe the poet's function is to try
to divert the course of history and advocates a wise passiveness in the
face of unpalatable events. Those who have died or been murdered in
the Troubles think little of the poet's efforts to 'atone upon this bed'
(VIII). Joyce, in the final poem (XII), says, 'What you must do must be
done on your own // . . . let others wear the sackcloth and the ashes.'

What is so very curious about this middle section of *Station Island*,
considering the great build-up for him in 'The King of the Ditchbacks',
is the almost total absence of Sweeney, except as the reprobate old
gardener in the first poem. Only in St John of the Cross's poem
does religion trespass beyond the boundaries drawn by the myopic St
Ronan. The conclusion must be that the rewards of the Lough Derg
pilgrimage are limited to what can be grasped by St Ronan – at best 'the
dazzle of the impossible'. Since Lough Derg is a failure, and Sweeney
largely an absentee, we turn to the final section of the book, 'Sweeney
Redivivus', to find out what happened to the young man of 'The king
of the Ditchbacks' on what must now be regarded as his alternative
pilgrimage, 'leaving everything he had / for a migrant solitude'. The
poet-disciple has declared his identity with the trespasser-master ('If
I stop / he stops'). So, how has the spirit of the *peregrinus* informed
the poet, either in his life or in his thinking?

It's a dusty answer, as the poet steps 'from a justified line / into the
margin' ('The First Gloss'). The trouble lies in Sweeney's credentials,
as Heaney has presented them. The fine delineation of Sweeney as a
pilgrim, forsaking convention and society and undergoing the greatest
privation as a penance, and being led towards true understanding,

collapses into the betrayal of his ultimate surrender to the orthodoxy he has challenged. Was the whole enterprise ever anything more than a poet's dream?

> And there I was, incredible to myself,
> among people far too eager to believe me
> and my story, even if it happened to be true.
> ('Sweeney Redivivus')

The poems are 'voiced for Sweeney'. But we sometimes find the poet narrating, sometimes Sweeney. Who is speaking in 'Alerted'? Who is in the end 'rooted to the spot, / alerted, disappointed / under my old clandestine / pre-Copernican night'? It could be either. In the end there is nothing left for both men but what St Ronan provides, described with such savage scorn at the close of 'The Cleric'.

> Give him his due, in the end
>
> he opened my path to a kingdom
> of such scope and neuter allegiance
> my emptiness reigns at its whim.

The spiritual freedom glimpsed in 'The First Flight' ends in 'the old rules' dispensed by that old rook in the tower, who has taken over from Sweeney the title of 'The Master' (in the poem of that name).

In 'An Artist', the narrator must be the poet, who admires the soaring imagination of his fellow poet of the Middle Ages who created Sweeney, rather than the dedication and devotion allegorised in those imaginings.

> I love the thought of his anger.
> His obstinacy against the rock, his coercion
> of the substance from green apples.
>
> The way he was a dog barking
> at the image of himself barking.
> . . . .
> His forehead like a hurled *boule*
> travelling unpainted space
> behind the apple and behind the mountain.

Whatever respect there may be here for visionary poetry, there is also an amused condescension for the stuff of visions. The 'forehead' inevitably brings to mind the immense brow in the portraits of the visionary William Blake 'who beat upon the wall / Till truth obeyed his call',[35] while the comic idea of its being hurled seems to follow the linkage which Heaney saw between the Sweeney poetry and the insane patter of Shakespeare's Edgar. When Lear imagines that his daughters' dogs are barking at him, Edgar says, 'Tom will throw his head at them.' There is certainly something mad about the artist who tries to paint the substance of green apples.

It is the final poem of *Station Island*, 'On the Road', which meets and fully answers our question, whatever happened to the alternative pilgrimage? I find it a deeply sad and saddening poem. We learn that all roads are one, including the road on which 'the rich young man' asked his question, *Master, what must I do to be saved? – Sell all you have and give to the poor. And follow me.* The young man was 'up and away' like a human soul ballooning from the mouth of a character in a medieval manuscript. But it's a short flight, and he comes to earth on the roof of the church he had escaped from, 'scaling heaven / by superstition'. Then, very strangely, he follows his aerial master's command to follow him by saying he would 'migrate' to a subterranean chamber (reminiscent of Lascaux[36]), where there is a rock carving of a deer, with a 'strained / expectant muzzle / and a nostril flared // at a dried-up source'. Then the poet says he would 'meditate / that stone-faced vigil' –

> until the long dumbfounded
> spirit broke cover
> to raise a dust
> in the font of exhaustion.

The first thing which this 'dust in the font of exhaustion' makes me think of is the 'eternal fountain' in the boyhood translation from St John of the Cross –

[35] W. B. Yeats, 'An Acre of Grass'.
[36] Helen Vendler, *Seamus Heaney* (Cambridge, Mass.: Harvard University Press, 1998), p. 56.

> And its current so in flood it overspills
> to water hell and heaven and all peoples
> although it is the night.

The second thing I think of is Blake's 'Infant Sorrow', in which the
new-born babe leaps into the dangerous world 'like a fiend hid in a
cloud', but –

> Struggling in my fathers hands
> Striving against my swadling bands:
> Bound and weary I thought best
> To sulk upon my mothers breast.

The third thing I think of is the end of St Matthew's story. When the
young man heard what was demanded of him 'he went away sorrowful:
for he had great possessions'.

As I said earlier, I find Heaney's interpolation of Moling's jest at
the end of *Sweeney Astray*, indicating that he has 'limed' the bird-
man for the Holy Ghost, an unwarranted deviation from the spirit of
Buile Suibhne, at least of O'Keeffe's translation of it, which suggests
that Moling accepts Sweeney's access to a higher vision of Christ
than his own, or Ronan's. Yet the submission, which makes Sweeney
reconcile himself to a church and its theology he has spent a lifetime
rejecting, impels *Station Island*, rendering rebellion futile and reducing
Sweeney's vision to a poetic fancy, while doing nothing to repair the
limitation and inadequacy of Ronan's concept of Christianity.

Carleton, Kavanagh and Heaney have all experienced the rigours of the
Lough Derg pilgrimage, pondered its rewards and doubted its claims.
W. B. Yeats, so far as I know, never 'did' the pilgrimage, though he
said in 1919 (when he was 55), 'If I were four-and-twenty . . . I think I
would go – though certainly I am no Catholic and never shall be one –
upon both of our great pilgrimages, to Croagh Patrick and to Lough
Derg.'[37] A poem of Yeats that specifically mentions the Lough Derg
pilgrimage, 'The Pilgrim', was published in *A Broadside* (October
1937), and in *New Poems* (1938).

---

[37] Yeats, *Explorations*, p. 266. Quoted in part by Daniel Albright in his note to 'The
Pilgrim', in the Everyman edition of *The Poems* (London: Dent, 1994), p. 794.

The theme of *New Poems* would seem to be 'tragic joy', so nobly expressed at the end of the first stanza of the first poem, 'The Gyres'.

> Hector is dead and there's a light in Troy;
> We that look on but laugh in tragic joy.

Tragic joy is the mysterious elation experienced after moving through and beyond the turmoil and heartbreak of catastrophe, its confusion and loss. It is hardly serenity, more a wry detachment: something, Yeats claims, which came in the end to Hamlet and to Lear – truth which 'the mill of the mind' can never reach.[38] This tragic joy is, to say the least, an elevated and precarious shelf to rest on; it is not thought of as a comfortable and secure philosophic position. There is a reduced level of it in the many 'refrain' ballads in *New Poems* (of which 'The Pilgrim' is an excellent example). The mood here is a kind of resigned acceptance of the inevitability of misfortune and upheaval, coupled with a refusal to draw conclusions or provide explanations. 'How goes the weather?' asks the refrain of 'The O'Rahilly', a poem of violence and death. 'Day-break and a candle end' is the cryptic reply of 'The Wild Old Wicked Man'. More lucidly, each stanza of 'The Curse of Cromwell' ends with 'O what of that, O what of that / What is there left to say?' And, more lucidly still, the refrain of 'What Then?', a poem deriding worldly aspiration and ambition, goes '"What then?" sang Plato's ghost, "what then?"'

The speaker in 'The Pilgrim', wanting to know what life means, has been led to an imagined haven of drink and sex. But there is no wisdom available *there*; only the meaningless mantra of 'fol de rol de rolly O'.

> I fasted for some forty days on bread and buttermilk
> For passing round the bottle with girls in rags or silk,
> In country shawl or Paris cloak, had put my wits astray,
> And what's the good of women for all that they can say
> Is fol de rol de rolly O.[39]

---

[38] See Yeats, 'An Acre of Grass'.

[39] I quote from Macmillan's revised edition of *The Poems*, edited by R. J. Finneran (1989; 2nd edn, London: MacMillan, 1991), which is closer to the text appearing in *New Poems* (1938), both in punctuation and the non-use of italics for the refrain.

Pursuing a better answer, he goes to the other extreme, first of fasting, then of renunciation and penance at Lough Derg. 'Round Lough Derg's holy island I went upon the stones'. His prayers bring him nothing, and an old pilgrim beside him, praying also, can offer him only the solace of those empty syllables once more: 'fol de rol de rolly O'. But, knowing 'that all the dead in the world about that place are stuck', the speaker attempts to commune with the dead. 'I swear to God I questioned them.' And all he got from them was that meaningless burble yet again, 'fol de rol de rolly O'. This seems to be the most important moment in the poem, a deliberate opposition of nothingness to the very full accounts which Yeats had given of his own questioning of the dead; in particular, what he had got from his 'instructors' during the seances after his marriage in that great system of things recorded in *A Vision*. The relationship of the living to the dead, and the shape taken by the dead in Purgatory, is described in all its complexity in Book III of that work. Is Yeats, in these two lines of 'The Pilgrim', doing battle with himself? Are we to take it that the terse nonsense which the pilgrim hears from the dead has equal validity with what Yeats records, or is it that this pilgrim was incapable of listening and understanding – was guilty, in short, of spiritual deafness? This is the crucial question posed by the poem.

We must not say that Yeats was incapable of a debate of this sort. In these late poems he was always challenging himself. At one point in *A Vision*, his 'instructors' said that so far from providing him with a universal system 'we have come to give you metaphors for poetry'.[40] But even metaphors could fail, and in 'The Circus Animals' Desertion' Yeats acknowledged that when all his 'ladders' were gone he must lie down 'in the foul rag-and-bone shop of the heart'. The greatness of Yeats's later poems is often in those moments when all systems and stoical consolations are momentarily punctured by the rawness of experienced life; the 'intolerable music' at the end of 'News from the Delphic Oracle', the cry of the 'stricken rabbit' at the close of 'The Man and the Echo'. I have always thought that the 'gratitude' in that wonderful four-line poem, 'Gratitude to the Unknown Instructors',

[40] Yeats, *A Vision* [1925 and 1937] (London: Macmillan, 1962), p. 8.

is largely ironical. The first two lines give them thanks for providing a comprehensive system ('What they undertook to do / They brought to pass'), while the last two salute an utterly different cosmos, of contingency, uncertainty and tremulous possibility, in which 'All things hang like a drop of dew / Upon a blade of grass'.

In the fourth stanza of 'The Pilgrim', the speaker is in the boat, leaving the island, and 'a great black ragged bird' appeared.

> A great black ragged bird appeared when I was in the boat;
> Some twenty feet from tip to tip had it stretched rightly out,
> With flopping and with flapping it made a great display
> But I never stopped to question, what could the boatman say
> But fol de rol de rolly O.

The pilgrim, who had questioned the dead (to no avail) 'never stopped to question'. Question whom? The boatman presumably. I think the sense of the following phrase is: 'For what could the boatman say?' The pilgrim 'never stopped to question' the boatman, because he had learned not to expect any other answer to his questions about hidden truths than 'fol de rol de rolly O'. This failure to enquire is a pity, because there seem to be two legends about that bird. In writing about *The Wanderings of Oisin* in 1959, John Unterecker noted that Yeats had used P. W. Joyce's version of the Celtic *immram*, the Voyage of Maildun.[41] The voyagers came to an island with a lake, and towards this lake, which contained the waters of life, an immense ancient bird was flying. After three days, the sailors saw this bird fly away again, completely rejuvenated. So the pilgrim's bird might be a good omen, signifying that Lough Derg had the power to grant what only Tír-na-nóg could grant, eternal youth. But years later, in 'If I were Four and Twenty' (1919), Yeats wrote that he would like to 'memorialise bishops to open once again that Lough Derg cave of vision once beset by an evil spirit in the form of a long-legged bird with no feathers on its wings'.[42] So the bird might be of ill-omen. But the pilgrim, unfortunately, never stopped to raise any question about it.

---

[41] John Unterecker, *A Reader's Guide to William Butler Yeats* (London: Thames and Hudson, 1959), pp. 54–5.
[42] Yeats, *Explorations*, p. 267.

As a result of his experiences at Lough Derg, the pilgrim goes back to the public house and is prepared to meet any woman, or any man –

> Now I am in the public house and lean upon the wall,
> So come in rags or come in silk, in cloak or country shawl,
> And come with learned lovers or with what men you may
> For I can put the whole lot down, and all I have to say
> Is fol de rol de rolly O.

Surely, this pilgrim is all too easily satisfied that he has received the answer to his enquiries about ultimate verity. All along the line he has been rebuffed, so his conclusion is that such knowledge is simply not available. He retires to the public house, complacent and confident that he knows all the answers, namely, that nothing is to be known.

There are three possible interpretations of 'The Pilgrim'. First, that it acknowledges and approves of a complete agnosticism about ultimate value; second, that it repudiates the speaker for his failure to understand messages from the other world, and, indeed, his failure even to 'question'. But there is a third interpretation. The poem is an acknowledgement of the difficulty of hearing and interpreting messages about the unknown, and, by implication, a questioning of the interpretations by others of supposed messages. There is something to be said for the pilgrim's failure, in spite of his efforts, to get through to an authoritative voice. But in the end, he is rash and arrogant in his agnosticism, a terrible example of the confident complacency of the doubter. Yeats is hardly weighing 'fol de rol de rolly O' against *A Vision* when it comes to finding out the truth about the dead. But if the pilgrim is found wanting for hearing nothing from them but an incomprehensible muttering, perhaps Yeats in that stanza admits his own temerity in having so confidently interpreted what *he* heard from the spirit-world.

'The Pilgrim' is not an attack on pilgrimage. Far from it. This individual who has chosen pilgrimage as a possible route to straighten out his life shows a good deal more understanding of what the rite really means than many of the pilgrims mentioned in this chapter, and his failure is more in his temperament than in the rite itself.

Yeats is a striking absentee from the ghosts who surround the poet as he contemplates the Lough Derg pilgrimage in Heaney's *Station Island*. He deserves a place, for he had encompassed the alternative pilgrimage which seems to me to be lacking in Heaney's poems. Yeats's poem 'Sailing to Byzantium' is as near as one can get to the act of pilgrimage without the conviction of faith, without accepting what is offered or implied by the penitential rites of Lough Derg.[43] The poem tells of an old man who, contemptuous of the 'sensual music' of the 'dying generations' around him, sails the seas to Byzantium. The old man pleads with the 'sages standing in God's holy fire' to free him from his physical life.

> Consume my heart away; sick with desire
> And fastened to a dying animal
> It knows not what it is; and gather me
> Into the artifice of eternity.

He asks that when he is 'out of nature' he may become an artefact such as 'Grecian goldsmiths make / Of hammered gold and gold enamelling', and, as an artefact of that kind – perhaps a bird 'upon a golden bough' – re-enter the living world, as its historian, its recorder, its prophet.

> Or set upon a golden bough to sing
> To lords and ladies of Byzantium
> Of what is past, or passing, or to come.

The old man's journey is the poet's journey of the mind to an imaginary city, hoping to create by his craft the 'artifice of eternity' which might be a guiding light for the unimaginative generations he has abandoned. Yeats creates in his beautifully wrought poem the concept of going outside the world in order to speak to the world. The poem is his gift to the dying generations from beyond their ken; it comes from the artifice of eternity which is the true poet's domain. The making of his poem about a pilgrimage is itself the pilgrimage.

---

[43] See the excellent discussion by R. F. Foster in *W. B. Yeats: A Life*, vol. II: *The Arch-Poet* (Oxford: Oxford University Press, 2003), p. 326.

Romeo called his kiss of Juliet his 'prayer's effect'. His mode of supplication – kissing the statue of the goddess – was also the boon he expected from his goddess. So, in a way, Yeats's poem is the prayer of the old man, whose request to be released from the physical world so that he may return to it as a mentor is also the effect of that prayer, a boon to us from the mysterious region where art is made.

CHAPTER 9

Doubting Castle

Bunyan's *The Pilgrim's Progress* (first published in 1678) is the great classic of pilgrimage literature, of world-wide fame and immensely influential. It was the culmination of a long line of allegorical writings on human life as a pilgrimage (most or all of them unknown to Bunyan) going back at least as far as Guillaume de Deguileville's widely read *Le pèlerinage de l'homme* in the fourteenth century. It is a paradox that that form of Christianity which destroyed images and pilgrimage should have created a fictional pilgrimage of such power and influence as the *Pilgrim's Progress*. However severe and narrow its doctrinal holdings, Bunyan's presentation of the ragged and tormented hero, with a book in his hand and a great burden on his back, who 'brake out with a lamentable cry; saying, *what shall I do?*' (p. 8),[1] then his alienation from his wife and family and all around him, his determination to pursue his dangerous journey towards eternal life, and the vicissitudes of that journey, provides *images* of the greatest vividness and the widest appeal.

Quite late in his journey, Christian misleads Hopeful out of their proper track and they find themselves in the grounds of Doubting Castle, whose owner is Giant Despair. The giant and his wife Diffidence thrust the intruders into a dungeon, beat them horribly, then advise them to make away with themselves. When they don't take this advice, they are shown the bones and skulls of those whom Giant Despair has already despatched, and he undertakes to tear them to pieces similarly within ten days. Back in their dungeon the two victims begin to pray, and continue in prayer all night.

[1] Text and page numbers from the second Oxford edition of *Pilgrim's Progress*, edited by J. B. Wharey, revised by Roger Sharrock (Oxford: Clarendon Press, 1960).

Now a little before it was day, good *Christian*, as one half amazed, brake out in this passionate speech, *What a fool, quoth he, am I, thus to lie in a stinking Dungeon, when I may as well walk at liberty?* I have a *Key* in my bosom, called *Promise*, that will, (I am perswaded) open any lock in *Doubting-Castle*. Then said *Hopeful*, That's good news; good Brother pluck it out of thy bosom, and try. Then *Christian* pulled it out of his bosom, and began to try at the Dungeon door, whose bolt (as he turned the Key) gave back, and the door flew open with ease, and *Christian* and *Hopeful* both came out. (p. 118)

It is a strange kind of despair, and a strange form of doubting, that can be so suddenly ended. What is this key called Promise? The Oxford editors helpfully refer us to *Grace Abounding*, §§ 246 ff, where it is made clear that 'the Promise' means one of the assurances of future blessing recorded in the Bible, that book which Christian was holding in his hand, that book whose truth 'is confirmed by the blood of him that made it' (p. 12). In particular, Bunyan mentions in *Grace Abounding* the sixth chapter of St John's gospel (verse 37), which he renders as *And him that comes to me, I will in no wise cast out*. Bunyan also recollects that 'many a pull hath my heart had with Satan, for that blessed sixth of *John*'. So, Christian's 'forgetting' in the dungeon of Doubting Castle must mean diffidence or mistrust or doubt that the biblical promise of acceptance referred to the pilgrims. This is one of the very few places in *The Pilgrim's Progress* where the cornerstone doctrine of election is implied.[2] If the courage and determination of individual Christian effort was to be saluted in that work, then the divine choice of election or reprobation, made before the beginning of time, which might annul all effort on earth, had to be minimised or suppressed. There is a very interesting moment in *Grace Abounding* (§§ 53–9), concerning Bunyan's early doubts, when this tussle between human endeavour and divine decree is made painfully clear. He had a vision of the poor people of Bedford enjoying the sunshine high on a mountain. But there was a wall round the mountain which

---

[2] Gordon Campbell remarks: 'the doctrine of election was . . . crucial . . . to Bunyan's theology . . . and yet it does not affect the Christian of *The Pilgrim's Progress*'; see *The Pilgrim's Progress: Critical and Historical Views*, ed. V. Newey (Liverpool: Liverpool University Press, 1980), p. 257.

prevented him from joining them. Eventually he found a gap in the wall, 'very strait and narrow', and after a great struggle, 'me-thought I at first did get in my head, and after that, by a sideling striving, my shoulders, and my whole body: Then was I exceeding glad, and went and sate down in the midst of them.' But after a time he began 'to be assaulted with fresh doubts about my future happiness; especially with such as these, *Whether I was elected* . . . I evidently saw, unless that the great God, of his infinite Grace and Bounty, had voluntarily chosen me to be a Vessel of Mercy, though I should desire, and long, and labour until my heart did break, no good could come of it. Therefore this would still stick with me, *How can you tell you are elected?*.'[3]

So that is the doubt which afflicts Christian in his dungeon, doubt whether one has been accepted by God, doubt which can be instantly resolved, not by any demonstration or logic, but by the conviction that God meant what he said, that 'God had a bigger mouth to speak with, than I had a heart to conceive with.'[4] This present chapter is about doubt, but doubt on a very different level. Bunyan's Doubting Castle is not a place for questioning the truth of Christianity. Those who doubt, for example, the resurrection of the body, are contemptuously 'dashed all to pieces' from 'the top of an Hill, called *Errour*' (p. 120). The character *Atheist* is treated more kindly. Christian and Hopeful meet him going back home, with his back towards Mount Sion. Hopeful simply says, 'What! no Mount *Sion*? Did we not see from the delectable Mountains the Gate of the City?'

It is the haunted figure at the beginning of *The Pilgrim's Progress*, whose neighbours thought that 'some frenzy distemper had got into his head' (p. 9), who wept and trembled, and cried 'What shall I do?', the man not yet called a pilgrim,[5] that is the better image of doubt. As Christian hears from Evangelist about the wicket-gate he 'began

---

[3] John Bunyan, *Grace Abounding to the Chief of Sinners*, ed. J. Brown (Cambridge: Cambridge University Press, 1907), pp. 21–2.

[4] *Ibid.*, § 250, p. 76.

[5] The metaphor of pilgrimage does not appear in the early part of the story at all; the first reference is on Hill Difficulty (44).

to run . . . crying, Life, Life, Eternal Life' (p. 10). His neighbour Obstinate calls him a craz'd-headed coxcomb, a brain-sick fellow, a mis-led fantastical fellow (pp. 11, 12). We have seen in that wonderful early medieval Irish work *Buile Suibhne* that every year the madmen of Ireland, including Sweeney, assembled in Glen Bolcain. We have a kind of Glen Bolcain in this chapter, with those who have gone mad, those who are thought to be mad and those who pretend to be mad: Bunyan's Christian, Shakespeare's Hamlet and his Edgar, and Suibhne. All four qualify, in my view, as pilgrims: Christian obviously, Hamlet by reason of the ballad sung by Ophelia, Edgar because of a self-definition of disputed meaning in a line of disputed text and Suibhne/Sweeney because his translator, Heaney, twice calls him one. Fragile foundation for the last three, perhaps, but they are true *peregrini*.

To recapitulate on definitions: I take the controlling meaning of 'pilgrimage' to be the journey to a shrine, for penance, for thanks, for intercession, for relief, for instruction, above all perhaps for renewal. This meaning is enormously expanded by the derivation of the word 'pilgrim' from the Latin *peregrinus*, which, meaning one who travelled from afar to sojourn in a particular country, was used metaphorically in the New Testament to describe Christians living as it were in exile on earth and travelling towards their own country, heaven. The concept of alienation from the surrounding society became rooted in the entire concept of pilgrimage, and pilgrimage expanded to include not only the journey to a shrine for illumination, but also the journey onwards from that illumination: a renewed life of service in preparation for eternal life. Pilgrims of this second kind I have generally been calling *peregrini*. We have seen in the earlier chapters of this book a good deal of doubt about the value of the New Testament metaphor of pilgrimage – from Langland, Vaughan, Christina Rossetti and Emily Dickinson, who feel either that their own vision of Christ and Christianity is compromised by the forward-march implied by the metaphor, or that the metaphor is unequal to rendering the great mystery of death and the uncertainty of an after-life. A deeper doubt about the value of pilgrimage itself comes into some of the literary accounts of the Lough Derg pilgrimage. What I want to do now is to return to Shakespeare via Bunyan and the author of *Buile Suibhne* to locate an idea of pilgrimage which is founded on doubt.

Common to all four works I am now looking at, *Hamlet*, *King Lear*, *The Pilgrim's Progress* and *Buile Suibhne* or, as I shall now call it, *Sweeney Astray*, is the pilgrim's alienation, his apartness from society (all four are men), and the association of this 'alienation', as we would expect from the nineteenth-century history of the word, with madness. Alienation is the starting point and substance of pilgrimage in this group. With Christian it is first his wife and family (to whom we shall return), then almost everyone around him, Mr Worldly-Wiseman, for example, who dwelt in the town of Carnal-Policy, and Legality, who lived in the village of Morality, and had a son called Civility. The contempt of Christian and the few who think like him for the 'normality' of the lives and understanding of the rest is best shown in the passage of Christian and Faithful through Vanity Fair (pp. 88–98). In the allegory, pilgrims to heaven must pass through this fair, but in real life it is the society in which they have to live. One of the witnesses at the trial of Faithful had heard him affirm, '*That Christianity, and the Customs of our Town of* Vanity *were Diametrically opposite, and could not be reconciled*' (p. 93). Everything in the town was for sale: Honours, Preferments, Titles, Wives, Husbands, Children, Lives, Blood, Bodies, Souls and what not. When the pilgrims said '*We buy the truth*', they called them 'Bedlams and mad' (p. 91), imprisoned them and did violence to them, and brought Faithful to a cruel death.

In different images, the passage of pilgrims through ordinary life is first the encounter with Apollyon and then the traverse of the Valley of the Shadow of Death (pp. 56–65). The hideous monster Apollyon is the lord and owner of the dominions in which Christian was born, and he demands his continued service. Christian defeats him with the sword which has been given him, and then must struggle to keep to his 'exceeding narrow' track through the Valley of the Shadow of Death. Here there is 'a continual howling and yelling, as of a people under unutterable misery; who there sat bound in affliction'. The valley is as dark as pitch, but filled with flame and smoke coming from the mouth of hell. Sometimes Christian thinks 'he should be torn in pieces, or trodden down like mire in the Streets'. But he keeps his faith in God, and gets through.

The second condition common to all four pilgrims is asceticism. Christian's most difficult trial comes early on: his abandonment of his wife and children. When he first told them of his fears, and the need for escape, they thought he was out of his mind. After he had met Evangelist, he ran from his own door, with his fingers in his ears to their cries for him to return (pp. 10, 26). And he does not return; he is very much on his own, at least as regards women, for the rest of his journey. Of course he meets women, and, at the house called Beautiful, Charity cross-questions him: '*Have you a family? Are you a married man?*' (p. 50). Christian says he has a wife and four small children, and when Charity asks him why they are not with him he bursts into tears and replies that they were 'utterly averse' to his going on pilgrimage. Charity presses him. Did he do enough to persuade them of the reasons for his journey and their need to accompany him? 'Yes', said Christian, 'over, and over, and over.' In the end Charity commends his action, and says '*thou hast delivered thy soul from their blood*' (p. 52).

In 1938 Patrick Kavanagh was asked to give a radio talk in a series entitled *I Liked This Book*. He spoke on *The Pilgrim's Progress* and called his contribution 'I Hated This Book'. His reason was 'that it was unchristian of Christian to leave home'.[6] There is a problem here. Christian is the hero of an allegorical fiction, who falls into the Slough of Despond, gets imprisoned by Giant Despair, goes though the river of death, walks through the gates into the heavenly city. Nothing of this was meant to apply *literally* to the aspiring Christian for whom Bunyan was writing. Bunyan's fictional hero clearly left home without his wife and family. What was he recommending for his reader? Was this to apply literally? Christian's distress at leaving his wife is strongly emphasised. When in the second edition of his book Bunyan brought in Mr Worldly-Wiseman, the first question he made him ask Christian was '*Hast thou a Wife and Children?*' Christian replies, 'Yes, but I am

---

[6] Antoinette Quinn, *Patrick Kavanagh* (Dublin: Gill and Macmillan, 2001), p. 108.

so laden with this burden, that I cannot take that pleasure in them as formerly: methinks, I am as if I had none' (p. 17). The marginal gloss refers to 1 Corinthians 7:29, where St Paul, pointing out that 'the time is short' (that is, before the end of the world), recommends that 'they that have wives be as though they have none'. This appears to mean that sexual intercourse is to be avoided. Bunyan also added the quotation of Christ's words from Luke 14:26, 'If any man come to me, and hate not his father, and mother, and wife, and children, and brethren, and sisters, yea, and his own life also, he cannot be my disciple' (AV).

In the allegorical fiction, Christian, who in spite of his errors and divagations becomes the best of Christians, leaves his recalcitrant wife and goes alone to meet his maker. After the initial pages of the book nothing is said about the grimness of a divided home, with discord reigning for years on end. Kavanagh was simply in disagreement with Bunyan when he said it was unchristian to leave home. Given the circumstances of Bunyan's fiction the most Christian thing for the hero to do was to leave home, a true *peregrinus*, tackling the perils of the wilderness alone. Decoding the allegory, the reader may well decide that the message for the ordinary wayfaring Christian was that it might be necessary also for *him* to leave his unsympathetic wife in order to live his new spiritual life to the full. If we look for enlightenment at the second part of *The Pilgrim's Progress*, meant to sweeten the rigours of the male-dominated first part, we are not much helped. It is never clear whether, when Christiana talks of her husband having left her because of his convictions, we are talking about what 'really' happened, or are meant to decode this as signifying a rupture in their views which made their married life a misery. Whatever Bunyan thought about the sexual relations of married couples in a home divided by religious disagreement, the tenor of his epic allegory, the first part of *The Pilgrim's Progress*, is to forsake compromise and endure separation, however great the heartache on either side, in the spirit of Luke 14:26.

The apartness of Sweeney, the bird-man, hardly needs exposition. Heaney has been criticised for using 'astray' to translate '*buile*'. In his Glossary, O'Keeffe translates '*buile*' as 'frenzy, ecstasy, madness, vision'. Suibhne is also called '*geilt*' (e.g., 19, 83) of which O'Keeffe says 'a madman . . . applied specially to a crazy person living in the woods'.[7] Anyway, Sweeney is, like Bunyan's Christian, considered out of his mind by normal people, and he is content to accept this appellation as a mark of his difference: 'I am the madman of Glen Bolcain' (21). His asceticism is obvious too. Whether we see his life of expiation among the trees as chosen or enforced, his laments for what he has lost are equally sincere, and the company of women ranks high among his losses. At one point he goes back to see his wife, Eorann (30–2). When he 'deserted his kingship', she went to live with his kinsman Guaire. Sweeney reminds her of 'the great love we shared' – 'but you have broken trust'. Eorann frankly welcomes him, 'my first and last and favourite'. She would gladly go with him to the wild, but Sweeney refuses to contemplate her sharing his life of hardship. 'I am yours no longer. / And you are another man's . . . And yet I hold no grudge, / my gentle one. / Christ ordained my bondage.' Much later Sweeney visits Eorann again, but this time she repels him (55–6), saying 'Why don't you go away and leave us in peace?' Sweeney launches into a Hamlet-like attack on women in general; 'betrayal such as mine by Eorann / is second nature in a woman'. He says elsewhere (43), 'Human love has failed me.' When he is dying from the spear of the absurdly jealous swine-herd Mongan, Sweeney looks back on his life among the trees in the wild.

> There was a time when I preferred
> the mountain grouse crying at dawn
> to the voice and closeness
> of a beautiful woman.   (83)

As I have said, *The Pilgrim's Progress* evinces no doubt about the fundamentals of the Christian religion as Bunyan perceived them. I also argued in the last chapter that what seems to me the most important feature of the ending of *Buile Suibhne* is muted in Heaney's translation, namely, that Sweeney's long life of ascetic dedication in

---

[7] *Buile Suibhne*, trans. J. G. O'Keeffe (London: Irish Texts Society, 1913); Seamus Heaney, *Sweeney Astray* (London: Faber and Faber, 1984). Reference numbers to quotations from *Sweeney Astray* refer to the marginal section numbers, not to pages.

the wilds, away from human society, was recognised by St Moling and his followers as giving him a spiritual insight superior to that in their own church and ministry. Here are Heaney's own words for the reaction of an eye-witness to the killing.

> Whoever struck here will live to regret
> killing the king, the saint, the holy fool.
> . . . .
> He was a king, he was a madman.
> His grave will be a hallowing of the earth.
>
> (80)

Almost immediately after this (in Heaney's translation) Sweeney, in his death-poem, goes back to his time in the wild 'when I preferred / wolf-packs yelping and howling / to the sheepish voice of a cleric / bleating out plainsong' (83). It is language like this, coupled with St Moling's admiration for Sweeney and his humble admission of his own insufficiency (75), which helps us to see the poem's quiet contempt for the limitations of the Christianity practised by the irascible rule-ridden cleric, St Ronan. Most certainly Sweeney's submission and his acceptance of the rites of the church do not indicate doubt about Christianity, but Heaney's identification of him as a pilgrim is absolutely right: Sweeney is a fierce *peregrinus*, lacerating himself in his separation from human society in order to find a truer relation with 'his' Christ than that which the church offered him.

Turning now to a work which questions every religious consolation, an epic of doubt, Shakespeare's *King Lear*, I want briefly to reconsider the role of Edgar as *peregrinus* in a world of disbelief.[8] At 2.3.11–12, Edgar appears as a hunted fugitive trying to escape recognition. He has been falsely accused by his half-brother Edmund of seeking to murder his father, the Earl of Gloucester, who has threatened to execute him when he is found. He resolves to reduce himself to the filthy state of a Bedlam beggar, that is, one who pretends to be a lunatic from Bethlehem Hospital.

---

[8] W. R. Elton's classic study *'King Lear' and the Gods* (San Marino, Calif.: Huntington Library, 1966; Lexington: University of Kentucky Press, 1988) is still the best account of the religious attitudes and expectations of the play's characters.

And with presented nakedness outface
The winds and persecutions of the sky.

He greets himself with his new identity, Poor Tom: 'Edgar I nothing am.' Exiled from himself, he is also Sweeney and Christian. In adopting his naked madness the earl's son is performing a double deception, for a Bedlam beggar was one who took on the frightening guise and behaviour of a lunatic and went among the poor to 'enforce their charity'.

In Shakespeare's plays and poems the word 'truth' scarcely if ever means 'eternal verities', though we can find 'the light of truth' in *Love's Labour's Lost*. The word usually means (besides 'that which is true') fidelity, constancy, loyalty. Truth, that is, is largely a question of personal conduct, committing oneself to someone who seems to embody rightness. Truth as ultimate truth is a misty concept, inaccessible and undiscussed. It is chiefly known by its violation. A kind of manichean system seems to be in operation, with two rival kingdoms struggling for dominance. Those who carry out the work of the devil in this great contest for power pay their opponents the enormous tribute of copying them exactly, so that the unprepared are quite unable to distinguish the true from the false – 'th' equivocation of the fiend / That lies like truth'.[9] So competent are these deceivers in aping the followers of truth that it is really a matter of faith for the well-intentioned to believe anyone's integrity, as Macduff puts it in *Macbeth*.

> Angels are bright still, though the brightest fell.
> Though all things foul would wear the brows of grace,
> Yet grace must still look so.   (4.3.22–4)

The metaphor for truth in the world is kingship, and true kingship is almost never to be found: it is corrupted either by the unsteadiness of the occupant of the throne or, more often, by the usurpation of the throne by an illegitimate aspirant. A further metaphor, for these lookalike contenders for power, legitimate and illegitimate, is the strife of brother and brother, as in *Hamlet*, and here in *Lear* with the contention of Edmund and Edgar. Shakespeare's grim insistence on the

---

[9] *Macbeth*, 5.6.43–4.

vital importance of true descent and legitimate inheritance jars on most of us today, but what is really being talked about, in terms of the concerns of this exclusive aristocratic society, is the continuance of truth. In the present play, the wicked have fed upon the shallow thoughtlessness of those who have inherited authority (Lear and Gloucester) and redirected authority into their own hands. It is the task of the dispossessed children, Cordelia and Edgar, to mend the breach and restore true authority.

Edgar is the godson of Lear (2.1.91), so he has a double task in this restoration. When he reappears as Poor Tom in the hovel in the storm, his 'explanation' of himself is a brilliantly demented rendering of the human condition – struggling to escape the clutches of the foul fiend. In his parody of the ten commandments (3.4.78–80), he substitutes 'Take heed o' the foul fiend' for 'Thou shalt have none other gods but me.' In his grand question, 'Is man no more than this?', Lear is quite wrong in taking Edgar's image of devil-tormented man as the reality of a poverty which he has overlooked. Since he takes Poor Tom as his 'philosopher' he would do well to note Edgar's insistence that 'the prince of darkness is a gentleman'. It is a member of the aristocracy who is quite literally hunting him down.

Edgar's recognition of his role as not so much to escape the wrath of his pursuers as to turn the tables on them and undo the harm they have done comes with the inspired snatch of a supposed ballad: 'Child Rowland to the dark tower came.' (Browning built his whole poem on that line, expanding it into the knight's terrifying pilgrimage directed by 'that hoary cripple', with its utterly enigmatic conclusion. In many ways the poem is an inspired commentary on Edgar's new life as a *peregrinus*.) When, later in the play, Edgar meets his father brutally blinded, his reaction is of the greatest importance.

> World, world, O world!
> But that thy strange mutations make us hate thee,
> Life would not yield to age. (4.1.11–13)

Edgar's first main task will be to prevent his father, distressed in body and mind, conscious of the wrong he has done in trusting Edmund and exiling Edgar, from carrying out his plan to commit suicide. Yet here he is, saying that the world is so evil that we would certainly commit suicide, except that . . . What is it then that stops us committing suicide? The supposed 'canon 'gainst self-slaughter'? No, it is that the 'strange mutations' in the evil of the world – such as that which he has just become a witness of, the blinding of his father – 'make us hate thee'. I take it that Edgar's cry is one of 'no surrender!' One's hatred of the viciousness of the world is such that one must stay alive to do battle with it and conquer it. ('O cursèd spite, / That ever I was born to set it right.')

The length and complexity of the scene in which Edgar tricks his father into thinking he has thrown himself off the cliff at Dover betokens its importance. 'Why I do trifle thus with his despair', says Edgar, 'is done to cure it.' Edgar is not the only character who assumes a semi-divine role in believing he can cure despair. Duke Vincentio in *Measure for Measure*, pretending to be a friar, decides not to tell Isabella that he has contrived to keep Claudio alive.

> I will keep her ignorant of her good,
> To make her heavenly comforts of despair,
> When it is least expected.   (4.3.109–11)

Edgar knows the risk he is taking – that his father might die from shock (4.6.42–7) – but goes ahead to tell his completely bewildered and blind parent that he has fallen from the cliff above and that his life has been saved by a miracle, adding that he (Edgar) has *seen* the devil who inhabited Poor Tom leaving his father at the cliff-top.

> Think that the clearest gods, who make them honours
> Of men's impossibilities, have preserved thee.
>   (4.6.73–4)

When the battle takes place and it looks as though the forces of Cordelia and Lear are losing, Edgar comes in to move Gloucester to safety. Gloucester demurs, but Edgar insists.

> What, in ill thoughts again? Men must endure
> Their going hence even as their coming hither.
> Ripeness is all. Come on.   (5.2.9–11)

We learn later from Edgar that he told his father the whole course of 'my pilgrimage' (as the Quarto text has it), but that Gloucester's heart gave out, unable to bear the 'two extremes of passion, joy and grief', and he died – naturally. Edgar's vision of life as a continued and necessary endurance of evil, from beginning to end, accords with his earlier words which I interpreted as meaning that we stay alive in order to fight the world we hate. But what is 'ripeness'? The concept is the justification of Edgar's pilgrimage, as it is of Hamlet's. It seems to indicate the moment of mature understanding, of judgement and of readiness, the moment that can only be achieved by endurance, the moment when a person 'stands in judgement on his soul',[10] the moment for decisive intervention.

Edgar's moment of ripeness may be when, clad as Child Rowland, he stands over the defeated and dying Edmund, and makes his confident adieu.

> The gods are just and of our pleasant vices
> Make instruments to plague us:
> The dark and vicious place where thee he got
> Cost him his eyes.   (5.3.171–4)

It is remarkable that anyone should say of the events in *King Lear* that the gods are just, and the evidence that divine justice has shown itself in punishing Gloucester with blindness because of sexual impropriety puts Edgar into an extreme puritanical position which it is hard to defend. But it is his position, and it is consonant with his autobiography of Poor Tom, who was led into lust and lechery by the foul fiend. It seems self-righteous and arrogant all the same, and it reveals the weakness of Edgar and Shakespeare's *peregrini* in their self-appointed tasks of redressing the evil of the world. It is one thing to identify the presence of the foul fiend; it is quite another to script the voice of God.

Lear's moment of ripeness must be when he is reunited with Cordelia and the two of them go to confinement as prisoners of war.

---

[10] W. B. Yeats, 'The Man and the Echo', in *The Poems*, ed. R. J. Finneran, 2nd edn (London: MacMillan, 1991), pp. 345–6.

When thou dost ask me blessing I'll kneel down
And ask of thee forgiveness. So we'll live
And pray . . .
And take upon's the mystery of things
As if we were God's spies.   (5.3.10–12, 16–17)

The play demonstrates the uselessness of this moment as of Edgar's moment. Before Edmund made his pronouncement about his half-brother, Edmund had ordered the execution of Lear and Cordelia, and Cordelia has already been hanged. Lear comes on stage with his dead daughter in his arms. The mystery of things – the secret meaning of human destinies – has eluded him as it eludes Edgar, if in any way they thought to justify the ways of God to man. I repeat what I said in my earlier chapter, that Edgar's failure to put the world to rights must surely make him refuse Albany's invitation to join with Kent in sustaining order within the 'gored' kingdom. Kent turns away, contemplating like so many pilgrims a journey to death, and Edgar may do so too, thinking of the failure of his other pilgrimage. So, as the Quarto has it, Albany is left to end the play with his awkward truisms.

We might not take Edgar as one of Shakespeare's pilgrims if Shakespeare had not written *Hamlet* some years earlier. Though his assumption of bruised and lunatic nakedness as his disguise in the extremity of his exile allies him with our Glen Bolcain group, and his determination to cleanse the world and right its wrongs places him alongside Hamlet, he lacks the essential experience which initiates Hamlet's pilgrimage, his communication with the dead, and lacks the essential accompaniment of Hamlet's experience, doubt. The doubt is there, but it is in the author's mind, not Edgar's (unless it is in his final silence). So Edgar is a kind of honorary pilgrim, gaining his membership from the fuller definition Shakespeare had provided in *Hamlet*.

Hamlet at his entry, shattered to the point of suicide by the sudden and untimely death of his father and his mother's remarriage to his uncle, who has assumed the throne of Denmark, is incomprehensible except in terms of the great metaphors which I outlined above, the metaphor of true kingship and true descent, and the metaphor of the brows of grace, which 'all things foul would wear'. Hamlet is instinctively aware that the world has gone awry; that 'my father's brother, but no more like my father / Than I to Hercules' is a false simulacrum of kingship (1.2.151–2), and that his mother has given warrant to the falsity by accepting Claudius as king and husband. A pilgrim should visit a shrine to pray for guidance and to plead for those in Purgatory, but in the play Purgatory itself visits Hamlet in the person of his dead father's spirit.[11] Hamlet's question of the Ghost, 'What should we do?', is the ultimate question for every pilgrim: what are we all to do, in this world that is out of joint, this distracted globe? Hamlet's vows to obey the Ghost's commands are summed up in his dedication to 'remember' him, that is, to rescue and continue the tradition of values embodied in the true king. Hamlet's immediate consciousness of alienation, and his adoption of the garb of madness to indicate this, is striking. 'O day and night, but this is wondrous strange', says Horatio, hearing that the 'honest ghost' has spoken with Hamlet. 'And therefore as a stranger give it welcome', replies Hamlet (1.5.164–5).

The violence of his alienation is visited on Ophelia; a symbol, poor girl, of the sexual ties which Hamlet renounces as a weakness towards a frailer sex and as an impediment to his greater cause. His transformation into madness causes exactly the consternation he wants in Claudius. The two other most notable things in Hamlet at this time are, first, the extension of his role far beyond the execution of the Ghost's behests, and, second, the birth of doubt. First, the Ghost has scarcely left the stage when Hamlet bursts out with –

> The time is out of joint: O cursèd spite,
> That ever I was born to set it right.
> (1.5.188–9)

What the Ghost has commanded is already seen to be but a part of the wider scope of cleansing the world. Hamlet's interpretation

---

[11] Although for many years in many places I have advanced essentially the same views of *Hamlet* as are here expressed, it was my interest in the subject of pilgrimage, and then Stephen Greenblatt's major work *Hamlet in Purgatory* (Princeton and Oxford: Princeton University Press, 2001), which made me realise I had never sufficiently acknowledged the importance of the concept of Purgatory in interpreting the play.

of that wider scope will mean a positive contradiction of the Ghost's injunction to leave Gertrude to heaven; Hamlet is determined to rescue and reform her. Second, the propriety, the wisdom and the value of the Ghost's first command, to avenge his own murder, which can only mean removing Claudius from the throne and killing him, is what perplexes and torments Hamlet until the very end of the play. The Ghost may have been the foul fiend: 'the devil hath power / T'assume a pleasing shape' (2.3.599–600); it may be 'a damnèd ghost that we have seen' (3.2.82). Hamlet's doubt concerning the Ghost inevitably brings into question his duty as a divinely appointed missionary. The play-scene confirms the Ghost, and leads to the extraordinary opportunity of killing Claudius at prayer, yet Hamlet does not take it, for what must be a complex mix of reasons. In part perhaps he refrains because of his inflated picture of himself as a controller of Claudius's eternal fate:

> Up sword, and know thou a more horrid hent,
> . . . .
> Then trip him that his heels may kick at heaven . . .
> (3.3.88, 93)

In part, he refrains because it is his intense preference to ignore the Ghost's command, and go to his mother to commence her reclamation (see 3.2.392); in part it is a sense of the futility of the act of killing (curiously both overcome and confirmed a minute later when he drives his sword through the arras and kills the wrong man).

Hamlet's verbal cruelty to Ophelia in the nunnery scene, and his killing of her father, drive her out of her mind, and in that insanity, I suggested, she has the all-important flash of insight into her former lover as a pilgrim. We ignore Ophelia's hint at our peril. But what kind of a pilgrimage is this? Hamlet both accepts and rejects the Ghost as the emissary of heaven; he both endorses and challenges the Ghost's injunctions, and in either case feels free to alter and extend those injunctions; he feels he has a commission to change the world, and he wishes to leave the world altogether; he is both a person under divine instruction and a person creating his own instructions.

On those occasions when Hamlet is convinced he has a divine mission, he can speak like this, of the killing of Polonius.

> For this same lord
> I do repent; but heaven hath pleas'd it so,
> To punish me with this and this with me,
> That I must be their scourge and minister.
>
> (3.4.172–5)

Yet, when he has contrived to get back from the voyage to England – 'I am set naked on your kingdom' (4.7.43) – his words to Horatio indicate a torment of indecision and uncertainty, and, even at this moment, his need for assurance about his course.

> Does it not, think thee, stand me now upon –
> He that hath killed my king, and whored my mother,
> Popped in between th'election and my hopes,
> Thrown out his angle for my proper life,
> And with such cozenage – is't not perfect conscience
> To quit him with this arm? And is't not to be damned
> To let this canker of our nature come
> In further evil?[12]   (5.2.63–70)

These are strong words. Not only does Hamlet say it would be 'perfect conscience' to kill Claudius, but he believes that to disobey a command of heaven communicated by the ghost of his father, and thus allow a criminal and illegal king to continue ruling in Denmark, might incur the penalty of eternal damnation. It is impossible not to see Hamlet's conception of his role in life at this point as one that involves both the future of society and the state of his eternal soul. But he has left it too late. Events have overtaken the resolution of his uncertainties. Claudius and Laertes have conspired to kill him and he is fatally wounded with the poisoned rapier before he takes his final wild revenge – which delivers the Denmark he had sought to retrieve into the hands of the foreigner Fortinbras.

---

[12] The crucial final sentence of this passage is not in the earlier Quarto text, and appears in the later Folio. It is possible that Shakespeare added it to confirm Hamlet's sense, at this moment, of divine authority for his mission.

When the mad Ophelia sings her confused snatches from the Walsingham ballad, identifying her 'true love' with a pilgrim, to be recognised by 'his cockle hat and staff / And his sandal shoon', she is told by the other pilgrim that he's dead, and the image of her dead lover coalesces with the image of her dead father. She is granted a sight of the end of her lover's pilgrimage. Hamlet's attempt to assert truth, after he has painfully sought to guarantee a divine sanction for his action, is worse than fruitless. As in the later play, *King Lear*, the champion of truth, or what he considers to be truth, is outclassed by the champions of 'the foul fiend'. The defeat of Hamlet by the iniquity of Claudius is truly tragic. If it is fair to call his communication with his father in Purgatory, and his subsequent wrestle in apartness and pretended madness with his interpretation of that communication, a pilgrimage, then Shakespeare has given pilgrimage a definition in indefiniteness that contrasts very strongly with the certainty of *The Pilgrim's Progress*.

CHAPTER 10

Epilogue – Therapy

The subject of David Lodge's novel of 1995, *Therapy*, is Laurence Passmore, aged fifty-eight, his problems and his therapy. Passmore is the writer of a highly successful television sitcom, *The People Next Door*. He has a house in Rummidge, near where his wife Sally lectures, and a flat in London. His psychiatrist Alexandra (she calls herself a cognitive behaviour therapist) suggests he write down a list of the good and bad things in his life.

Under the 'Good' column I wrote:

1. Professionally successful
2. Well-off
3. Good health
4. Stable marriage
5. Kids successfully launched in adult life
6. Nice house
7. Great car
8. As many holidays as I want.

Under the 'Bad' column I wrote just one thing:

1. Feel unhappy most of the time.

A few weeks later I added another item:

2. Pain in knee.[1]

The mysterious recurring pain in his knee, which can't be diagnosed or treated, becomes the objective correlative of his mysterious

---

[1] David Lodge, *Therapy* (London: Penguin, 1996), p. 23. Subsequent quotations and page references are from this edition; the novel was first published by Secker and Warburg in 1995.

unhappiness, and is equally resistant to treatment. He doesn't tell each of his therapists of the others: Roland the blind physiotherapist on Mondays, Alexandra on Tuesdays, Miss Wu for acupuncture or Dudley for aromatherapy on Fridays. On Wednesdays and Thursdays he is in London for rehearsals, and sees Amy, the 'caster' of his sitcom, with whom he has an intimate but platonic relationship – 'a sort of therapy too, I suppose' (p. 15).

The entire relation of this moving and very funny novel is by Laurence himself, mostly from the journal he starts keeping. He came from a working-class home in London, and had the misfortune to win a place at a snob grammar-school, where he was grossly under-educated, and has been catching up ever since; he is obviously a very gifted writer. It is chance that throws Kierkegaard in his way, but he perseveres with him because he comes to feel that Kierkegaard is the only person who understands him. He dips into the 'dog's breakfast' of *Either/Or*, and there finds 'The Unhappiest Man'; he felt 'he was speaking directly to my condition' (p. 100). Kierkegaard tells him he is hoping for the wrong things, remembering the wrong things and (above all) not understanding that, whatever decision or choice he makes, he will regret it. It is his absorption in Kierkegaard, intensifying his normal self-absorption, which makes him fail to listen when his wife tells him she wants a separation. She has to make a second announcement.

Book 2 is a series of brilliant monologues spoken by the people Laurence desperately turns to in his efforts to counteract Sally's departure. It later turns out that these are written by Laurence himself, initially as a form of therapy suggested by Alexandra to improve his always low but now rapidly falling self-esteem. They turn out quite differently, as merciless and humiliating self-portrayals which serve not Alexandra but Kierkegaard; they are part of the process by which Laurence chooses himself and makes his existential affirmation. His thoughts are now going back to a new remembering, and a new kind of remembering, of Maureen Kavanagh, his very first girl-friend, when they were both at school, he at his traditional grammar-school and she at the Sacred Heart convent school in Greenwich. It is his aromatherapist's lavender oil that brings her back; it suddenly reminds him of the scent of lavender in the Woolworth stationery she used. 'The smell of lavender brought her out into the open – the lavender and Kierkegaard' (p. 221). He feels he must write about their relationship, and the memoir (which now follows) turns out to be something major in his life, different from anything else he had ever written. It is a teenage version of the 'Seducer's Diary' of *Either/Or*; Maureen is Kierkegaard's Regine, and the climax of the story is a ruthless betrayal. Laurence has wormed his way into the Immaculate Conception parish youth club, and in the nativity play is acting Herod to Maureen's Virgin Mary. When Maureen has qualms (priest-inspired) about continuing their innocent enough necking and petting while she is playing Mary, the offended Laurence brutally ends the relationship and never sees her again.

And to see her again is now all he wants. He finds her husband, Bede Harrington, who is a perfect example of the limited orthodox Catholicism of the St Ronan kind. But she seems to be away in Spain, on her own. 'On a sort of tour, is she?' asks Laurence. Bede replies, 'No, . . . a pilgrimage' (p. 271).

Their son Damien, Maureen's favourite child, had been shot and killed in Angola while on an aid mission. Bede had not found his faith any help at this time, and had rejected a counsellor who thought he might be suffering from guilt, 'because you're alive and he isn't' (p. 276). Maureen had insisted on going off on 'this absurd pilgrimage' to Compostela; she was doing it on foot, alone, and was suffering. Laurence sets off for Spain and eventually finds and confronts the astonished woman. When he tells her he wants 'to get absolution' (p. 297), he is at first hurt by her having almost forgotten the forty-year-old betrayal, and dismissing it as only one of the disappointments of her early love-life. But he becomes absorbed in Maureen's pilgrimage. Laurence spares no detail of how much older, travel-worn and nearly disabled the pilgrim is, compared with his fantasy recollection of his first love, and no detail of the noisy and smelly traffic, and of the crowds on their way to Santiago. But everything is now transformed. He realises that he hasn't felt a twinge in his bad knee.

This is Maureen's pilgrimage; Laurence's share in it is entirely vicarious. Maureen is not explicit about her own motives. The pilgrimage is an offering-up for Damien, and she has found solace in the total absorption in the challenge of the journey, with all its hardships, and its fulfilment. She thinks of the millions who have preceded her. 'They must have got something tremendous out of it, I thought to myself, or people wouldn't have kept on going' (p. 303). The pair reach the shrine, and onlookers make way for the dust-stained pilgrim to kneel and pray.

Just before they reach Santiago, they come across an English television crew, and Laurence is pushed in front of the camera to explain what he meant by saying, 'I'm not a true pilgrim', a true pilgrim being 'someone for whom it's an existential act of self-definition . . . a leap into the absurd, in Kierkegaard's sense'. So Laurence goes on to explain that those crowding towards Santiago might be divided into the three stages of development described by Kierkegaard, the aesthetic, the ethical and finally the religious. The aesthetic type were basically on holiday; the ethical type conformed to everything that was expected of them. The true pilgrim was the religious pilgrim – in Kierkegaard's sense of religion.

To Kierkegaard, Christianity was 'absurd': if it were entirely rational, there would be no merit in believing it. The whole point was that you chose to believe without rational compulsion – you made a leap into the void and in the process chose yourself. Walking a thousand miles to the shrine of Santiago without knowing whether there was anybody actually buried there was such a leap. (p. 305)

Lodge does not say whether Maureen heard Laurence's theory of pilgrimage. Presumably she would have put it very differently. Her faith was too entire and certain for it to be considered a leap into the 'absurd'. Laurence has only a small share in Maureen's experience and its meaning for her. But the combination of Kierkegaard, and his part-share in Maureen's pilgrimage, bring about his first successful therapy. 'For I do feel I've reached the end of something. And, hopefully, a new beginning' (p. 286).

A good many years ago I too was trying to read Kierkegaard and finding the experience much as Laurence Passmore described it.

Reading Kierkegaard is like flying through heavy cloud. Every now and again there's a break and you get a brief, brilliantly lit view of the ground, and then you're back in the swirling grey mist again, with not a fucking clue where you are. (p. 109)

There was a really electrifying break in the clouds when I was reading *Fear and Trembling*; it concerned the 'leap' that Passmore is talking about, and it seemed to me to light up the conundrum of Hamlet's indecision. This is what I wrote in 1983.

I have for several years suggested to my students that the central dilemma in *Hamlet* is that which Kierkegaard describes, concerning Abraham and the intended sacrifice of Isaac . . . Abraham believed that he had heard God and in obedience was prepared to murder his beloved son. This indeed is faith. It is the idea of the wager again – betting that there is a God[2] – and that trusting in what we hear enables us to fulfil a demand of the absolute, although we outgo the laws of worldly ethics.

Kierkegaard tries out many scenarios for the intense but skeletal drama provided in Genesis. What would Isaac say when he heard Abraham's explanation of his extraordinary conduct towards him? 'So you were prepared to kill me because a voice told you to?' And so on. There *can* be no certainty. Isaac was not killed, but Abraham was ready and willing to kill him. Either he was a murderer, or he was an obedient child of God. Faith, says Kierkegaard, is 'a paradox which is capable of transforming a murder into a holy act well-pleasing to God'. But, he asks, 'If the individual has misunderstood the deity – what can save him?'

The *mistaken* conviction of the individual that he can be above the universally accepted ethics of society, Kierkegaard calls the 'demoniacal'. He speaks of 'the knight of faith who in the solitude of the universe never hears any human voice, but walks alone with his dreadful responsibility'. Dreadful, because he may be eternally lost, for following the demoniac and not the divine. Either way, he seems mad to the world; at the very least, the world 'denounces as presumption his wanting to play providence by his actions'[3] . . .

Is Hamlet's sense of mission divine or demoniac?[4]

---

[2] Earlier in the essay I had mentioned Lucien Goldman's use of 'the notion of Pascal that man has to wager that God exists, for he is a hidden God whose presence is not indisputably known and whose voice is not unequivocally heard'.

[3] Søren Kierkegaard, *Fear and Trembling*, trans. W. Lowrie (1941; New York: Doubleday, 1954), pp. 64, 71, 90, 95.

[4] Philip Edwards, 'Tragic Balance in Hamlet'. Quoted from *Shakespeare Survey* 36 (1983), 50.

Laurence Passmore believes that Maureen's pilgrimage is justified to herself as a leap of faith, 'absurd' but necessary in Kierkegaard's view. He does not himself, so far as we hear in the remaining few pages of the novel, accept the leap, but he accepts its possibility, and he shares to some extent in what Maureen has achieved or has been granted. So far as I understand it, Passmore's position at the end of the novel is a willing suspension of disbelief, and that would make him an ideal reader of pilgrimage literature. We might try him out as a spectator at a performance of *Hamlet*. He might say that Shakespeare, an intensely religious but also an intensely sceptical writer, had created a hero who was eventually and after great internal torment convinced of the possibility of divine intervention and of human assistance in that intervention. Hamlet made the Kierkegaardian leap. Whether Shakespeare also made it is another question. Hamlet and Edgar are second-guessing a God whose credentials are not wholly convincing, but at least we accept the possibility that they could be right. We suspend our disbelief.

Most of us, reading pilgrimage literature, remain in Doubting Castle, rooted to the bank, trembling on the brink, accepting the *possibility* of a conviction we cannot share. The history of pilgrimage is the history of constant hope and constant doubt; the practice has no meaning for those who do not believe, and is corrupted by those who think they believe, but it is constantly re-invented in the face of constant discrediting. In the literature of pilgrimage – pilgrimage as both reality and metaphor – the pressure of both doubt and hope is co-existent and extreme. The idea of a very difficult journey through unfamiliar terrain to a shrine where a ritual of self-examination leads to a knowledge of incalculable value not elsewhere to be obtained remains stubbornly inviting, even when poet after poet shows the inadequacy of available pilgrimage metaphors to convey the sense of an encounter with the sacred.

This book is really about possibility, as one of Emily Dickinson's best-known poems expresses it.

> I dwell in Possibility –
> A fairer House than Prose –
> More numerous of Windows –
> Superior – for Doors –

Of Chambers as the Cedars –
Impregnable of Eye –
And for an Everlasting Roof
The Gambrels of the Sky –

Of Visitors – the fairest –
For Occupation – This –
The spreading wide my narrow Hands
To gather Paradise –
                    (Johnson 657/Franklin 466)

The rejection of 'possibility' is brilliantly shown in the carefree and cocksure hero of Yeats's poem 'The Pilgrim'. The most outrageous acceptance of possibility, and its extreme cost, is in Sweeney the bird-man soaring above the limitations of St Ronan's comfortable orthodoxy. In between are all the hesitations and rephrasings I have tried to outline, including Purchas's brazen redefinition. One cannot help being impressed by the constant searching of writers among all the metaphors of search to assess the value of images which try to apprehend contact with the sacred, the moment that transforms our otherwise meaningless round of routine and violence. Their concern with pilgrimage as an idea is a strong protest against the reduction of the word to its present colourlessness, meaning only a visit to a famous place, or to the birthplace of a famous person. Writers keep the word alive, as Robert Crawford does in his poem 'Pilgrim', printed in the *London Review of Books* in February 2002,[5] the last line of which captures so well the 'possibility' which is inherent in the insecurity of pilgrimage.

Lighter than a snail-shell from a thrush's anvil,
Glimpsed in grass cuttings, whiffs of splintered light,

But knee-tough, toddler fierce and undeflected,
Slogging between Arbilot and Balmirmer

Where the Arbroath road shoggles in the heat,
All plainchant and sticky willie,

---

[5] Reprinted in Robert Crawford, *The Tip of My Tongue* (London: Jonathan Cape, 2003), p. 7. Quoted by permission of the author and The Random House Group Limited.

E-babble and cushie doos,
A soul, like the signal from a mobile phone,

Heads south where muscadine light
Slurs long, dwammy midsummer breakers,

And sings out, blithe, by a kirk whose bell-rope
Hangs, a frayed leash that's attached to the whole of the sky.[6]

---

[6] 'Shoggles' means shimmers; 'sticky willie' is goose-grass or cleavers; 'cushie doos' are wood pigeons; 'dwammy' means dream-like.

Index